CW00328984

THE BEST OF THE
GALLUP
MANAGEMENT JOURNAL
2001 - 2007

THE BEST OF THE

GALLUP

MANAGEMENT JOURNAL

2001 - 2007

Edited by Geoffrey Brewer and Barb Sanford

GALLUP PRESS
New York

Gallup Press
1251 Avenue of the Americas
23rd Floor
New York, NY 10020

Manufactured in the United States of America

First printing: 2007

10 9 8 7 6 5 4 3 2 1

Library of Congress Control Number: 2007933137

ISBN: 978-1-59562-019-4

TABLE OF CONTENTS

CUSTOMER

BRAND

LEADERSHIP

INTRODUCTION

You are holding in your hands the highlights of an ongoing conversation that the *Gallup Management Journal* has been having with its readers — executives, managers, and highly engaged employees — since 2001. While it's difficult to sum up seven years' worth of work in a sentence or two, we'd like to give it a shot: In its essence, the *GMJ's* purpose is to give leaders actionable insights into managing the human side of their businesses — their employees and customers. It continues to be our hope that those insights help make your business more productive and profitable.

If you've been a regular reader of the *GMJ* since we launched the publication in March 2001, or if you're reading it for the first time in this volume, one thing should be very clear: When we write about the "human" side of business, we're not talking about something "soft" or "warm and fuzzy." On the contrary, the *GMJ* — and Gallup consulting in general — has been committed to showing you how to engage employees and customers, build world-class brands, develop future leaders, and continually improve your company's performance, in *measurable* ways. It's not enough to say that an engaged employee is a more productive and profitable employee; we have to *prove it*.

And so, every *GMJ* article, whether it's written by one of Gallup's leading experts or scientists, or by an executive from a successful global company, or by Gallup's very own CEO, must have three elements for us to publish it: a strong point of view, real-life stories that bring that viewpoint to life, and deep and solid research that supports it. There isn't a viewpoint or perspective in this volume that isn't backed by decades of Gallup management research, or at the very least, research that's been approved by Gallup.

The reason for this rigor is straightforward: Business has been entering a new era in recent years, and executives are still struggling with the transition. Most of you have reengineered and reorganized your companies numerous times. Applying principles such as Six Sigma and Total Quality Management, you have improved, refined, and almost perfected your business processes. Many of you have wrung the excess costs, waste, and redundancies out of your companies. But what remains is your biggest challenge of all: improving and perfecting your relationships with customers and with the employees who engage them. More than anything, executives and managers need quantifiable, measurable strategies for making the "intangible" side of their business as productive and profitable as it can be.

For years, "hardheaded" business leaders and gurus have said that it's impossible to measure these intangibles. *GMJ* would argue that not only is it possible to do so, it's essential — and leading-edge companies have been doing it for a long time. In this volume, you'll find proof. The many articles and interviews here cover topics such as winning fickle customers for life, why customer satisfaction is the wrong measure, the best way to get meaningful employee feedback, the 12 elements of great managing, why most advertising doesn't work, and the impact of positive leadership. The volume includes a range of voices from within and outside of Gallup. A Ritz-Carlton executive tells how his company is reinventing its world-class brand, while a leader at Ann Taylor describes how the retailer invests in talent. Nobel Prize winner Daniel Kahneman probes how customers think, while one of the inventors of the Internet, Vinton Cerf, speculates on the future of his creation.

These are highlights of the first seven years — *GMJ* has many years to go. The conversation will continue. But for now, we hope you profit from this collection of articles as your business stakes its claim and engages employees and customers in an ever-more competitive, and all-too-often uncertain, global economy.

Geoffrey Brewer, Editorial Director

Barb Sanford, Managing Editor

Larry Emond, Executive Publisher

EMPLOYEE

FEEDBACK FOR REAL

by John Thackray

March 15, 2001

A series of simple workplace questions can spark employee-management action with measurable results. The effects are local and team-based, but they can be repeated across the entire company for bottom-line gains.

"The positive effect of feedback on performance has become one of the most widely accepted principles in psychology," write professors Angelo S. DeNisi and Avraham N. Kluger in the February 2000 issue of the Academy of Management *Executive*. No surprise then that feedback gathering, whether in the form of 360-degree evaluations, employee opinion polls, or numeric "voting" pads at large executive gatherings, has spread like kudzu across the corporate landscape.

But there is a dangerous flaw in much feedback methodology. An analysis by the two professors of 131 studies on feedback effectiveness found that "In more than a third of the cases where it was possible to assess the effectiveness of feedback, providing feedback actually hurt subsequent performance." Poor design and participation are obvious culprits, but the biggest source of failure in the feedback effort is surely that employees' volunteered input unaccountably evaporates. The individual has his or her moment of self-expression — a fleeting participation in the great collective search for truth — then silence, nada, frustration as the status quo prevails.

Five years ago, Gallup decided to create a better feedback process for employers large and small: an opinion-based tool that would both release and direct the powers of feedback. The primary goal was to identify and measure the elements of worker engagement that are most powerfully linked to improved business outcomes — be they sales growth, productivity, customer loyalty, and so forth — and the generation of value.

To identify the elements of worker engagement, Gallup conducted hundreds of focus groups and many thousands of worker interviews in all kinds of organizations, at all levels, in most industries, and in many countries.

From these inquiries, researchers pinpointed, out of hundreds of variables, 12 key employee expectations that, when satisfied, form the foundation of strong feelings of engagement. The result was a 12-item survey in which employees are asked to rate their level of agreement with each item on a scale of one to five.

Results have shown a strong link between high survey scores and worker performance. That, Gallup research shows, is linked to business outcomes. Thus, from the employer's standpoint, addressing the issues that boost worker engagement is a logical pathway to higher profits. Of course, this correlation is not new. It has been discussed in general terms by managers for decades. The Gallup method differs by creating a methodology that bridges the "soft" values that pertain to worker morale and employee engagement, such as recognition and desire to contribute, with "hard" and measurable outcomes.

Employees respond to the 12 engagement items using a scale of one to five, based on their weak or strong agreement. But the Q^{12} process (companies that use the process devise their own internal term for it) is far more than a baseline litmus test of the degree of existing worker engagement. It deploys a feedback methodology for improving engagement by creating a factual base for discussion and debate of the causes behind the numbers. It yields actionable input from staff and managers for changes in attitude, conduct, policies, and processes. Follow-up surveys over the years track long-term progress — or backsliding — on the 12 items, each time releasing another wave of feedback. And because the terms of discussion are always grounded in data, the energy and the truths of this feedback do not evaporate unheeded but, to the contrary, foster positive change in the work arena.

In recent years, this tool has been used by more than 87,000 divisions or work units within corporations, and approximately 1.5 million employees have participated. For companies that were able to provide data across units, comparisons of engagement scores reveal that those with high Q^{12} scores have also experienced lower turnover, higher sales growth, better productivity, better customer loyalty, or other manifestations of superior performance.

Dozens of managers and employees from four companies that have adopted and gotten results from Q^{12} — International Paper; Swissôtel; B&Q, a UK retailer of do-it-yourself and gardening supplies; and Best Buy, the electronics retail chain — have offered insights and observations for this story. The number of employees involved in the Q^{12} interventions detailed here was large — more than 20,000 at B&Q alone.

THE 12 ELEMENTS OF GREAT MANAGING

To identify the elements of worker engagement, Gallup conducted many thousands of interviews in all kinds of organizations, at all levels, in most industries, and in many countries. These 12 statements — the Gallup Q^{12} — emerged from Gallup's pioneering research as those that best predict employee and workgroup performance.

- I know what is expected of me at work.

- I have the materials and equipment I need to do my work right.

- At work, I have the opportunity to do what I do best every day.

- In the last seven days, I have received recognition or praise for doing good work.

- My supervisor, or someone at work, seems to care about me as a person.

- There is someone at work who encourages my development.

- At work, my opinions seem to count.

- The mission or purpose of my company makes me feel my job is important.

- My associates or fellow employees are committed to doing quality work.

- I have a best friend at work.

- In the last six months, someone at work has talked to me about my progress.

- This last year, I have had opportunities at work to learn and grow.

How about we write the schedule, boss?

Feedback releases energies that increase engagement. And behind and within the feedback there lies — what? Excitement? Hope? Mindfulness? Determination? Yes, these and a dozen more human attributes. When given their Q^{12} scores, many managers and subordinates appear galvanized, possessed of that quite incredible feeling that yes, they can make a difference to the team's culture — they can improve processes, enrich skills, and do whatever is necessary to give the workday more meaning. The yearning to escape feelings of meaninglessness is why, at heart, we identify with the goals of the organization when it comes to performance, quality, and similar values.

Each Q^{12} element has a common ingredient: remediability. It addresses a condition that is within the capacity of managers and workers to change together, as a team initiative. Fate and acts of God are sidelined. Previously occluded truths are, in turn, laid bare. John Pearson, Manager of the Sunderland branch of B&Q, observes, "We'd all like to think that our management style is fair/reasonable and that it encourages the staff to buy in. But when you see hard Q^{12} numbers about key management performance indicators, it makes you look at yourself and how you manage."

Three years ago, Swissôtel Atlanta Security Chief John Sheffler, a former drill sergeant, ran his department like an army platoon and refused subordinates' appeals for more flexible work hours to accommodate their family, school, and other obligations. When confronted with the news that his eight-person team's Q^{12} responses totaled up to the worst Q^{12} score among hundreds of work units in the Swissôtel chain, he saw the light. "I opened myself up to criticism and asked them to tell me what was upsetting them, what I was doing wrong as a manager," Sheffler recalls.

The guards discussed his over-controlling nature, in particular his domination of the schedule. Sheffler worried that if guards had more choice of hours, they'd all pick day shifts, and there'd be nobody for night work. No, they shot back: They would take responsibility for total coverage, if given more flexibility. "We sat and listened to what we really didn't want to hear, and slowly the management style changed," says Sheffler. A year later, his group registered a perfect score. "We went from the bottom all the way up to the sky," he says.

"He took a huge risk that worked out brilliantly," says Janis Cannon, the facility's General Manager.

Big deal, you might say: Fewer than a dozen security guards feel great about their new work environment. But imagine such events multiplied for hundreds of teams and nearly 3,000 employees who participated from 13 Swissôtels, and the magnitude of the impact should be clear (the questionnaire was translated into nine languages for the diverse workforce). More than is perhaps recognized in most corporate boardrooms, small teams and workgroups have strong diagnostic powers and self-correcting abilities, which, when allowed purposeful expression, create culture change on a huge scale. The locus of power — the leadership initiative — is with the whole team, only guided by the manager.

Opportunities for change are first presented when managers sit down with their teams to study the Q^{12} scores. This is the moment when the manager gets a first reading on what's happening beneath the everyday rhythms. Mark McMullen, Manager of a B&Q Newcastle outlet, was at first puzzled as to why his employees had not given a top score for the second item: "I have the materials and equipment I need to do my work right." Scores on most other items were very high. "The big thing that came across in our discussion was uniforms. They were saying, 'No, I'm not going to give a high score on that because I don't have a new uniform. I have a tatty one that I've had for a year and a half,'" McMullen recalls, adding, "It is easy to make assumptions before you ask them what the reasons might be. Sitting down with the group, you do get the complete facts and the meat on the bones of what the problems really are."

Start small, then build

The Q^{12} is a barometer of local conditions that a worker can see and touch. At first, some of the employees of International Paper's Mansfield Mill in Louisiana saw in the survey a chance to take shots at the company. According to Mill Manager Tommy Joseph, "It is easy to slip into a victim's role when you answer these questions, looking at the whole company. People so often feel they have no control, and this [answering the questionnaire] is a chance to vent those feelings. So we said, 'Guys, forget about the company, forget about the mill's management. Focus on the team that you interact with every day; think about yourselves as a team.' The Q^{12} is pretty granular."

At one of Mansfield Mill's paper-making machines, teams have registered improvements in "just about every measure that we look at: acceptance of the product, higher efficiency, lower levels of customer returns, and fewer complaints," Joseph says. He gives the lion's share of the credit to the Q^{12} framework. "The process that they go through is more important than the actual questions," he continues. "It gets them talking to each other, questioning each other. It opens up boundaries where it is okay to talk about things that had not been talked about before. The feedback is where the value is." Team dialogue made these workers aware of shortcomings. They "came forward and asked for help on team training techniques, conflict resolution, problem solving, and better communication."

Aggregate Q^{12} results challenge the conventional view on the determinants of worker morale. We are inclined to think that objective work conditions determine job contentment: Someone with a dangerous and dirty job will obviously feel less engaged than a professional with a sunny corner office. That view is flat-out wrong, according to Gallup results. Workers experiencing the same lousy pay, intolerable noise, physical hardship, speed of the production line, and so forth can manifest abysmal or exceptionally high engagement scores. It depends on how their managers strive to build a strong foundation for better engagement.

What goes into that foundation depends on local conditions and circumstances — the view from the unit level, not the view from the corporate bridge. Efficiency, in this view, largely depends on the distinctive culture of small teams. Lieske Robbert, Head of Human Resources for Swissôtel, says some of the highest engagement and customer satisfaction scores for the entire chain are to be found in the laundry operation in Istanbul and in the room-service operation at the Swissôtel Cairo. But each laundry operation and room-service crew in the hotel chain has to strive in its own way.

"Whatever those people in Istanbul room service are doing, I guarantee that it would not be acceptable for room service in New York City to imitate it," Robbert says. "We like to share successes, but we don't want people to copy others' behavior. Because if model behaviors were simply reproduced, it could give the wrong message. We want people to do it [find improvements] themselves, in a way that is natural, instinctual — not to follow a process."

Interpretive feedback is not orderly, and at times, may verge on chaos. It entails wheel spinning and digressions and ambiguities. Some worker suggestions can be just plain wacko, which is why managers using Q^{12} quickly learn how to keep feedback from straying into irrelevance. Says McMullen of the B&Q Newcastle store, "If anyone puts forward something that is unachievable — for example, that we should have a color scanner or printer — it is important that the idea is knocked on the head immediately, and that I don't say, 'Maybe' or 'We'll see what we can do.' But we still give reasons why."

The best get better

Each work unit is typically asked to develop action plans to improve its two worst and two best Q^{12} scores. Working on the laggards makes sense, but what is the point of pushing in areas of proven excellence? Because success begets success. The potential gains are highest in the top-performing groups.

Best Buy, the giant electronics retail chain, has found that while the engagement and performance of all stores have increased as a result of the Q^{12} process, the better stores have improved faster and more dramatically. "Though we have been able to get the water level to rise in general, it has been easier to get the better ships to rise higher than it has been to transform the ones at the bottom," says Brad Anderson, Best Buy's President and Chief Operating Officer. In a recent Gallup study, the top group registered roughly double the performance scores on key customer values: shopping experience, store atmosphere, employee knowledge of the products, and time spent with customers. Sales on a per-square-foot basis almost doubled in the better ranked outlets.

"Unlocking skills and talent is a difficult thing to do," Anderson concedes. "If it wasn't difficult, we'd have made more progress." The key triggering event, as he sees it, "is to unlock the confidence that people have in their own skills. If you are at a school like MIT, you are expected to make a big contribution. At a lesser school, you're not expected to make such a big contribution. My suspicion is that expectations have a huge impact on the kind of contribution people actually do make. Our good stores are much more like an MIT."

The most vulnerable part of the feedback loop is the manager's willingness to rigorously interpret the results and hew to team input. The framing of the Q^{12} results in numbers is important because it offers less opportunity for the evasion that is inherent in dialogue. "That's the biggest benefit: getting direct feedback from your people on a scored basis," says Greg Wanta, Manager of International Paper's Texarkana Mill in Texas.

But what if a line manager doesn't buy into this process? He or she should be free to decline, just as any worker can refuse to fill out the questionnaire. "It is not surprising that some people have not done much with it," says

International Paper's Tommy Joseph. "In any organization where you have 600 to 700 people, there is always going to be 5% to 10% — no matter how hard you try — who will never get on board. My philosophy is to expend as much effort as I can with the people in the middle and at the top."

Similar thoughts are shared by Matthew Brearley, Director of Retail Personnel at B&Q. "I definitely believe that the managers who are good will improve more and more on their Q^{12}s. They will keep driving for improvement. Managers who are average, less than average, or who don't have what it takes regardless of how much you measure them, will need real help if they are to improve. To get those stores to be top performers, we'll have to build better management capabilities," he says.

Companies that adopt the Q^{12} program go to a lot of trouble to sell it to the troops. Considerable effort also goes to reassuring participants that it's okay to criticize superiors. "I tell my people, 'If there is something I'm doing that is bothering you, let me know,'" says Mike Ralston, Manager of the Whitehall, Pennsylvania, Best Buy outlet. "And I tell them, 'There will be no retribution.' Over the years, people have learned to trust me on this. They realize that there is no retribution."

Not all workers want to get with the program, so there can't be pressure on those who don't care to participate. Another Best Buy store's General Manager, Doug Carter of Orlando, Florida, emphasizes, "We want to make sure that everyone in our store is aware, to the degree of their interest, how our business runs. But we certainly don't want to over-communicate and lose an employee who has no interest in how my job, or the store as a whole, works. We are simply trying to identify an interest in some individuals and amplify it to the greatest level."

The degree of interest can be raised through leadership strategies that are hinted at in the statements — recognition, support, and the like. "We need to incorporate the needs that are expressed in the 12 questions into our personalities as leaders," says Carmen Fulchini, Best Buy's General Manager at a new outlet in Woodbridge, New Jersey. "I check my managers on this sometimes and ask, 'What did you do to give feedback to people recently? Give me some examples, good or bad.' If they struggle to remember, I immediately stop them and say, 'If you have to think about it, then you did not give them quality feedback. If you had, it would have stood out in your mind, because it came right from the heart, spontaneously, and when you walked away, you felt good about it.'"

Explaining what makes a great building, architect Mies van der Rohe famously said that "God is in the details." And that is the beauty of Q^{12}. It operates at a level of detail that is vivid to an individual employee but often not to his or her supervisor. Cumulatively, across the workforce, this detail is a force that can increase efficiency, becoming a bottom-line factor no less important than the macro things top management does.

"There are so many little things that are easily overlooked when you are managing a large shop, and which the Q^{12} exposes," says Steve Fowler, General Manager of the B&Q Huddersfield, Yorkshire unit. Consider the little matter of staplers. The Q^{12} survey asks about materials needed for doing one's job, meaning anything from a computer to a forklift. For the checkout staff at this B&Q store, an absence of staplers turned out to be pretty significant. Fowler explains, "To a girl who works only 16 hours a week, it can make a difference. If you ask for feedback on her greatest frustration, back it comes about the embarrassment she feels when a customer asks to have the credit card slip stapled to the invoice and she has to say, 'Sorry, actually I can't do it. There is a stapler three checkout counters away, but there are no staples in it.' That hits at so many different issues, such as 'I have the opportunity to do my job properly' and 'I can do what I do best' and 'I can offer customers good service.'"

That one little missing stapler, according to Fowler, "affects so many indices of engagement." Correct the problem and bingo — this worker's feelings of engagement soar, because she has been given a voice, was heard, improved the working conditions of other checkout workers, and did her bit to boost customer service. Such value generated for B&Q shareholders could be created no other way.

See Related Article
"Taking Feedback to the Bottom Line" (page 16)

TAKING FEEDBACK TO
THE BOTTOM LINE

by James K. Harter

March 15, 2001

**Research involving 200,000 employees across 36 companies shows
how engagement drives real business outcomes**

"People are our most important asset" is one of the oldest aphorisms in business. Words to that effect have been uttered by practically every CEO. But ask that CEO how his or her people differ from the competition's, and the answer will be that they are just, well, better. Ask how worker psychology contributes to economic value, and the response is likely to consist of bromides about loyalty, empowerment, creativity, and motivation. Much of business is like this: We know in our bones that something is true but do not understand the particulars.

EFFECT OF ENGAGEMENT ON TURNOVER IN
HIGH- AND LOW-TURNOVER COMPANIES

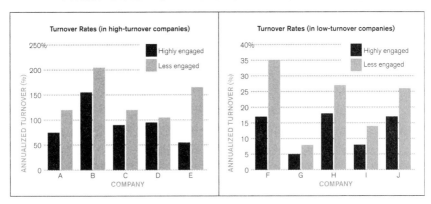

Since the beginnings of "scientific management" a century ago, researchers have been struggling to understand how the many aspects of human relations in the workplace affect the bottom line. Advances in the past decade have been pretty dramatic. In the 1990s, Gallup accelerated its work in the field and began to study the effect of workers' attitudes, emotions, and behaviors on performance.

Previous studies had suggested — in line with common sense — positive relationships between job satisfaction and achievement on the job. A more "satisfied" employee is likely to be more cooperative, more helpful to colleagues, and more punctual. The satisfied employee makes better use of time, shows up for more days of work, has longer tenure, and earns higher performance ratings. But the key questions for business are: What conditions govern the increase and decline of satisfaction within a company and its workforce? If these can be identified, can they be influenced? Do workgroups with higher rates of satisfaction generate significantly higher performance outcomes? If linkage could be established, companies could work to increase satisfaction and generate profits that would otherwise be left on the table.

These were the questions that Gallup addressed as we zeroed in on top-performing teams and individuals. At hundreds of focus groups across different industries, high-performance non-managers and managers discussed the things that caused them to experience well-being at work and, conversely, that made them angry and turned off and hurt productivity. As one might imagine, this yielded a rich soup of observations. Out of this often chaotic and contradictory input, we identified the major satisfaction generators, the key elements that supervisors might significantly influence and control, as distinct from those they might not have the power to do anything about — such as rates of pay, hours of work, and the like. Finally we developed 12 simple statements to identify respondents' feelings about the key satisfaction elements. High scores around the 12 items indicate the presence of deep worker "engagement," which is the condition that engenders satisfaction and other emotional outcomes like loyalty and pride. Engagement leads to measurable business outcomes, as our research shows.

The sources of worker engagement

Simple and straightforward on the surface, the statements are nonetheless freighted with psychological power. They reveal deep and eternal human needs. The human psyche's wants are constant, irreducible. Classical psychology has often looked through a morbid lens, identifying what is wrong with people and society. But lately, a growing number of thinkers are studying the other end of the spectrum. These "positive psychologists" argue for a serious accounting of the elements that govern well-being and success — for the individual, the group, and the organization.

EFFECT OF ENGAGEMENT ON LOYALTY, SALES, & PROFITS

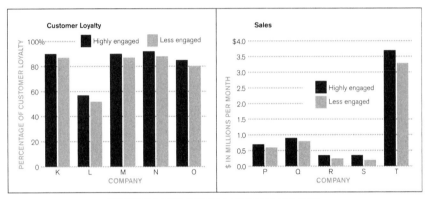

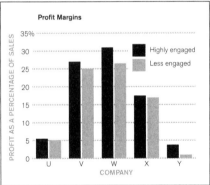

Most of us crave meaning as well as money through work, and in a work-obsessed culture, much of that craving will be persistently manifested in the office and factory. When emotional needs are met, worker attention, cognition, and performance should increase. Conversely, an alienated or depressed state can eat away at memory function and the capacity to perform complex tasks. The moral is simple: If you satisfy their deep wants, employees become more cognitively and emotionally engaged and will perform better. And this is true across national and corporate cultures, in all occupations, regardless of rates of pay — because the underlying needs are universal.

Obviously the statements do not capture the full cause of a worker's sense of engagement. No survey could. But they do cover most of the factors behind a feeling of engagement that can vary with great sensitivity to changes in the workplace. As of the last iteration, 198,514 workers within 36 companies in 21 industries, such as finance, manufacturing, retail, services, transportation, and public utilities, had responded to these statements at least once, sometimes two or three times.

Robust links to the bottom line

We used a statistical technique called meta-analysis to combine the results of many diverse studies, because it provides the strongest test of true relationships and their consistency across organizations. We collected employee engagement scores and business unit outcome data (profitability, sales, employee retention, customer satisfaction) for 7,939 business units, teams, or workgroups in 36 companies. We then correlated engagement results with business outcome data to assess whether business units with high scores on engagement had higher business outcomes and if those with low scores had lower outcomes. The correlation was positive and substantially meaningful to success across different businesses: Highly engaged individuals were most often found in the high-performance units.

This research points to but does not establish cause. (Gallup has conducted individual case studies that yield evidence of cause and effect.) Employee engagement is far from the only driver of desirable business outcomes. Management tactics, procedures, and human invention also contribute to improved revenues, customer loyalty, higher productivity, and so forth. What we claim is that this picture of the nexus between engagement and economic performance is robust, in part because of the huge research database and the different industries and work situations. It is new knowledge, a foundation on which to build a big advance in the understanding of the connection between human elements and economic outcomes.

The study found variability in degrees of engagement within companies from unit to unit, which tells us that the factors influencing employee engagement are mostly local and proximate to workers, not pan-corporate. It is true that manufacturing work teams and groups had lower engagement scores than professional or white-collar varieties. Yet within the manufacturing category, there are many teams and workgroups with extraordinarily high engagement scores. They were high because these workers and managers had taken the initiative and modified practices and behaviors. And that, according to our meta-analysis, is positively linked to business outcomes. The bottom line: On the production line as at the shop counter, basic human needs for self-validation, whether they are satisfied or thwarted, determine degrees of engagement and hence the value that is created or destroyed for the company.

To learn more about the Gallup Q^{12} items, see graphic "The 12 Elements of Great Managing" in "Feedback for Real" (page 7)

THE MANAGER'S DUTY   *by Rodd Wagner*

November 5, 2001

Front-line supervisors can play a crucial role in the battle against terrorism

My grandfather was a supervisor of a power station in Idaho during World War II. After Pearl Harbor, he also assumed the duties of an Air Force observer. "If a plane came over," he wrote, "I would call Pocatello, giving directions of flight and any other information possible."

My grandmother was one of four women from the remote town who were, as the local newspaper reported, "armed with guns and the ability to use them." She helped guard the power plant against sabotage.

They were a small part of the war effort, but a part of it nonetheless. As it did for many people, the war blurred the line between their duty to their company and their duty to their country. The home front miracle of World War II was how many small acts of hard work, sacrifice, neighborly compassion, and good management combined to out-produce the Axis powers.

Some managerial triumphs of the war are legendary. Andrew Jackson Higgins invented and his employees built 20,094 landing craft of all types, including the "Higgins boats," the craft that made it possible to land the D-Day troops on the beaches of Normandy. Henry J. Kaiser and his managers employed women welders and automotive assembly line techniques to speed 1,490 Liberty and Victory ships into action.

But the United States also enlisted its first-level supervisors. The War Production Board distributed an "official plan book" outlining how managers could solicit ideas and rally support from their work teams. "The urgency of tomorrow must be felt in every shop and factory producing war goods, in every home and every farm," wrote President Franklin Delano Roosevelt in the introduction to the manual.

Together, these efforts worked. "The astonishing acceleration in the American productive effort," wrote Paul Johnson in *A History of the American People*, "was made possible by the essential dynamism and flexibility of the

American enterprise system, wedded to a national purpose which served the same galvanizing role as the optimism of the Twenties."

The parallel to today is unmistakable. Fresh from the optimism of the '80s and '90s, a horrible galvanizing event confronts the United States. As U.S. armed forces fight, police investigate, and security is tightened, how can American managers contribute to the battle against terrorism?

Managing an economic recovery

During World War II, U.S. citizens made great sacrifices to divert production to the war effort. In this very different war, the short-term threat appears to be that fear could slow the economic machine that affords us everything from unemployment benefits to stealth bombers.

For more than 50 years, The Gallup Organization has studied the effects of good and bad management, as perceived by the employees, on the ability of a company to succeed. The most important discovery: Top executives are less important, and front-line managers are more important, than usually supposed.

Top brass are important for articulating a corporate vision and determining business strategy, but only the men and women who share the day-to-day struggles with employees — their direct supervisors — can translate the company's mission into performance. Only managers make it personal.

Great managers engender higher productivity, higher safety, fewer resignations, fewer lost days, and higher customer loyalty. Before the attacks, Gallup estimated that "actively disengaged" employees cost the U.S. economy between $292 billion and $355 billion per year. By motivating their employees and managing them toward excellence, great managers have the potential to make a tremendous difference in the United States' ability to rebound economically from this threat.

Defending free enterprise — and freedom itself

A corny ad for Royal Typewriters during World War II oversimplified the war by suggesting that Americans were fighting for the right to "buy anything you want." It's not as eloquent as Adam Smith, but the sentiment is the same.

Nine days after the attacks, the London-based *Economist* magazine editorialized: "Those who criticize America's leadership of the world's capitalist system — a far from perfect affair — should remember that it has brought more wealth and better living standards to more people than any other in history." With the free-market system under attack, managers should not be shy about defending it.

In choosing the World Trade Center as one of their targets, the terrorists showed their contempt for that success and reinforced Osama bin Laden's charge to "kill the Americans and plunder their money wherever and whenever they find it." Terrorists killing a company's employees are now among a manager's worst nightmares. We saw that as we watched New York managers and executives grieving over the loss of their people.

A new definition of duty

What are a manager's responsibilities in these very different times? And will managers galvanize themselves and fulfill their pivotal role — a role that research suggests is uniquely theirs?

The terrorists have left thousands of Americans unemployed. Will managers launch the new projects, build, design, invent, and create demand for improved products and services that require more workers at their firms?

The terrorists seek to intimidate American workers, and they may attack again with deadly efficiency. Will managers reassure their associates, inspire them to greater personal achievements, set higher goals, and forge ahead in spite of their fears?

The terrorists want to destroy the wealth of our free nations. Will managers redouble their efforts — work harder and smarter — to preserve it?

We do not know what this new national crisis will require of our business managers. Greater vigilance, maybe. Higher productivity, perhaps, like their World War II predecessors. Calm in the face of another attack, if more attacks come. A commitment to inclusiveness when racial and religious tensions are high. And when it's needed, wisdom and compassion in the difficult discussions that determine who is laid off and who is retained. As business improves, discretion in the crucial decisions of whom to hire. A steadying influence that looks forward to the next quarter, the next year, to employees' career goals, to what customers want — all the previously routine aspects of management that built, and will rebuild, the free world's economic strength.

It can be intuitively difficult to imagine the cumulative force of many modest workplace improvements, such as making sure teams have the right tools, recognizing and developing employees, coaching, or team building.

It's easier to see it in reverse as we get reports of the economic damage done when the United States stopped in its tracks for the better part of a week. But the effect does in fact work both ways. One of the best ways to make up for one week lost is 51 weeks of extra effort. Recently it's been in vogue to say a company works 24/7. Now we need a series of "9/11" days — days of especially focused managerial and employee effort — to answer the events of September 11.

A stewardship to fulfill

The events of September 11 forced America to reexamine what it seeks to defend: religious freedom, free markets, representative government, "domestic tranquility," and life itself. Managers are not bystanders to the drama, responsible only to their boss and the bottom line. They have powerful stewardships over the democratic way of life. The inherent principles of management stem from the direct connections between political liberties and economic freedom.

If you are a manager, your job suddenly is more important. The stakes are higher now. You serve your country well by managing well.

TO LEVERAGE DIVERSITY,
THINK INCLUSIVELY   *by Jack Ludwig and Vijay S. Talluri*

December 15, 2001

Inclusiveness is good for the corporate balance sheet as well as the corporate soul

White men were once a majority in America's workforce, but for decades, their numbers have been dwindling. According to the Bureau of Labor Statistics, by 2005, white males will make up only 38% of the workforce, and by 2008, women and people of color will account for about 70% of new workers. In other words, knowing how to manage diversity gains more importance with each passing year. Yet most corporate diversity programs simply shield companies from legal penalties under federal nondiscrimination statutes, when what's really needed is a way to move beyond the defensive goal of expunging discrimination toward the next step — inclusiveness.

Inclusiveness is a strategy to unleash the power of diversity to generate business value. It involves creating opportunities throughout an organization so that the talents of all employees can be fully realized. And it extends beyond strictly embracing legal dictates associated with the "protected categories" of discrimination law, which include race, gender, religion, age, and disability.

Of course the issues surrounding protected categories are important. Gallup surveys show that many members of these categories, particularly African-Americans, feel discriminated against in the workplace. In the fall of 2001, for example, we conducted a poll of 2,004 randomly selected adults in the United States. The poll revealed that 44% of blacks but only 10% of whites feel that blacks are treated unfairly on the job.

But protected categories represent a relatively narrow subset of differences among workers; diversity covers the entire spectrum of human differences, including physical characteristics, educational backgrounds, experiences, and preferences. As a tool to leverage diversity, inclusiveness focuses on using the unique strengths of each employee to increase the productivity and profitability of an organization.

How does an executive exercise the power that comes from these strengths? As the old business adage has it, "If you don't measure it, you can't manage it." In 2000, a mid-size healthcare services company asked us to design a survey to measure inclusiveness. Analysis of the results showed that attitudes about inclusiveness varied across the company and that workgroups with the lowest inclusiveness scores had lower productivity and retention scores than those with higher inclusiveness scores.

Our research in this case and in other surveys conducted since then is laying the foundation for a system to measure an organization's success at creating and maintaining inclusive environments. Based on thousands of employee interviews, we identified a list of 10 questions that, when asked of employees, indicate how inclusive a company is and how effective it is at managing diversity.

THE GALLUP I[10]

1. Do you always trust your company to be fair to all employees?
2. At work, are all employees always treated with respect?
3. Does your supervisor keep all employees well informed?
4. Do you feel free to express your views at work?
5. Does your company treasure diverse opinions and ideas?
6. At work, are you encouraged to use your unique talents?
7. Do you always feel valued in your company?
8. Is your supervisor open to new ideas and suggestions?
9. Does your supervisor always make the best use of employees' skills?
10. Does your company delight in making the best use of employees' backgrounds and talents?

The I[10] items are protected by copyright of Gallup, Inc., 2001. All rights reserved.

By regularly auditing employees' answers to these questions, an organization can assess the degree to which employees feel included. It can also garner valuable information about legal compliance issues, even though the I[10] does not address such issues directly. The research shows that answers to the I^{10} correlate strongly with perceptions of fairness in hiring and promotion.

More to the point: Once such regular audits are in place, organizations can begin to study their progress in inclusiveness and how it relates to positive business outcomes. And that's the key. Studying the measurable links between inclusiveness and positive business outcomes (such as retention, profitability, and productivity) is the secret to harnessing the business value of workforce diversity.

To further explore these links, we recently conducted a poll using the I^{10} in a random nationwide survey of 2,014 working Americans. Employees who felt most included — those in the actively inclusive category — were nearly three times as likely as those in the not inclusive category to strongly agree with the statement that they "planned to be with their current company one year from now." What's more, while only 3% of not inclusive respondents gave strong endorsement to the statement "I would recommend my company as a place to work to friends and family," 86% of those in the actively inclusive category strongly agreed.

INCLUSIVENESS INDEX

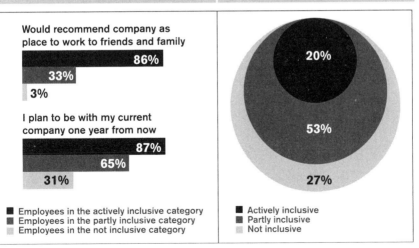

THE MOST INCLUSIVE WORKPLACES GENERATE THE MOST LOYAL EMPLOYEES	BUT ONLY 20% OF AMERICAN EMPLOYEES CONSIDER THEIR WORKPLACES AMONG THE MOST INCLUSIVE

Would recommend company as place to work to friends and family
86%
33%
3%

I plan to be with my current company one year from now
87%
65%
31%

20%
53%
27%

■ Employees in the actively inclusive category
■ Employees in the partly inclusive category
▨ Employees in the not inclusive category

■ Actively inclusive
■ Partly inclusive
▨ Not inclusive

Corroborating these powerful links between individual feelings of workplace inclusiveness and important business outcomes is the finding that 85% of actively inclusive respondents are engaged in their job. (Gallup measures engagement, a feeling of being fully involved in one's job, through responses to the statements that make up the Q^{12}.) More than a decade of Gallup research demonstrates that engagement leads to measurable improvement in business outcomes, including lower turnover, stronger customer loyalty, higher sales, and better profit margins. So the strong link between inclusiveness and engagement makes the story simple: The bottom line stands to gain when an organization turns its attention to leveraging diversity.

In the business environment of the 21st century, companies that rely on defensive antidiscrimination programs to handle differences, or worse, ignore them, will lose opportunities for growth. With periodic inclusiveness audits, corporate executives can leverage for business success what the global economy is teaching us to appreciate as a valuable end in itself: the diversity of the workforce and our population at large.

Results of Gallup's National Survey of Workplace Inclusiveness are based on 2,014 telephone interviews conducted July 26–August 23, 2001, in English, with a randomly selected sample of employed adults (except the exclusively self-employed) in the continental United States. Results were aligned to relevant U.S. Department of Commerce estimates of demographic characteristics. For results based on a sample of this size, one can say with 95% confidence that the margin of sampling error for percentage estimates is not greater than plus or minus three percentage points.

See Related Articles
"Feedback for Real" (page 7)
"Taking Feedback to the Bottom Line" (page 16)

UPEND THE TREND

March 15, 2002

The longer workers stay in their jobs, the more disheartened they become

Meet Joe the company man. Joe has been with the company for nearly 25 years. While in high school, he worked summers in the mailroom. During college, he helped out the analysts as a researcher. And when he graduated from college, he became an analyst. From there, he moved up to associate, and now a wife and two kids later, Joe is a vice president of the company.

But here's a secret: You would think that loyalty to one company for so many years would be a sure sign that Joe is a happy employee. But Joe hates his job. And he's not alone.

Through analysis of its database of 1.4 million employees in 66 countries, Gallup researchers have identified an inverse relationship between employee engagement, or the degree to which a worker is fulfilled by his or her job, and length of service, or the number of years he or she has been with the company. That means that, for most employees, the first year on the job is their best. It's downhill from there for the worker and for the company as well, because disengaged employees are a drag on profit, sales, and overall satisfaction among customers. (Gallup measures engagement through the Q^{12}, a 12-item survey that asks employees to rate the quality of their workplace.)

Frankly, this finding surprised Gallup researchers. We expected to see an increasing sense of belonging over time. New hires, we figured, would be tentative — unsure of what to expect from their jobs, their managers, and their coworkers. But we assumed that their uncertainty would diminish as time passed, and companies would see engagement ratings rise as managers helped new workers identify their talents, learn skills, and move into roles that drew on their particular strengths. But that's not what happens.

The problem, it turns out, is this: Though companies may recognize how crucial it is to engage their workers and may even acknowledge that it must be an ongoing process, the essential principles of employee engagement have not become ingrained in management practices. It's one thing to accept that employees aren't interchangeable cogs in a wheel, but it's quite another to make sure that every part of an organization is set up to appreciate their specific talents and to direct those talents to best serve the company's objectives.

Clearly, the inverse relationship between engagement and length of service suggests a disconnect between how businesses intend to treat their workers and how workers feel about their jobs. That implies that much of the time and money companies invest in developing their employees and managers may be counterproductive. Instead of honoring and capitalizing on the strengths of employees, companies continually remind workers of their shortcomings through training programs that focus on fixing an employee's weaknesses. And this can lead to a disengaged workforce.

Great managers drive engagement up over time by developing employees around their strengths. They do this by providing employees with a clear mission and by helping them think about how to apply their strengths to those outcomes. The best managers figure out strategies for managing a weakness so that it isn't a barrier to achieving the outcome.

Take Bill, a supervisor in the claims department of an insurance company. After three years as a supervisor, Bill felt that he had slowly become less engaged, and he was close to leaving the company. He was constantly being criticized by his manager for not spending enough time with his staff. Although Bill did a great job with the claims work, his manager continued to focus on this one shortcoming. Just as Bill was ready to quit, he got a new manager.

The new manager asked for a meeting at which Bill confessed that although he liked the people on his staff, he was having difficulty finding time to connect with them. The only advice he had ever received from his old boss was to try harder. The new manager asked Bill to describe some of the things he did each day. He quickly discovered that Bill was a list maker who zeroed in on his list every day until each item was checked off. His new manager's simple solution was to add one staff member's name to the top of that list each day. Bill's job was to check in on that person before the end of the day to see how things were going. This worked beautifully.

Today, two years later, Bill is still with the company and feeling more engaged than ever.

The new manager helped Bill move from being disengaged to being fully engaged in his work. But the manager is not the only one who bears responsibility for capitalizing on each person's strengths. Since fit, or positioning someone based on their strengths, is about identifying organizational needs and exercising employee strengths, it's also up to the employee to figure out how best to apply his or her talents to become more fully engaged at work.

For instance, as a territory manager for Stryker Medical, Tom Dillis sells hospital equipment in the Pittsburgh area. He's good at it, he knows it, and he recognizes why his strengths account for his success. "My strength is my ability to form personal relationships," says Dillis, "and I use that strength with my customers." For many workers like Dillis, understanding personal strengths raises engagement. And once employees know what they do best, they can guide their managers in creating the right opportunities for them.

To beat the odds of the inverse relationship between employee engagement and length of service, make sure your managers understand the idea of human strengths. Make sure they enable every employee to identify his or her natural talents. And then don't be surprised to find that employees take pride in exercising their strengths to make their unique contributions to the organization.

If the challenges of managing human assets have taught us anything, it's that standardizing human nature doesn't work. If you want the productive talents of your employees to work for you over time, start by understanding those talents rather than quashing them.

To learn more about the Gallup Q^{12} items, see graphic "The 12 Elements of Great Managing" in "Feedback for Real" (page 7)

CREATING AN EMPLOYEE-CENTRIC
CALL CENTER

by Teresa J. Tschida

October 13, 2005

It's essential for companies to energize the people who have the most direct contact with customers

A walk through an automobile manufacturing plant can assault the senses. Thousands of moving parts whiz and whir, pieces and parts shift and shake, and the entire operation seems to be in a state of constant motion. Call centers often have an equally intense feel: They hum with the cacophony of hundreds of voices in one room, technology is running at full tilt, and there's often a rising sense of tension to match the commotion.

Managing a call center can be a lot like managing an auto manufacturing plant. There are seemingly thousands of moving parts to this complex operation, and all must be carefully tended to, from phone systems and voice-over-Internet calling to computer platforms and staffing levels, and much, much more.

But like the best auto plant supervisors, great call center managers know that the most important "moving part" is the people who work there. Managers who supervise high-performing call centers are realizing that the next step to success is focusing on human capital, because the customer experience happens one-on-one — on the phone between the customer and the agent. And for employees to interact with customers in productive, positive ways — and to keep those customers coming back — employees need to feel good about where they work and what they do.

Conversations with managers of leading call centers reveal three key factors in increasing agents' dedication, enthusiasm, and customer focus: measuring employee engagement, hiring the right managers, and keeping things fun.

1.   Measure employee engagement

Measuring the engagement level of call center employees can give management crucial insights about what helps and hinders them. Companies should take a baseline measurement to find out what hurts employee productivity, then enact change to correct any problems they uncover. According to Gallup Organization research, an improvement in worker engagement of just 5%-10% can result in an increase of approximately 1,227 to 2,454 more available call minutes per agent per year.

Another benefit to companies is that turnover decreases as engagement levels rise. For example, one Gallup client found that turnover among its least engaged employees (those in the bottom quartile, as measured by responses to a 12-item engagement survey, the Q^{12}) was about 20 percentage points higher than turnover among its most engaged employees (those in the top quartile). This difference held true for full-time and part-time employees. This can mean substantial savings in hiring and training costs — typically a major expenditure for call centers.

At the call center at ASB, a leading bank in New Zealand, listening to what employees have to say has resulted in changes that have dramatically improved the quality of life for employees. For starters, the company began asking agents what changes they wanted to see. "Many managers don't want to ask because then you might have to actually follow through," says Logan Munro, national manager of business development. "That's not how we see it. We haven't got our heads in the sand. We want to know how the environment could be made better."

One example of how ASB is doing things differently is that they removed the leader boards that flashed how many calls were holding. Now, only the call center managers — not the agents — have call displays, and it is the managers' responsibility to get the right number of agents on the phones to reduce the customer wait time. This eliminates pressure on agents so they are free to deliver quality service to the customers — a radical but effective solution for the call center industry.

2.   Hire the right managers

Managers make all the difference in creating the right kind of environment at a call center. Working as a call center agent can be a lonely position, and sitting in a cubicle with nothing but a telephone and perhaps a few photos of friends and family for hours on end can be hard on morale. But when companies hire managers who can know each employee as an individual and help them grow and develop as a team, the dynamic can change completely.

Gallup research shows that fostering the close relationships between call center location members pays off. When asked to rate the Q^{12} item "I have a best friend at work" on a scale of 1-5, locations with 10% or more employees who rated this item with a 5 were much more productive than locations with fewer than 10% of employees who rated this item a 5. Agents with the strongest response to this question answered .73 more calls per hour than their peers. This difference could result in substantial increases in productivity — and decreases in costs — for a call center.

Tom Rogers, senior department manager for Discover Financial Services, actively promotes the idea of having a best friend at work by encouraging managers to get to know their employees. At Discover Financial Services, new front-line managers attend training to learn two things: "basic management skills 101" and how to become great managers by getting to know their employees individually. The first thing newly hired managers are taught is how to build a rapport and dialogue with their direct reports by learning employees' "hot buttons" and finding out what their best day at work would look like. "Establishing a relationship with your employees comes before everything else," Rogers says. "That is the foundation for engagement."

When Rogers seeks new managers, he looks for applicants who understand that people are messy. "Managers who are process- or project-driven get frustrated managing people because they're more focused on efficiency and getting the job done," he says. "People are never finished — so these types don't make good managers." Instead, Rogers looks for people who are great at finding out what makes an individual tick, then developing that talent. "A manager's role is not to transform people into being different but to discuss what outcomes are needed and release [employees] to use their unique talents to reach those outcomes," he says.

For Rogers, managers can make all the difference in how employees feel about their workplace. "Most managers don't understand the significance they have in the lives of their employees, both inside and outside of work. The right kind of manager can make employees feel better when they leave to go home and feel better about coming back," he says. "They realize that every day is a day to make an impact on employees, either positively or negatively. And if that impact isn't positive, that's a day lost."

3. Don't forget the fun

Making work fun can be a great way to help employees feel good about where they work and what they do. At a call center, this can directly affect an agent's attitude and how he or she handles customers.

At ASB's call center, teams are encouraged to gather socially after work. For instance, some join in group sports such as cycling or kayaking. Attendance isn't required; employees go voluntarily. This is the "best friend" item in action. These team members are building relationships that extend beyond work — they build trusted friendships and help employees make real connections with one another.

The managers at ASB take their work — but not themselves — seriously. Recently, they dressed in pink tutus and wings, in the spirit of a team event. Munro says he could never envision a business model where employee engagement didn't matter: "We want our customers to be engaged with us, so the only way to have that is through engaged employees," he says.

The big winner: your company

Creating a more pleasant atmosphere helps employees create bonds and enjoy their workplaces that much more — an attitude boost that can have a significant impact on the level of customer service that employees provide. But ultimately, the big winners are companies, because taking these steps to create a great work atmosphere helps them retain more customers — and improve the bottom line.

AT WORK, FEELING
GOOD MATTERS

by Jerry Krueger and Emily Killham

December 8, 2005

Happy employees are better equipped to handle workplace relationships, stress, and change, according to the latest *GMJ* survey

For centuries, philosophers and social thinkers have postulated that the highest goal of human existence is to be happy. And many great thinkers have suggested that human happiness includes elements such as self-respect, material well-being, good health, meaningful work, and supportive families and communities.

Until recently, research on happiness and well-being has mainly been the bailiwick of psychologists and social scientists. But thanks to the pioneering work of researchers such as Daniel Kahneman, Ph.D., a professor of psychology and public affairs at Princeton University and winner of the 2002 Nobel Prize in economics, economists are becoming increasingly interested in the question of happiness and how it affects business performance. Kahneman states, "Business is more about emotions than most businesspeople care to admit."

Other research on happiness in the workplace suggests that worker well-being plays a major role in organizational performance. In a survey conducted by the American Psychological Association in 2004, nearly two-thirds of all respondents indicated that their work lives had a significant impact on their stress levels, while one in four had called in sick or taken a "mental health day" as a result of stress at work. What's more, healthcare expenditures are nearly 50% greater for workers who report high stress levels, according to the *Journal of Occupational and Environmental Medicine*.

Organizations that understand the connections between worker stress and health and well-being can help their employees manage stress and find balance in their work and personal lives. When they do, productivity and engagement improve.

The role of supervisors

The *Gallup Management Journal* surveyed U.S. employees to probe their perceptions of how happiness and well-being affect their job performance. Gallup researchers examined employee responses to see which factors differed most strongly among engaged employees (27% of respondents) and those who were not engaged (59%) or actively disengaged (14%).

THE THREE TYPES OF EMPLOYEES

ENGAGED employees work with passion, and they feel a profound connection to their company. They drive innovation and move the organization forward.

NOT-ENGAGED employees are essentially "checked out." They're sleepwalking through their workday, putting time — but not energy or passion — into their work.

ACTIVELY DISENGAGED employees aren't just unhappy at work; they're busy acting out their unhappiness. Every day, these workers undermine what their engaged coworkers accomplish.

Previous Gallup research — as well as results from this survey — show that supervisors play a crucial role in worker well-being and engagement. When respondents were asked to respond to the statement "My supervisor focuses on my strengths or positive characteristics," 77% of engaged workers strongly agreed with the statement. Just 23% of not-engaged and a scant 4% of actively disengaged workers strongly agreed that their supervisor focused on their strengths or positive characteristics. Interestingly, not one engaged worker disagreed with this statement.

When survey respondents were asked how they would characterize their interactions with their coworkers, 86% of engaged employees said their interactions with coworkers were always positive or mostly positive. The findings for less engaged workers showed significantly different results: 72% of not-engaged workers characterized these interactions as always or mostly positive, compared to just 45% of actively disengaged workers.

These findings indicate that a positive relationship with the supervisor has an important effect on engagement. These findings also suggest that people with higher levels of job engagement enjoy substantially more positive interactions with their coworkers than do their less engaged counterparts.

Feeling challenged?

When American employees were asked how often they feel challenged at work, a majority of engaged workers (61%) said they feel challenged very often, while 35% said they sometimes feel challenged. In contrast, just 49% of not-engaged and 24% of actively disengaged workers indicated that they very often feel challenged at work; 39% of not-engaged workers and 42% of actively disengaged workers sometimes feel challenged. It appears that while most American workers do perceive their jobs as being at least somewhat challenging, engaged employees lead the way in this respect.

But if most workers do feel challenged sometimes or very often at work, is that good or bad? To plumb this issue further, respondents were also asked how often they feel frustrated at work. Here, the differences were even more striking. Almost 4 in 10 engaged employees (39%) indicated that they rarely or never feel frustrated at work, while only 13% very often feel frustrated. In contrast, 6 in 10 actively disengaged workers and 26% of not-engaged employees said they very often feel frustrated. These responses suggest that while engaged workers do feel challenged at work, they view these challenges in a much more positive light than do less engaged workers.

The *GMJ* also wanted to find out if workers' feelings of self-worth had an effect on their engagement. They do. When asked how difficult it would be for their employer to replace them, 54% of disengaged employees said it would be extremely or somewhat difficult for their employer to replace them, compared to 76% of engaged employees. Engaged workers also felt significantly more secure at their workplaces: 54% of engaged workers felt more secure at work than they did a year ago, but only 36% of not-engaged workers and just 18% of actively disengaged workers agreed that they felt more secure at work than they did a year ago.

Taking stress home

To probe the connection between happiness at work and happiness outside the office, the survey asked respondents how much happiness they experience at work. The contrast in responses given by workers in each engagement group was quite noticeable. A clear majority of engaged workers — 86% — said they very often felt happy while at work. Among low-engagement respondents, only 11% of actively disengaged and 48% of not-engaged employees stated that they, too, were very often happy at work.

In response to the question "How much of the happiness you experience overall would you say comes from your work life?" 45% of engaged employees said they get a great deal of their overall happiness from their work life, compared to just 19% of not-engaged and 8% of actively disengaged employees. These findings suggest that while most workers experience varying degrees of happiness and well-being at work, engaged workers get the most from these feelings.

Not surprisingly, engaged workers also reported higher levels of overall life satisfaction. Five in 10 engaged workers (53%) strongly agreed that they had gotten the important things they want in their lives, compared to just 13% of actively disengaged workers; and 44% of engaged employees strongly agreed that the conditions of their lives were excellent, in contrast to just 9% of actively disengaged workers.

Negative feelings at work also seem to spill over into actively disengaged workers' home lives. The survey asked respondents if they had three or more days in the past month when work stress caused them to behave poorly with friends or family members. More than half (54%) of actively disengaged workers and 31% of not-engaged workers answered yes to this question, while just 17% of engaged workers answered yes. These results are similar to those reported in previous surveys.

The results of the *GMJ* Employee Engagement Index survey show a strong relationship between worker happiness and workplace engagement. Happy and engaged employees are much more likely to have a positive relationship with their boss, are better equipped to handle new challenges and changes, feel they are more valued by their employers, handle stress more effectively, and are much more satisfied with their lives.

Results of this survey are based on nationally representative samples of about 1,000 employed adults aged 18 and older. Interviews were conducted by telephone October 2000–May 2005 by The Gallup Organization. For results based on samples of this size, one can say with 95% confidence that the error attributable to sampling and other random effects could be plus or minus three percentage points. For findings based on subgroups, the sampling error would be greater.

See Related Articles
"What Were They Thinking?" (page 84)
"Are You Happy Now?" (page 90)

YOUR JOB MAY BE
KILLING YOU

Interviewed by Jennifer Robison

April 13, 2006

Workplace stress apparently can be linked to heart disease. A leading management expert explores this and other astonishing findings that connect workplace disengagement to health problems.

A *GMJ* Q&A with James K. Harter, coauthor of "Manage Your Human Sigma" (*Harvard Business Review*, July-August 2005)

The high cost of health insurance has prodded many American businesses to use creative strategies to encourage healthier habits among employees, from on-campus gyms and weight-loss programs to healthy food in the cafeteria; some businesses even employ on-site nurses.

But wellness programs can't be mandated, nor can good health. There's only so much an organization can do to promote healthy habits among employees. Furthermore, it's an uphill battle: As workers age, they become more expensive to insure and treat. But recent research suggests that businesses may be overlooking an important cause of ill health and high insurance costs: workplace stress.

We all know that stress can be hard on one's health, but recent research suggests it can actually be deadly. James K. Harter, Ph.D., Gallup's chief scientist of workplace management and well-being, has been studying well-being and the workplace for the past 20 years, and some of the recent research on the workplace and health has astonished even him. One finding that has grabbed his attention: Workplace stress apparently can be linked to heart disease — the number-one cause of death in American men and women over 35 — in a large proportion of workers. Worse yet, heart disease in these employees is separate from other health factors, such as weight, diet, smoking, or family history.

Considering the billions of dollars business invests in health insurance and the negative impact on revenue from lost productivity and absenteeism due to employee illness, reducing stress should be a crucial focus for any organization. Dr. Harter thinks that there's an often-overlooked answer: workplace engagement. He bases his theory on what Gallup research has uncovered about the connection between the quality of the workplace and stress and what scientists are learning about stress and illness. In this interview, Dr. Harter discusses the connection between health, engagement, and profitability — and what managers can do to increase all three. Read on — it'll do your heart good.

GMJ: What effect does physical well-being have on psychological well-being in the workplace?

Dr. Harter: Well, there have been a few studies on that, and researchers are finding that there's a significant interaction between work stress and health. In other words, if people are in an ongoing work situation that is negative or stressful, they have a higher potential for negative health consequences.

There's still a lot of work to do to understand the connection between work stress and health problems. That's why we need to dig into it and study it in more depth, so we can help organizations understand why doing what you do every day has an effect on worker health.

We already know that engagement is related to organizational outcomes like profitability and workgroup productivity, retention, and absenteeism — all of which have an impact on the bottom line of an organization. So understanding the linkages between well-being, health, and engagement is particularly important. I think we could understand that at an even more granular level as we learn more about psychobiology.

GMJ: So what are the relationships between health, stress, and engagement?

Harter: Scientists in our field are finding very substantial relationships. People who are engaged in their work have much lower self-reported stress than those who are disengaged.

A recent study in Germany, reported in *Psychosomatic Medicine*, for example, suggests that cortisol levels are higher among people with high self-reported levels of stress at work in comparison to people with lower self-reported stress. Cortisol, which is secreted by the adrenal glands, is a hormone necessary for the functioning of almost every one of our body parts. It's released in response to physical or psychological stress. Too much or too little leads to a variety of physical health symptoms and disease states. Extreme stress causes higher than needed levels of cortisol to be released.

Studying cortisol levels in the body is one way scientists can objectively measure stress and its consequences to one's physiology. In particular, the research in Germany revealed connections between chronic work stress and morning cortisol levels. People with high stress and high levels of cortisol are more likely to miss days of work and will probably be less productive each day.

We also know that people with poor work environments report more stress. If you're not as engaged in your work, you're less likely to be productive, and you're less likely to help the organization achieve the outcomes it wants to achieve. You may be less able to function in a team context.

We don't know yet if stress causes disengagement or if stress is a result of disengagement. There's a lot to study. But research suggests that the quality of the workplace can have a direct impact on the stress that people feel, which subsequently affects cortisol levels, which could then contribute to health problems like heart disease. It isn't a one-to-one formula, but the workplace and stress seem inseparable. There are many potential ramifications for organizations, including healthcare costs and lost productivity.

GMJ: So how stressed is work making us?

Harter: In the United States, 30% of the working population reports that there have been three or more days in the last month when the stress of work has caused them to behave poorly with family or friends. Among actively disengaged employees, an alarming 54% agreed that work stress had caused them to behave poorly with family or friends, while only 17% of engaged employees reported that stress had caused them to behave poorly. The percentages are similarly high in other countries.

GMJ: What are the linkages between stress, cortisol, and heart disease?

Harter: There's an interesting study from England that was recently reported in *Archives of Internal Medicine*. Researchers looked at 6,442 men in civil service departments who had no prevalent coronary heart disease at the baseline of the study. The researchers measured various aspects of the work environment directly related to quality of management, including getting criticized unfairly by their boss, getting information from their boss, how often their boss was willing to listen to their problems, and how often they received praise for their work, things like that.

Then they tracked the incidence of coronary heart disease for an average of 8.7 years and found a 30% lower likelihood of coronary heart disease for employees with positive perceptions of their work environment compared to those with unfavorable perceptions of their work environment. The findings remained consistent even when the researchers controlled for age, ethnicity, marital status, educational attainment, socio-economic position, cholesterol level, obesity, hypertension, smoking, alcohol consumption, and physical activity.

This 30% difference in coronary heart disease incidence is just shockingly important when you consider that Gallup research, which covers 4.5 million employees in 112 countries, indicates that fewer than one in every two employees feels strongly that they have a supervisor at work who cares about them as a person. And fewer than one in every three employees feels strongly that they have someone at work who encourages their development.

GMJ: So a major explanation for the 30% difference in who got heart disease was a bad workplace?

Harter: The research would seem to suggest that. Thirty percent is a much higher percentage than I would have guessed. The questions that people will instinctively ask are: Is the difference just due to the fact that these people have difficult lives in general? Don't they take care of themselves? Are these people just fatalistically flawed in some way? But the researchers actually controlled for the many other known predictors of heart disease. They found that in addition to all these other factors that are typically examined, the workplace environment contributed 30% to the risk of heart disease. That's a lot.

GMJ: How many people are affected by heart disease?

Harter: According to various sources, every minute, one American dies from a coronary event related to coronary heart disease. Thirteen million Americans have heart disease, and many more are at risk of getting it. And it's expensive to treat: Heart disease costs the American economy billions of dollars a year. And it's the leading cause of death for all Americans 35 and older, men and women.

GMJ: So what control do managers have? What can managers do to reduce these risks?

Harter: They can do a lot to prevent bad stress, the kind that can be a contributing factor to heart disease — or, as the study in England suggests, the kind that can *cause* it in some people. Gallup research has found that managers have direct influence over whether people are praised, whether people feel appreciated, whether people get the information they need to do their jobs. Managers can create environments that facilitate independent thinking and teamwork. These are all factors that managers often control — and even if they don't have direct control over them, they can influence people who do have control of them. So managers control or can influence the factors that create productive employees; they also control or can affect the things that keep employees engaged, lower employees' stress, and can keep health costs down in their companies.

GMJ: Well, that's kind of a God-like position, isn't it?

Harter: Kind of. We've known that managers are profoundly important in the workplace. For example, when we do research for the first time in an organization, we find wide variation in engagement levels from workgroup to workgroup, and we also find wide variation in productivity from workgroup to workgroup. Some day, I think we'll know how much variation exists on things like cortisol levels and heart disease risk and other factors; this early research indicates that managers may have a direct bearing on that as well. We *do* know that engaged employees have 27% fewer unexcused absences than actively disengaged ones, and that's a big sum in lost salary — salary that isn't turned into productivity in organizations.

GMJ: So what can you do if you think that your manager is giving you a heart attack — literally?

Harter: Well, you can either realize the importance of the relationship with your manager and confront the issues that are causing stress in your life, or you can get a different manager. You might realize that your relationship with your manager affects things other than just your work. It may affect your health. That may stimulate some people to redefine their relationship with their manager or to find a different manager. In fact, many employees do find another manager: Employee turnover is substantially higher for poor versus good managers.

Organizations need to take the workplace environment and the quality of employee/manager relationships seriously, because the health of employees may have an enormous effect on the bottom line in lost productivity, absenteeism, and insurance costs.

GMJ: What should senior executives do if they know some of the managers un-der them are creating disengaged employees? It might be difficult to go to the CEO and say, "I think some of our managers are killing people."

Harter: [Laughs] I'm laughing because it's such a strong statement, but it could be true. One of the things we found is that there is a cascade effect in organizations. If you're a manager of managers, your level of engagement has a relationship to the level of engagement of the people you manage, which then has a relationship to the engagement of the people they man-age. So if you're a manager of managers, you can set the tone. You can have an effect on whether the culture is positive — whether the culture pro-motes engagement. Through example, you can show that it's important to praise people when they do good work or that it's important to give people the right tools for the task when you ask them to do something.

As a side note, we found that the Q^{12} item with the highest relationship to stress at work might seem like the most boring of the items — "I have the materials and equipment I need to do my work right." [The Q^{12} is Gallup's 12-item employee engagement survey.] But if you think about it, that statement provides important clues to employee engagement and employee stress. Think about the last time you were asked to complete an important task, but you weren't given the materials you needed to do the work right. You probably thought something like, "Okay, they asked me to do this job, and I want to do it, but they're not giving me what I need to do it. They're tying my hands." That can cause enormous stress.

So I think that managers of managers can have a direct bearing on pro-moting employee engagement — and preventing stress — because they're in charge of getting employees what they need and providing other crucial kinds of employee support. How they manage their managers sets an ex-ample for how the rest of the organization should function.

GMJ: A lot of companies have wellness programs — gyms and diet programs are two examples. Do you think that programs like these have as much or more impact on health than increasing workplace engagement would? If you have a limited amount of dollars, where do you put them?

Harter: I think both are important. I can't tell you which has more impor-tance because the research has shown that both are important, and we're still learning about how each one contributes independently, but they in-teract considerably. Both require that someone take action. I think that there are ways that organizations can encourage people to take care of themselves. There's a lot of potential for creative thinking in this area.

In any case, whether you're a manager in a position to increase engagement in the workforce or an employee who can influence engagement within your own role, you need to take engagement — and stress — seriously. Executives and managers want to help their company reach their financial goals, and many employees do as well. But to tell people that the quality of the workplace may affect their risk of coronary heart disease . . . well. It hits home a little quicker. And that's one area where scientists should focus future research.

Additional Reading

Schlotz, W., Hellhammer, J., Schulz, P., and Stone, A. (2004) "Perceived work overload and chronic worrying predict weekend-weekday differences in the cortisol awakening response." *Psychosomatic Medicine, 66*, 207-214.

Kivimäki, M., Ferrie, J., Brunner, E., Head, J., Shipley, M., Vehtera, J., and Marmot, M. (2005). "Justice at work and reduced risk of coronary heart disease among employees." *Archives of Internal Medicine, 165*, 2245-2251.

See Related Articles
"Feedback for Real" (page 7)
"Taking Feedback to the Bottom Line" (page 16)
"At Work, Feeling Good Matters" (page 36)

To learn more about the levels of employee engagement, see graphic "The Three Types of Employees" in "At Work, Feeling Good Matters" (page 36)

CAN MANAGERS ENGAGE
UNION EMPLOYEES?

by Steve Crabtree

May 11, 2006

Business leaders offer insights into overcoming labor-management conflicts

If management takes a more active role in engaging its unionized workers, does that reduce the need for organized labor? Will unions view systematic efforts by management to keep employees happy and fulfilled as an attempt to undermine their own support? If so, how can companies defuse the situation by working *with* unions to support employee engagement?

Executives and managers tackled these and other questions at a recent Gallup roundtable discussion on engaging union employees, which took place in Washington, D.C. The 25 participants came from companies in a variety of industries, but all either had a large proportion of union employees or must account for the influence of unions in their labor market.

Public attitudes toward unions

James K. Harter, Ph.D., Gallup's chief scientist for workplace management and well-being, got the event started with a review of recent Gallup data on labor unions. He stated that Americans are less likely to belong to labor unions than they were 50 years ago. In the 1940s and 1950s, about one in six Americans told Gallup pollsters they belonged to a union; today the number is about one in ten. Unions still enjoy public support, although Americans' likelihood to say they approve of them has also declined somewhat in recent decades. Currently, 58% of Americans say they approve of unions, while 33% disapprove. A slight majority, 52%, say they've tended to sympathize with unions in labor disputes over the last two or three years, while 34% say they've sympathized with the companies.

From a manager's perspective, the crucial question is how the presence of a union colors his or her relationships with employees. Gallup's data suggest that union employees are, on average, less engaged than non-union employees. And, the percentage of actively disengaged employees is considerably higher among unionized than non-unionized employees in the same company.

In some cases, the sizeable differences may be because union employees tend to have different roles within the company than other employees. For example, at a power utility, the electricians may be unionized but not the administrative staff. However, the roundtable participants agreed that union membership itself can contribute to an "us versus them" mentality that can also diminish employees' sense of rapport with their companies. One participant, who said her company's approach was to partner with unions, said that "There are more adversarial relationships in some areas, and those are reflected in our employee engagement scores."

In discussing Gallup's data with roundtable participants, Harter stressed two other points. The first, gleaned from a Gallup Poll of the U.S. working population conducted in October 2005, is that unionized employees are more likely to say they will stay with their companies throughout their careers, but they're slightly less likely to recommend their companies to family and friends as a place to work. In other words, the sense of security their union affiliation gives them may encourage unionized employees to stick around — but that feeling doesn't translate into a greater emotional attachment to their jobs.

The second point is that the relationship between engagement and productivity is equal in union and non-union environments. Gallup's research with companies suggests that it may be harder to engage employees in a union environment, but engagement has just as profound a relationship to productivity in union and non-union environments.

Key insights

The averages notwithstanding, Harter notes there are many unionized workgroups that rank highly in Gallup's database of workplace engagement studies. Though it can be a challenge to build strong emotional connections with unionized employees, many companies do it. The roundtable discussions produced a number of useful insights into how they pull it off:

- **Make the engagement-building process open, inclusive, and non-threatening.** If union employees perceive an employee engagement survey and subsequent impact-planning processes as secretive and threatening rather than constructive, the effort is essentially doomed from the start, the roundtable group said. Employees are less likely to provide unbiased responses, and the union is more likely to do whatever it can to keep its members from participating.

When a government agency decided to focus on engaging its front-line employees as part of a broader effort to raise customer satisfaction, one of the first issues it needed to address was to ensure that the process was open and non-threatening. "[The union's] biggest concern was that the surveys not be used to promote a witch hunt," said an analyst attending the roundtable. "They wanted to know it was part of a learning environment, that it was non-threatening." Once that orientation was clearly established, the union threw its weight behind the agency's efforts to improve engagement.

- **Involve union officials in the survey and resulting change processes.** The same government agency went on to win union officials' full support by offering them input in the development process of the employee engagement survey. Beyond the survey's core engagement questions, additional items were negotiated between the agency and the union so both had a stake in the survey's outcome. The survey has been a success, the agency's representative said; the resulting impact plans have boosted employee engagement, and customer satisfaction is slowly but steadily rising.

Several of the roundtable participants also mentioned that it's important to emphasize that the company is not trying to undermine the union's role. Attempts to raise engagement in a union workplace should include close communication with union representatives, and, ideally, their active support is enlisted.

As one participant stated, "That all sounds nice," but union officials are often highly skeptical of, and sometimes downright hostile to, employee surveys of any kind. How can companies overcome that resistance? One manager suggested that safety concerns can be a good initial connecting point. Gallup research shows a strong relationship between employee engagement and workplace safety in a variety of settings. "The relationship between engagement and [workplace] safety is hard to argue with," the manager said. "It's an easy starting place for agreement, which can then flow into other areas."

But participants also sounded a note of caution against allowing the union to hijack the engagement program for the union's own purposes. They underscored the importance of being highly informed about both the union's local and national agenda — and realistic about its politics. Though it's seldom easy, one participant said, managers who understand union leaders' point of view may be able to use employee engagement as a rallying point to build trust between the company, its employees, and the union.

- **Use action planning to develop new lines of communication with employees.** One reason union-management relations can be contentious is that it's hard to get everyone to agree on what's best for workers. Several of the roundtable participants described how their companies have used engagement efforts as opportunities to find new ways to let their employees speak for themselves.

One of the roundtable participants is an executive at a large service-based company in an industry where employee burnout and turnover tend to be very high. Yet the organization maintains high levels of employee engagement and, in fact, has been able to halt several union attempts to organize employees at its facilities. The company's leadership recognizes that employee engagement is particularly critical in their industry, the executive said. Managers conduct regular action planning with all employees to address their facilities' engagement levels.

What's more, executive-level leaders use that action-planning process as an opportunity to meet directly with groups of hourly employees in different locations. The resulting dialogue gives leaders powerful insights and employees a strong sense of connection to the company. As some participants said, being able to voice their opinions about important matters like health benefits and retirement planning can create valuable champions of engagement among front-line managers and employees. "Listening is important to them," said the service industry executive, "and the outcome is important to us."

Perhaps most importantly, as one participant said, using engagement programs can open up new lines of communication and increase the flow of creative ideas that serve to keep the organization vital. That participant, a manager at a large power utility, described special intranet sites designed to enable all employees to express their opinions and maintain a dialogue with the company's leadership. "The more engaged groups are submitting more ideas," she said, "and more of those ideas are being implemented. We've found that engagement fosters innovation throughout the organization."

- **Recognize that unions can help the company increase employee engagement.** The presence of labor unions can pose a challenge to companies that intend to raise employee engagement, but it may also present opportunities. When union-management partnerships can come together to focus on aspects of engagement, such as growth and development opportunities, all employees may benefit.

Best of all, the devotion some unions inspire in their members can serve as a model for companies seeking to achieve a similar connection with employees — particularly, as one roundtable participant said, when it comes to communicating a clear, consistent purpose. "People want to belong to something they can believe in," the participant said. "The organization needs to talk about purpose, mission, and values — and then align them with behaviors. That's fundamental to engagement, and historically, unions have done better at that [than businesses]."

To learn more about the levels of employee engagement, see graphic "The Three Types of Employees" in "At Work, Feeling Good Matters" (page 36)

DISCOVERING THE ELEMENTS
OF GREAT MANAGING   *Interviewed by Jennifer Robison*

December 14, 2006

How fundamental aspects of employee psychology interact to drive success

A *GMJ* Q&A with Rodd Wagner and James K. Harter, authors of
12: The Elements of Great Managing

H.L. Mencken wrote: "There is always a well-known solution to every human problem — neat, plausible, and wrong." A dispiriting thought, to be sure. It would be so much easier to think that there's one pat answer, or a single silver bullet, that could solve every problem.

Forget it. Mencken was right. There isn't a neat, simple solution to any human problem, let alone the problems of managing humans. That's because business is an intricate dynamic, involving different people doing disparate things to achieve many goals. And if finding a single answer to the problems of people management is difficult, it's futile to think there's a single element that will make that complex dynamic perform at peak.

The fact is, there are 12 of them.

Rather, there are 12 basic needs that all humans need fulfilled at work. They include knowing what's expected of you, receiving recognition and praise for doing a good job, and believing that your opinions count. When those needs are met, the company benefits from dramatically increased employee engagement and organizational performance. So say Gallup's Rodd Wagner and Jim Harter, Ph.D., in their book *12: The Elements of Great Managing*.

12 — the sequel to the 1999 bestseller *First, Break All the Rules* — is based on decades of Gallup research, including interviews with more than 10 million managers and employees spanning 114 countries and conducted in 41 languages. *12* explores each of the elements and shows how companies create and sustain employee engagement through profiles of great managers in industries as varied as retail, manufacturing, hospitality, healthcare, and agriculture.

But how does it work? What are the 12 elements? What do they have to do with engagement, and why does engagement affect a company so much? In this interview, the authors of *12* explain some of their findings, including why human nature will always win, why legislating processes dooms the outcome, and why praising employees yields such high profits.

GMJ: The book is called 12: The Elements of Great Managing. *Why elements, and not edicts or laws — something more concrete?*

Rodd Wagner: The choice of the word *element* was intentional. The 12 elements are interdependent; none of them stands alone, and you can't create a highly profitable, productive, safe, customer-engaging workplace by focusing on just one. Instead, the elements of great managing come together to create an engaging workplace. The more of these elements you put together, the greater the compound you create, and the better it holds together.

James K. Harter, Ph.D.: Each of these elements predicts superior performance in an individual, in a workgroup, or ultimately — if you have enough engagement — in the company itself. And the 12 items we ask to assess employee engagement pass an empirical hurdle that hundreds of other items haven't. Saying the 12 items predict performance means that there's something about human nature, some pattern to what it means to be human in the workplace, that that particular item speaks to. And that's the part that I find fascinating: For some reason, those 12 elements do a pretty comprehensive job of describing what it means to be human at work.

GMJ: Why should managers know about the elements?

Harter: Because they predict performance. Workgroups that score higher on each of those 12 items tend to have higher performance. Engagement isn't everything; marketing initiatives and product offerings, for instance, have a big impact too. But in a highly competitive world, having your employees behind you is an important differentiator.

Wagner: Engagement has the greatest payoff or greatest incremental effect on profitability. Many things affect profitability, and many of them are outside the control of the firm. Airlines get hit by higher fuel costs; companies can be affected by weather; competitors take actions that catch your company unaware. But there are long-term strategic issues that are within the company's control, and employee engagement is one of the determinants of profitability that companies can really affect.

GMJ: You mention emotions constantly in the book — in fact, you say that between human nature and company policy, human nature will always win. What part does emotion play at work?

Wagner: There seems to be a bit of a dichotomy out there. You will hear comments to the effect that "our people are our greatest asset" or "this team is going to win" that suggest that a company understands how human nature can help them. On the other hand, in many cases there is an implicit antagonism toward human nature: that it needs to be harnessed, or legislated, or restricted and remolded, because if people are left to themselves, they'll do things that won't advance the company.

Harter: Yet when you delve into human nature, there's an awful lot that helps a company. People want to learn and grow, and to the degree that the company helps them do that, then they help the company.

People respond to praise and recognition. People enjoy having the opportunity to do the things that match their talents, and they get an intrinsic motivation and reward out of doing things that help the company. People reciprocate if they find friendships and support and encouragement at work. There's an awful lot about human nature that helps companies, yet there is skepticism about human nature from a lot of executives, and from a lot of managers.

GMJ: Why is that?

Wagner: I think it's because people are messy, and it seems messy and difficult to have to cater to people's emotions, because they seem unpredictable. But when we study great managers, it seems easy to them. They have a sincere approach to management — they're really in it for the people they manage. And for them, that makes it a lot easier than you might think.

GMJ: You studied managers in 114 countries. Why don't cultural differences contradict your findings on workplace engagement?

Harter: We saw some differences in how people respond to things; for example, how people respond to recognition differs according to the cultural norms and expectations in every country. But when you get down to what it takes to manage a worker, human beings are human beings. We found, even statistically, that how these elements sort workgroups — from productive to unproductive — is consistent across cultures.

Wagner: There are great cultural differences, but not necessarily differences in human nature. We're not all that far separated from each other in the things that make us react or that motivate us. It was interesting to see how people attribute things to their local culture that other people in other places would attribute to their local culture, but what they were really talking about was human nature.

GMJ: In the book, you say that paying people to execute a process instead of reaching an outcome is counterproductive. Can you explain that?

Harter: People want to make a difference and want to make an impact on the organization, but each person may have a different way of getting there. The best managers we studied help employees focus on the outcomes that are most important, then allow them to figure out the best way to get there.

Managers who try to legislate each step end up with workers who feel controlled and diminished, because they aren't able to put themselves into the job — they're basically being told what to do. And if you pay for process, you may not reach the goal, because the process becomes the goal. You also remove the employee's judgment and creativity, which might have helped get to the end result in a better way.

GMJ: Is it judgment or creativity that creates better processes, or both?

Wagner: Both. Companies always want their employees to take psychological ownership, to treat the company as though they owned it. Well, the real owner doesn't have to follow a manual, and the real owner gets to decide how best to take care of customers. Executives find themselves surprised that their employees aren't taking psychological ownership. Employees can't if their behavior is closely legislated.

GMJ: But I've heard executives say things like "I can't trust these people to run the cash register. How can I trust them to speak politely to a customer?"

Wagner: Then they've hired the wrong people.

Harter: Or they haven't really listened to their people. Or maybe both.

Wagner: You have to trust employees, because they are the interaction between the company and the customer. You've put them on that cash register; you've put them in the aisle of the retail store; you have entrusted them with the customer. So if you then shackle them with processes, you have handicapped them. You have to trust them, or you should get different people.

GMJ: One of the elements is recognition — that people need to be recognized for doing good work. Why is praise so important?

Wagner: One of the most pernicious thoughts out there is that paying people is praise enough. That runs quite contrary to everything we know about how humans learn and how behavior is reinforced.

People need that little dopamine surge that comes with recognition, that little tingle of excitement, fairly frequently. It's how we make sense of our world. In fact, people who don't have the proper mechanisms to release dopamine, such as people with Parkinson's disease, don't learn as quickly. Getting that little *zing* makes you want to do that thing again. When companies don't reinforce employees when they're doing the right thing, the employees' brains say, "There's nothing here, so let's move on and do something else."

GMJ: What are the financial benefits of praising employees?

Wagner: First, it doesn't cost that much. Research by Jim [Harter] and other scientists found that employees don't necessarily need a plaque or a trophy or something hugely expensive — unexpected words of praise are quite powerful. They don't cost anything, and people are then motivated to do the things that the company needs them to do, again and again. You can't buy recognition.

GMJ: Do you have to keep upping the ante with praise — a pat on the back, then a plaque, then a dinner? Or do people just need a steady drip of dopamine?

Harter: It depends on the person. Some want recognition in front of a group, while others are terrified by that. It's up to the manager to listen to each person to find out what's right for him or her, while thinking about what high performance is for that person.

But managers have failed much more often, not on giving too much recognition, but on giving too little. The ratio of positive to negative interactions needs to be high, about 5 to 1. If you get beyond 13 to 1, it may seem a little Pollyanna-ish, but no one ever does get to that level.

One of the things that bugs me is when managers ask someone else what their employees want: "What's the praise I ought to give my employees?"

Ask *them* what's meaningful to them. Buy them a cup of coffee and ask them, because they will tell you.

To learn more about the Gallup Q^{12} items, see graphic "The 12 Elements of Great Managing" in "Feedback for Real" (page 7)

CUSTOMER

THE CONSTANT CUSTOMER   *by Alec Appelbaum*

June 17, 2001

Holding onto a customer has never been harder — or more important. Proprietary Gallup research shows that the key to wooing customers isn't price or even product. It's emotion. Here's how to win over fickle customers and make them love you for life.

Within a five-minute walk of my Greenwich Village apartment, at least five restaurants serve strong coffee and excellent sandwiches at low prices. CEOs could learn a lot from the reasons I keep visiting my favorite — even if it's overflowing with customers every weekend. (It's true that multinational corporations have more moving parts than coffee shops, but bear with me.) My favorite place doesn't advertise, offer membership cards, or dole out rewards for frequent visits. But the waitresses candidly suggest the best quesadilla fillings, the owner has bused our table, and a waitress once let my wife borrow a cell phone when I was out and she'd forgotten her keys. It's not just that I know I'll get good value and a pleasant experience every time I'm there. I trust the staff with my time, my money, and my friends. I'm beyond satisfied with this brand: I miss it when I go too long without it. I'm attached.

Corporations have spent billions of dollars trying to make customers as loyal to their products and services as I am to that coffee shop. Ever since consumers on market research panels began weighing in on everything from cereal crunchiness to shampoo viscosity, companies have tried to tailor products to meet shoppers' preferences. More recently, as the Internet and other channels of electronic commerce became common market research tools in the mid '90s, businesses have tracked what individual customers buy — and don't buy. Now, with all that information at their fingertips, executives have been trying to figure out which business practices make faithful customers loyal. Yet an understanding of why customers stick with a brand is still evolving. Mainly, managers know what they don't know.

Today, the search for the ties that bind customers to brands has taken on fresh urgency. The equity markets are volatile, and venture investors are chastened, so loyal customers represent a company's best prospects for pumping capital into a business. Unlike stock appreciation, which can fluctuate wildly over the short and medium term, loyal customers can be counted on to build a solid base of revenues as well as to expand profits.

Such customers are likely to try new offerings and to provide strong word of mouth for a brand, saving companies advertising and product-assessment costs. So it's not surprising that customer loyalty ranked first among the management concerns of CEOs in this year's Conference Board survey, a widely watched gauge of hot-button issues across a range of industries.

But what is it that actually makes customers loyal? Simply satisfying them certainly isn't enough. Implicit in management legend W. Edwards Deming's call for continuous improvement — articulated in his 1986 work *Out of the Crisis* — is the idea that a customer who is satisfied today may have a different set of needs tomorrow. Since then, and especially in the past five years, marketing scholarship has established many times over that satisfaction scores alone fail to predict how customers will actually behave.

Part of the problem is that satisfaction scores measure only past experience. The American Customer Satisfaction Index (ACSI), for instance, plots whether a customer thought she received good value — whether, for example, a computer is as functional or a hotel room as clean as she expected it to be. The index reflects a rational assessment at a particular moment. But it fails to capture either the customer's intentions — whether she would recommend the brand to others — or emotions. People stay faithful to brands that earn both their rational trust and their deeply felt affection. That dynamic, which Gallup has studied extensively, turns out to be a better predictor of behavior than consumer satisfaction measures alone.

Return for a moment to my coffee shop. Shortly after I moved to the neighborhood, my wife and I tried a similarly priced competitor that had delicious omelets, fresh bagels, and attentive counter service; I would have given the place a high satisfaction score. Yet I've hardly ever been back. My emotional attachment to my favorite place — how it makes me feel, how I interact with its staff — matters more to me than whether I get better value elsewhere.

In the past few years, a marketing discipline has evolved to capture this distinction. Frederick F. Reichheld, author of the widely read *The Loyalty*

Effect: The Hidden Force Behind Growth, Profits, and Lasting Value, showed that making loyalists out of just 5% more customers would lead, on average, to an increase in profit per customer of between 25% and 100%. Reichheld's analysis showed that the cost of acquiring new customers was five times the cost of servicing established ones. The implication is that managers who depend on all manner of snazzy products and flashy ad campaigns to lure new buyers will always be playing catch-up with companies that concentrate on keeping established customers happy. Ever since, marketers have stopped looking for satisfied customers and have begun focusing on loyal ones. But how does a company forecast who will be loyal and who won't?

That's where Gallup's new 11-question metric of "customer engagement," called CE^{11}, comes in. CE^{11} measures rational formulations of loyalty according to three key factors (L^3): overall satisfaction, intent to repurchase, and intent to recommend. But it also adds eight measures of emotional attachment (A^8). "The total score, which reflects overall customer engagement, or CE^{11}, is the most powerful predictor of customer loyalty we know," says Gallup senior consultant John Fleming, Ph.D.

Gallup's research into the dynamics of rational loyalty (L^3) and emotional attachment (A^8) to a brand began with testimony from the customers of a world-renowned theme park. Gallup found that, despite agonizing waits for rides, high prices, and imperfect service, customers, by and large, remained loyal to the park. "Expensive food and long lines made me want to tear my hair out," said one customer, sounding exasperated with the park. "But when I looked down and saw the joy in my children's eyes, it was all worth it." That customer's emotions had trumped her reason; the brand had managed to create a sense of magic that transcended the park's shortcomings.

There is more to this, though, than just magic dust. When a brand inspires both rational loyalty and emotional attachment, customers will continually reward it with their business. Consider a Gallup study of a major hotel chain's affinity club. All members have rational incentives to spend more of their lodging dollar with the chain because they qualify for perks and discounts when they spend more. Yet some members spent more than others. Affinity club members who were strongly attached gave the chain 32% more of their total lodging dollars than did those who were not emotionally attached.

But CE[11] doesn't identify just attached customers of theme parks or luxury hotels. Its questions let customers of any product raise signs above their heads, declaring themselves the most eager buyers in the bazaar. The L^3 establishes a customer's rational disposition toward a brand. Then the A^8 captures what goes on in that customer's psyche when a product earns her confidence and coincides with something so useful or so delightful in her experience that it becomes a touchstone of her day. When L^3 and A^8 scores are high, the customer seeks out the brand even when she doesn't necessarily need to replenish her supply. The statistical science behind the A^8 captures the sequence in which that kind of emotional attachment develops.

Gallup developed the eight A^8 questions as paired indicators of four emotional states: confidence in a brand, belief in its integrity, pride in the brand, and passion for it. An analysis of responses to the questions revealed that customers develop emotional attachment to a brand in a cumulative way: Customers who agreed strongly with the first two statements of the A^8 were more likely to agree with the next two, and so on.

When customers agreed strongly with both statements about a brand's reliability — "This brand always delivers on what they promise" and "This brand is a name I can always trust" — they were demonstrating their confidence in the brand. Confidence normally precedes more intense feelings of attachment, because it determines whether a customer feels secure about a brand's utility.

A bank, for instance, will draw low scores on confidence if its monthly statements are sometimes inaccurate or if its tellers stare blankly when customers ask about the bank's investment or credit card offerings. And an offer to "fly the friendly skies" will inspire confidence only if the flight attendants remain friendly every minute the customer spends in the sky.

To build confidence, then, a manager needs to strive to keep a brand's marketing message in sync with the product or service the company delivers. Gallup found that among members of a hotel affinity club who said they got less from their membership experience than they thought they would when they enrolled, not quite 1 in 25 was confident in the brand. Compare that to the customers who said the membership matched their expectations: 1 in 4 was confident. The lesson is clear: When customers get less than they expect, they're unlikely to have confidence in the company — and we've seen that confidence is a precursor to long-term loyalty and emotional attachment.

$L^3 + A^8 = CE^{11}$: QUESTIONS THAT GET AT THE HEART OF CUSTOMER ENGAGEMENT

Traditionally, marketing images have associated passion for a brand with only a few items — cars, beer, and jewelry. Businesses like groceries and banking rarely try to appeal to consumers' passion. That's a mistake. Gallup surveyed 3,611 customers in six industries, using its CE^{11} metric. CE^{11} measures three key factors pertaining to a customer's rational assessment of a brand but also adds eight questions on emotional attachment. Across diverse industries, the proportion of emotionally attached consumers is remarkably consistent.

L^3

- Overall, how satisfied are you with [brand]?

- How likely are you to continue to choose/repurchase [brand]?

- How likely are you to recommend [brand] to a friend/associate?

A^8

CONFIDENCE

- [Brand] is a name I can always trust.

- [Brand] always delivers on what they promise.

INTEGRITY

- [Brand] always treats me fairly.

- If a problem arises, I can always count on [brand] to reach a fair and satisfactory resolution.

PRIDE

- I feel proud to be a [brand] customer.

- [Brand] always treats me with respect.

PASSION

- [Brand] is the perfect company for people like me.

- I can't imagine a world without [brand].

EMOTIONAL ATTACHMENT (A^8) IS CONSISTENT ACROSS INDUSTRIES (EXCEPT AIRLINES)

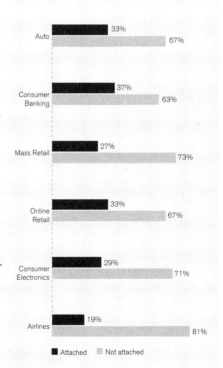

The CE^{11} items are protected by copyright of Gallup, Inc., 1994-2000. All rights reserved.

Belief in a brand's integrity — gauged by whether a customer feels fairly treated and by whether she expects a fair resolution to any problems she encounters — follows. That belief is reinforced when a customer feels she is dealing with a company that is not only competent and forthright, but also fair and ethical. It can be instilled, for instance, by a salesperson who steers the customer to a product she says she wants instead of dumbly pushing the most expensive merchandise. Similarly, if a desk clerk botches a room reservation, he should know to offer an upgrade or some other token of apology.

When such practices become commonplace — when a customer can count on getting reliable service and when she knows that someone will make amends if she doesn't — then she feels proud of the brand. (Pride, in Gallup's classification, reflects the customer's strong sense that the brand treats her with respect and that she, in turn, feels good about using it.) High scores on pride questions indicate that a customer has crossed a threshold of commitment to the brand. We can all think of brands with which customers proudly identify — luxury brands such as Rolls Royce, as well as discount brands such as the Sam's Club unit of Wal-Mart. It's no coincidence that both enjoy reputations for treating customers with deference and respect.

When a customer wears a logo on her backpack or drops a brand name in a cocktail party conversation, she has reached the highest rung of emotional attachment: passion. Customers with passion strongly agree with the statements "This brand is the perfect company for people like me" and "I can't imagine a world without this brand." They would never take a trip to the beach house without stocking up on their favorite soda; they will travel a little farther to find their preferred motor oil. That level of attachment corresponds to growing revenues: One Gallup study, for instance, demonstrated that a mid-size bank could add $265 million to its total of customer balances on deposit just by drawing higher attachment scores from 50,000 more customers.

Passionate consumers have been known to wage public campaigns protesting a change in a soft drink formula, indicating a depth of commitment that moves beyond loyal to fanatic. And that level of passion can by sparked by goods as everyday as hiking boots or potato chips. Indeed, Gallup research across a range of industries — from online retail to airlines to banks — found that roughly 1 in 10 customers in every industry is passionate.

So the excuse of being in a "boring" business no longer absolves managers from bonding with customers who make brands integral to their lives.

BONDING CUSTOMERS WITH BRANDS ACROSS INDUSTRIES

No matter what the industry, there's an emotional element to how a customer interacts with a brand. Consider the case of Southwest Airlines (below). Five times as many of its customers were fully engaged as were customers of United. The same dynamic occurs across many industries, including retailing, among competitors with similar prices and products.

Each of these brand pairs seems interchangeable from the point of view of traditional customer satisfaction measures. But when emotional investment is considered, winners emerge regarding the likelihood of attracting lifelong customers. — John Fleming, Ph.D.

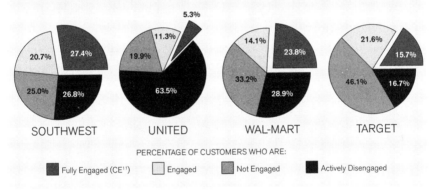

PERCENTAGE OF CUSTOMERS WHO ARE:

Fully Engaged (CE[11])   Engaged   Not Engaged   Actively Disengaged

When a brand communicates that it deserves consumers' trust, it can draw passionate believers even in a reviled industry. That's the lesson of Southwest Airlines. In another Gallup study, Southwest saw 27% of its customers fully engaged, compared with 7% for Delta and 5% for United. You'd expect a customer to feel emotionally attached to the car in his driveway (or the retailer he visits on weekends), but the airline delaying his trip home? Clearly, Southwest, like Wal-Mart, has managed to communicate an emotional appeal that its competitors lack — an appeal that has relatively little to do with the specific natures of their respective markets.

It's no coincidence that both brands focus on service in ways that can make an often frustrating experience pleasant for customers. Southwest, with its wisecracking flight attendants and small-city jet service, cultivates an image of fun in an industry that's full of delays and inconvenience. Wal-Mart banished the surly clerk who haunts so many discount retailers and replaced him with a friendly greeter, often a senior citizen instead of a resentful teen. Such service features often inspire high emotional attachment because they improve the odds that a customer will experience each of the four emotional states that drive A^8 scores.

At the top of the A^8 ladder, a passionate customer can — and will — shower dollars on a brand. But on the ground, a manager has to figure out how to persuade uncommitted customers to move up the rungs of that ladder, from provisionally satisfied to rationally loyal to emotionally engaged. Gallup's research has revealed three powerful ways managers can reach that goal: 1) creating products that are as flawless as possible; 2) training employees to act as ambassadors of the brand; and 3) transforming problems into opportunities to please customers.

Flawlessness may seem unreachable, but practical steps can be taken to come close. For banks, flawlessness includes ATMs that always work, customer service reps who offer up-to-date information on rates, and back-office staffers who rectify errors quickly and courteously. For airlines, flawlessness means on-time performance, clean and modern aircraft, and pleasant terminals.

One way to encourage the perception of flawlessness among customers is to instill in salespeople and customer service personnel the belief that the wares they offer are as close to perfect as possible — and always improving. Actually, a manager should instill this sense in all employees; it's just that sales and customer service people have more opportunities to cultivate it among customers.

Another strategic lever that emerged from Gallup's research calls on managers to direct front-line staffers — call center operators, desk clerks, floor salespeople — to communicate fairness and respect. A surly or clueless desk clerk can sour a customer on a hotel chain, especially if that chain advertises its comfort and friendliness. Managers should also make sure that front-line employees' behaviors and the promises they make on behalf of the brand are fully aligned with the company's marketing message. When an employee clearly doesn't buy into — or even understand — a brand's promises, it's hard for customers to become convinced that the brand has integrity. If managers select, position, and train employees to delight customers and reward them for doing so, customers will become emotionally attached simply by conducting business with the brand.

The third strategic lever is perhaps the most surprising. When customers experience problems — say, a service glitch or a faulty product — a funny thing happens. Companies that deal quickly and thoroughly with customers' problems tend to arouse passion in their customers just as surely as companies that never create problems at all. Southwest Airlines' customers, for example, say the airline effectively deals with problems in 77% of cases, compared with less than 50% for the four largest carriers. As a result, nearly half of those who say they are loyal to an airline identify Southwest as their favorite.

Great companies become great by cultivating distinct brand identities. CE[11] offers an analytical tool for gauging how that brand resonates in the marketplace. It enables a company to clearly see the path from its products and services to the hearts, minds, and wallets of its customers.

WHO'S ANSWERING THE PHONE?   *by Alec Appelbaum*

September 15, 2001

Your company's fortunes hang on it. (Yes, really!)

They are the conscripts of the Information Age. Lined up headset to headset, they make pitches, take orders, and provide technical support. They get sworn at, hung up on, sometimes even thanked. But what these telephone-wielding armies really do is tell people all about your business. Never mind the Super Bowl ads or the stadium sponsorships; what gets imprinted about your brand in the hearts and minds of your customers is how they're treated during those few minutes when one of your lowest paid representatives has them on the line.

If that scares you, it should. Millions of American workers make their living on the phone, capturing or squandering goodwill countless times each day. This corps of workers is exploding, and even if many consumers don't know what a call center is — that place where row upon row of workers answer and originate calls on a company's behalf — they can hardly escape its influence. Department of Labor data show that the number of call center employees grew by 39% between 1996 and 2000 — a period during which that traditional icon of phone work, the secretary, saw its population decline by 17%.

Employees of call centers aren't alone on the front lines of consumer contact, either. They're part of a legion of customer service representatives that also includes those who operate face to face in brick-and-mortar venues and on the Internet. But those on the phone may come to predominate. According to The Boyd Co., a location consultant firm in Princeton, New Jersey, call centers are now the fastest growing industry segment in the United States. By 2003, Boyd says, there will be 105,000 North American call centers employing 4 million workers — a dramatic increase from 70,000 and 2.5 million, respectively, in 1999.

But while communications technology is transforming our workplaces — who needs a secretary when you have voicemail and e-mail? — it is hardly supplanting the people who talk to customers. According to a biennial projection of employment trends from the U.S. Bureau of Labor Statistics, even the emergence of e-commerce stands to result in more, not fewer, call centers, as companies find a need to back up or supplement automated Web services.

All those millions of operators on the phone, connecting with so many American households every day, are making a statement about the value your company puts on the people who buy its products and services. But chances are, it won't be the message you intend, and the potential for harm lurks in every encounter. "Everybody expects to be satisfied, so if I call and you meet my expectations, you're just breaking even," says Mike McDonald, Gallup's director of call center retention, whose job it is to find and keep the right people to staff Gallup's own call centers. "If you dazzle me, I may tell a couple of friends. But if you make me mad, maybe I'll tell seven," he says.

That equation ought to keep senior executives awake at night. But, for the most part, they have other things on their minds. The cost-cutting potential of technology has proven irresistible to corporate boards, which have jumped at the chance to automate functions that real live human beings used to serve. To justify huge investments in computer networks and Internet operations, companies have tried to shave the expense of serving each customer. That hasn't slowed the rise in the number of workers manning call center phones, but it has tended to make call centers a low corporate priority. Minding customers has become a back-office function, and outsourcing has boomed.

That view of the call center as just another entry-level (or outsourced) necessity runs counter to the evolution of modern customer service. Once, taking care of customers was a matter of various clerical tasks — processing orders, handling routine complaints, and so forth — and it made sense for those functions to be overseen by a company's operations department. But as major industries deregulated and markets went global, those erstwhile clerks, now ensconced in call centers, assumed extra burdens.

Today, if a company is to grow, its people on the phone need to be trained to be persuasive and to adapt to customers' needs and whims; their skills ought to include salesmanship and relationship management. But corporate organizational charts rarely reflect that change in emphasis, says Bill McEwen, Ph.D., who runs Gallup's brand loyalty practice. "Often, marketing managers are told that managing customer service is not their job, that they should leave it to operations or HR."

That kind of stubborn orientation can be costly. In the 1990s, Wells Fargo & Company focused on efficiency and forged a reputation for ruthless mergers, cutting thousands of apparently redundant employees — many of them specialists in the care and feeding of customers — in the bank's branches as well as in its call centers. But while slashing expenses did improve profit margins, it also handicapped prospects for growth; the bank ended up losing customers in droves.

So Wells Fargo became a different company with a new mission, merging in late 1998 with Norwest, a company famous for its "high touch" customer service. "We [were losing] one of every five consumers every year due primarily to failures in our processes or in our attitude," explained new CEO Dick Kovacevich in his 2000 letter to shareholders. He resolved to cut the number of defections, thus reducing the cost of acquiring new customers and making it possible to sell additional services to a loyal base of established customers. By mid-August 2001, Kovacevich announced that customer defections had dropped to 17% from 20% in 1999 — the equivalent of keeping almost 200,000 households as customers.

Having seen the former Wells Fargo try to grow through acquisitions and technology, only to see rivals become even bigger, Kovacevich focused the new company on winning more business from current customers. And he trumpeted customer service as the tonic that would make it happen.

Whether or not Kovacevich achieves his goal, he at least recognizes the problem — and the opportunity. Other corporate leaders remain insulated from a part of their business — customer service in general, and call centers in particular — that, more often than not, is systematically alienating customers. In today's business environment, that can be a fatal flaw. The person sitting in that call center seat is ideally situated to cement relationships with customers and, by extension, to fuel a company's growth. Usually, though, these employees are poorly trained, minimally paid, and motivated by nothing more than a desire to finish their shift and go home. As a result, says Glenn Phelps, Ph.D., who directs Gallup's call center program, "Brand image suffers, bonds to customers fray, and value is destroyed." In today's worst run centers, Phelps suggests, "Some employees are so ill-suited to engaging customers that they would make more money for a company if it paid them to stay home."

Suppose, for example, that McEwen's bank has failed to record a deposit he made, and he calls to complain. The person in the call center didn't make the mistake, but she has the opportunity to calm him down and solve the problem. If that happens, he may end up feeling better about the bank than he did before the error occurred. However, if she hates her job or feels rushed to get him off the line — or is negatively affected in any of a million other ways — she'll miss her chance to appease him, and the bank will have made itself look foolish twice. McEwen is likely to take his business to the institution down the street and tell a few of his friends exactly why he switched.

At the heart of the Gallup approach to call centers is the idea that a well-run operation can build brand loyalty by making customers feel better, whatever the situation. It's literally what Gallup call center employees get paid to do — to get the most they can out of their minutes on the line with a customer. To make that happen in clients' call centers too, Gallup consultants show how to measure customer service, hire the kinds of phone reps and managers who can get the job done, and structure a workplace and compensation so that top performers can thrive. "Our method recognizes that people are crucial," says McEwen.

Paying call center reps for what they accomplish is akin to the way salespeople are compensated. When you're selling something, what you earn isn't based on how many clients you wine and dine, even though getting out and doing that is an essential part of the job. Rather, most of your pay depends on how many of those clients end up happy enough to make a purchase. But in most call centers, performance is a badly designed numbers game, where the quantity of customer contacts is all that matters.

Research by Jagdip Singh, professor of marketing at Case Western Reserve University's Weatherhead School of Management in Cleveland, suggests that productivity — which call center managers often measure in terms of such things as the number of rings before a response — doesn't always correlate to improved levels of trust or satisfaction among customers. So managers should develop metrics for evaluating what kind of mood an agent arouses in customers, not how many customers' moods an agent can change. For example, although an employee may be able to answer just as many calls when she's exhausted as when she's well rested, the quality of her interactions with customers is likely to suffer if she's tired.

Gallup's breakthrough methods for measuring quality let managers recognize and reward high standards of performance. In the organization's own call centers, top employees know how to keep respondents on the phone long enough to get through a questionnaire and how to explain the kind of responses that are needed. "If I fail to probe when someone says, 'Oh, five or six,'" says one Gallup worker, "then that survey will get thrown out," and he'll have wasted his own time as well as the respondent's. If, on the other hand, he's sufficiently charming and dogged to get people to complete surveys that other employees might fumble, his pay — based on how many surveys he completes in a month — and his satisfaction will rise accordingly. Gallup staffers who are exceptionally skilled at working with customers make a good living, earning more than three times as much as the industry average.

Phelps says that companies should make pay-for-performance a staple of call center operations. But it's not enough to tie compensation to productivity and customer loyalty. It's also essential for managers to give workers some control over their own schedules, so they will operate when they're most likely to be sharp; to respect their instincts for dealing with truculent or confused customers; and to provide a clear career path that enables customer service stars to prosper as they help their employers grow.

The Gallup approach also acknowledges that some people, no matter how well they are motivated and managed, just aren't cut out for call center work. In a sample of employees hired on the basis of uniform criteria — that is, workers who might be expected to perform about equally — the top 5% boosted customer loyalty scores by 27% over a 12-month period, while the bottom 5% didn't improve scores at all. To create relationships on the phone, representatives need to use not only factual knowledge but also personal grace. A manager's challenge is to separate employees who have that grace from those who don't.

Gallup's focus on the individual approach is especially valuable because of the sheer number of variables involved in call center operations. How can managers hope to exert meaningful quality control when there are thousands of employees on the line at the same time dealing in their own way with whatever situations come up? "If I go to a store, I'll see one of two or three people, but if I call my bank, I will talk to one of 3,000 people in its regional call center," says McEwen. And every one of those 3,000 needs to know how to promote products, justify company procedures, and often, cover for other departments' errors. A manager must be confident that the worker on the phone has the poise to handle any situation that comes up.

"This thing called customer service has a lot more to do with delivery than with content," says Mark Vondrasek, senior vice president of worldwide operations for Northern Trust, a Chicago money management firm. Vondrasek hired Gallup last year to help his company foster customer loyalty via the call centers of one of its businesses. In listening to tapes of conversations with clients who had filled out surveys, Vondrasek found that two workers may sometimes provide the exact same information to a very different effect. For example, clients often ask for special terms or favors, which may not be available. "The customer's reaction when you say you can't provide something is driven almost exclusively by employees' delivery," says Vondrasek. "Those who can put a difficult 'no' in front of a client with compassion and empathy are rated far better." That discovery has led Vondrasek to start building a pay-for-performance system that will help him reward the people in his call centers who create growth for the company.

In an industrial setting or a traditional corporate one, extra sweat leads to extra reward. The machinist who stays late earns overtime and becomes a foreman; the mailroom clerk who comes up with the CEO's missing document gets noticed and climbs the corporate ladder. But that's not necessarily how things work in a call center. There, both the employee and a customer shape every unit of work. "How willing you are to accept extra work is minor compared with how customers feel about you," says Vondrasek. It may be better to let an effective employee work fewer hours than to reward someone simply for working more.

But in the best of all worlds, your call center reps will complete as many calls as they can, knowing they'll be rewarded. And you'll be confident that in those intimate moments when they're alone with your customers, they'll know what to say. In a study of 5,000 call center reps, Phelps found that the strongest 25% improved the loyalty of 70% of the customers they talked to, while reps in the weakest quarter alienated more customers than they connected with, making those employees a revenue drain.

No company willingly operates its customer service in that bottom quartile; a brand's effectiveness depends on the human relationships formed around it. But more and more of those relationships succeed or fail on the phone. Every company that understands this will make sure that employees wearing headsets see their jobs not as dead-end work, but as opportunities in which meeting the company's goals pays off for them as well. For the rest — companies that continue to assume that call center workers are interchangeable and expendable — success may prove as elusive as the payoff from the millions of dollars it takes to put their name on a ball park.

WHY SPY?

by Scott Ahlstrand

December 15, 2001

There are ways to get into your customers' heads. Mystery shopping isn't one of them.

For a CEO who already has too much to manage, it may seem like a great idea: mystery shopping. Spot-checks in his company's stores by people posing as shoppers, with the aim of turning up useful information about which stores are surpassing company expectations for customer service and which are falling short. Clandestine? Without a doubt. Enlightening? Hardly.

If all customers were interchangeable or weighed different elements of the shopping experience equally or shopped at the same time of day, mystery shopping might have far-reaching value. But real customers don't fit those criteria. As a result, mystery shopping fails to reflect how a vast, varied customer base actually feels about a company's stores. And because it fails to capture customer experience, it has precious little to teach executives about improving customer service and is flawed as a predictor of customer behavior.

Unfortunately, mystery shopping is pitched as a tool for all those things. By 1999, the mystery shopping industry in the United States was estimated at $750 million in annual revenues and growing, according to the Marketing Research Association. Fortunately, there is a better way. But first, full disclosure: Gallup is in the business of teaching executives how to better understand customers. Unlike the proponents of mystery shopping, we operate from the premise that to know how customers feel, you have to talk to them. More important, we're sure that statistical evidence and plain common sense support Gallup's approach.

Consider, for example, these four ways in which mystery shopping fails to live up to its hype:

- Mystery shopping produces a sample that is too small to be statistically valid. Many companies use one shopper a month, or at most three to five. But it's not uncommon for a popular retailer to have thousands of transactions a day. To suppose that five or so visits a month approximates the typical customer experience is folly. To further assume that those visits can meaningfully inform crucial decisions on marketing or management only compounds the original error.

- Mystery shoppers cannot speak for your customers. Even if mystery shoppers are demographically similar to your customers, they do not share the aims or expectations of a real customer. Accordingly, they're not likely to have a real customer's take on such service variables as courtesy, attentiveness, knowledge, or promptness.

- Mystery shoppers are paid to notice things that real customers don't, resulting in a distorted picture of a customer's experience. Imagine walking into a fast-food restaurant. If it is clean, and the service is friendly and efficient — and the food is as you expected — you probably will continue thinking about whatever was on your mind. But if your hamburger is cold or your fries are soggy, the excellence of the other factors won't even register. As a customer, you would give the restaurant a definitive thumbs-down. A mystery shopper, however, would give high marks in all categories but the food. Customers are not that meticulous or forgiving. They notice when a store delights or appalls them — but not much in between.

- Mystery shopping cannot be used reliably to predict customer behavior or business outcomes. A retail giant that is one of Gallup's clients asked us to interview 500 customers, using the same questions a mystery shopper would use to evaluate a store. We analyzed the responses in relation to the customers' emotional attachments to a brand and their plans to stay loyal, and we found no statistically valid relationship. None. Anybody who implies that mystery shopping will unlock your customer's psyche is likely overpromising, to put it mildly.

In limited and tightly controlled circumstances, mystery shoppers can serve a purpose, however. At a major bank, for example, mystery shoppers test the wait time in lines and assess compliance with rules for hanging advertising posters. But even for such mundane tasks, managers must make sure that mystery shoppers are objective and that the elements of the shopping experience they evaluate are the same ones that real customers are likely to notice.

Mystery shopping has also been used to identify unfair and illegal business practices, such as gender or racial discrimination by brokers, lenders, cab drivers, and co-op boards. But the successful use of mystery shopping to expose civil rights violations is no reason to believe that it is appropriate as a gauge of customer service.

An alternative to mystery shopping is to elicit feedback from a statistically significant sample of real customers. For the amount of money spent on most mystery shopping programs, a more robust, reliable customer service system could be developed. A large organization could use Web sites or toll-free numbers to conduct customer surveys that would produce vastly more and higher quality data. Such computer and phone surveys are especially useful if a company has stores in many locations.

Or executives can opt for in-person customer interviews that are conducted, perhaps, as customers leave a location. This method is an especially useful data-gathering technique if you want to find out what customers think about a particular venue, such as a flagship location. The cost might be higher than mystery shopping, but such interviews yield real-time insights into customers' likes, dislikes, and intentions to visit the location again.

Whether from the Web, by phone, or in person, information garnered from real customers can be organized into a report card that will inform managers about what needs improvement. Armed with reliable data about what works and what does not, regional and store managers can be confident that their most important actions, such as educating employees, implementing operational change, and setting strategy, will be true to the needs of their customers.

Of course, companies must define their objectives and decide how best to meet them. Mystery shopping may show you how well your stores comply with quantifiable, objective standards, such as wait times. But to gauge the shifting truth of how customers feel and what they want, there's no substitute for asking them.

MARKETING TO THE
MASS AFFLUENT   *by Raksha Arora and Lydia Saad*

December 9, 2004

They've got cash to spare, they're growing as a group, and their social attitudes are complex. How do you target them?

In 1980, 15% of U.S. households had annual incomes of more than $75,000 (in 2003 adjusted dollars). Today, that figure is up to 26%, reports the Census Bureau. This means that one in every four households in the country now belong to the ranks of the mass affluent.

Smart marketers have been paying close attention to this growing and substantial demographic group, which was spawned in the 1980s — a period of rising inequality, according to the census. Educated, idiosyncratic, and flush with discretionary income, the mass affluent resist traditional segmentation. They move freely between what were once thought to be mutually exclusive customer segments: They buy their Dom Perignon from Costco and asparagus from a farmers' market. They pair a thousand-dollar Louis Vuitton handbag with yoga pants from Target. Their beverage of choice might be Vanilla Coke with a shot of Rémy XO.

Indeed, Gallup Poll data reveal that the mass affluent defy easy characterization. This article examines their values and political leanings.

Lean to the left, lean to the right

Not surprisingly, the mass affluent are more likely to be Republican than non-affluents. But don't assume that conventional political characterizations apply to this upscale segment. When asked to describe their social and economic attitudes in broad strokes, affluents are no more likely than non-affluents to say they are conservative on either dimension: 36% of affluents say they are conservative on social issues, while 37% of non-affluents say the same. On economic issues, 45% of affluents and 43% of non-affluents describe themselves as conservative. Also, the GOP-leaning mass affluents are no more likely than non-affluents to bemoan the worsening state of moral values in the country and are equally likely to be church attendees.

However, the two market segments begin to look different when we compare the views of affluents and non-affluents on *specific* issues. While affluents are not as monolithically conservative as one might expect, it is interesting to note that they are even more socially liberal than their non-affluent counterparts. For example, mass affluents are considerably more likely than non-affluents to perceive a host of controversial activities as "morally acceptable": doctor-assisted suicide, cloning animals, abortion, and homosexual behavior. Affluents are also more likely to be tolerant of sex between unmarried men and women and stem-cell research using human embryos.

Although these positions are associated more with the political left than the right, mass affluents adopt more liberal positions despite their majority Republican credentials. In contrast, non-affluent America, while more likely to be Democratic, subscribes to a relatively conservative value system where social issues are concerned.

In this context, then, it stands to reason that Kenneth Cole Productions, the upscale shoe and apparel maker, would blatantly tout its socially liberal values to entice mass affluent consumers into its stores. Bold ad campaign slogans such as "Women have the right to be pregnant, but not barefoot" may seem risky, given that affluents' brand and product habits often seem to be in conflict with their stated social positions. However, for Kenneth Cole, at least some part of this strategy has paid off, thanks to those among the mass affluent who have embraced his message.

Affluent and libertarian

Mass affluents and non-affluents do agree on some social values. Both income groups are tolerant of divorce and express widespread support for the death penalty and medical testing on animals. And large majorities of both groups consider suicide, human cloning, and extramarital affairs to be morally unacceptable.

Affluent men versus affluent women

Among the mass affluent, men and women differ regarding some social values. Affluent men, for instance, aren't very concerned about animal rights — the overwhelming majority find it acceptable to buy and wear animal fur (78%) and to conduct medical tests on animals (79%). In contrast, although *Vogue* Editor-in-Chief Anna Wintour might say that fur is in this season, many affluent women aren't entirely convinced — only 61% approve of buying and wearing fur, and 61% approve of conducting medical tests on animals.

Of course, 61% is still an appreciable majority. And clearly, the ranks of affluent women consist of fur-wearers as well as virulently anti-fur PETA supporters. Thus, although affluent women appear to lean to the left on a number of social issues, it should not be assumed that they do so on all of them.

Affluent men and women also differ sharply on the subject of having a child outside of marriage: 62% of affluent women find this morally acceptable, compared with 46% of affluent men. Both groups widely oppose cloning humans, but they have distinctly different reactions to cloning animals: 50% of men believe this is acceptable, compared with only 31% of women.

Differences on abortion
On the controversial issue of abortion, affluent women embrace a distinctly more pro-choice position than non-affluent women, who are least likely to be pro-choice. Only 45% of non-affluent women consider themselves to be pro-choice, compared with 64% of affluent women. Accordingly, while affluent women are nearly twice as likely to describe themselves as "pro-choice" as they are to describe themselves as "pro-life" (64% vs. 33%), non-affluent women are evenly divided at 45%.

Affluent Americans bridge the generation gap
Social conservatism generally correlates with age: Conservative attitudes are most prevalent among older adults. Not so with affluents. In fact, affluents aged 50 and older are more similar to young affluents in their social outlook than they are to other older adults.

This is seen in generational attitudes toward the prevailing moral climate in the United States. Typically, older Americans are more critical of the nation's moral climate than younger Americans, and this is true among non-affluents. Among affluents, however, older and younger adults share nearly identical perspectives. About a third of affluents aged 50 and older describe the state of moral values in the nation as poor; about a third of the younger adults in both income groups would agree. On the other hand, half of non-affluents aged 50 and older share this bleak view of American morality. Similarly, on the once-taboo issue of unmarried men and women having sexual relations, 57% of older affluents consider this morally acceptable, as do 68% of younger affluents and 63% of younger non-affluents. Only 37% of older non-affluents, however, share this view.

The same pattern is evident with respect to other touchy moral questions we've discussed, including doctor-assisted suicide, having children out of wedlock, homosexual behavior, and abortion. On all of these, older affluents are more similar in their views to younger adults — and both are more accepting of these behaviors than older non-affluents are. So whether we are looking at all affluents or older affluents, they can surprise us with their more liberal values.

Bottom line

Businesses strive to design a product experience that results in absolute customer engagement — a higher kind of loyalty that would make a customer say, "I can't imagine a world without my iPod" or "my Toyota Prius." And this emotional engagement between customers and the brands and products they idolize is based on core values that are common to customers and companies. The success of the Republican Party provides a classic example of marketing to the traditional values of blue-collar America. Brand managers and marketers who want to replicate that success among the mass affluent need to fine-tune their message to the core values of these mass affluent customers.

The marketing moral: While one might assume that the mass affluent support conservative, free-market economics, they are more liberal in their social views than you might think. So marketers should get to know the mass affluent value system — and not simply typecast them as right-wing traditionalists just because they lean Republican.

WHAT WERE
THEY THINKING?

Interviewed by Jennifer Robison

January 13, 2005

In the first of a two-part interview, a Nobel Prize-winning psychologist explains how context, perception, and faulty reasoning affect your customers — and maybe you

A *GMJ* Q&A with Princeton Psychology and Public Affairs Professor Daniel Kahneman, winner of the 2002 Nobel Prize in economics

Daniel Kahneman has started a quiet little revolution — one that may wind up blasting a big hole in the foundation of economics. For centuries, economists have based most of their theories on the "rational-agent model," which assumes that people make reasonable decisions and do simple cost/benefit analyses on the things they buy. But they don't. Dr. Kahneman's research shows that, probably more often than not, individual decisions are based on perception, context, and faulty reasoning — all of which can be manipulated.

Interestingly, Dr. Kahneman is not an economist. He's a psychologist — Eugene Higgins Professor of Psychology at Princeton University, a professor of public affairs at the Woodrow Wilson School, and a Gallup Senior Scientist, one of a cadre of leading scientists who lend their expertise to Gallup research.

But Kahneman belongs to an even more rarefied group: In October 2002, The Royal Swedish Academy of Sciences awarded him the Nobel Prize in economics "for having integrated insights from psychological research into economic science, especially concerning human judgment and decision-making under uncertainty."

Kahneman's insights are as relevant to the global economic scale as they are to the average shampoo purchase. What we think we know about our own decisions is wrong, and what we thought we knew about economics may be just as wrong. And anyone who hopes to create revenue for an organization will do well to learn from what Kahneman has discovered.

In the first of a two-part *GMJ* interview, Dr. Kahneman discusses how businesspeople should make high-level decisions, when and how people fall prey to cognitive illusions, and why everything *always* depends on context.

GMJ: A lot of your research has centered on the way people think, and you've identified two broad categories: intuition and reasoning. What's the difference?

Dr. Kahneman: Intuitive thoughts are those that come to you quickly and effortlessly, whereas reasoning is something that you've got to work at and is characteristically effortful and slower. Everyone does both — thinks intuitively and reasons. But usually we're guided by and operate at the intuitive level. We don't slow ourselves down to reason carefully most of the time.

GMJ: Is that true for every facet of life, from decisions about what we're going to have for supper to which car we should buy?

Kahneman: Well, that's tricky. We use intuitive thinking more often than we realize, but which car to buy is a much more complicated operation. In such a case, you have intuitive wishes, and you have an initial emotional response. Buying a car is never a purely intuitive, spontaneous, impulsive thing; you reason about the car. But the reasoning is superimposed on an emotional attitude.

GMJ: How often is that first system of thinking, intuitive thinking, wrong?

Kahneman: It's fine most of the time. You know, we're very highly skilled in what we do. Whenever you develop a skill, it becomes part of that intuitive system of thought. You drive your car intuitively — you don't think about every single operation as you do it — and we're awfully good at that. What is remarkable is that people don't check themselves. We give answers without thinking. And most of the time we're okay. But sometimes that habit of mind gets us into trouble.

GMJ: On the other hand, if you checked every decision you ever made . . .

Kahneman: . . . you couldn't possibly live. It would just slow you down too much. You know, we've got to act, and we are, in general, very skilled at what we do.

GMJ: One of the reasons that you were awarded the Nobel Prize is you showed that the rational-agent model of economics — that people buy things based on a careful, reasoned cost/benefit analysis, not intuition or emotion — isn't necessarily correct, right?

Kahneman: Sort of. The line of research that I've engaged in is called the study of bounded rationality. That is, people are reasonable, but their minds are limited. So it's not that people are necessarily driven by emotion — they're driven by mental computations that are incomplete or inaccurate, and they're susceptible to what we call cognitive illusions. And that's a different thing than being driven by emotions.

GMJ: What's a cognitive illusion?

Kahneman: It's an impression that you get at the intuitive, but not necessarily emotional, level that is wrong or misleading. Cognitive illusions are difficult to shake, and often we get them because these impressions come from accessibility. Accessibility refers to impressions based on the most accessible thought or explanation. For example, an easy question is one where the answer comes easily to mind — it's highly accessible. The answers to difficult questions are not so easily accessible.

GMJ: Are some thoughts more accessible than others?

Kahneman: Oh, yes. There are certain ideas that come to mind very easily for various reasons. If you're in a bad mood, then thoughts of bad events come easily to mind — the world will now seem like a more dangerous place, and you'll be more pessimistic about the future. Just being in a bad mood changes the accessibility of a whole lot of other thoughts. It's harder to imagine people laughing and smiling, and it's easier to imagine wakes and funerals.

GMJ: So if you can change someone's mood . . .

Kahneman: Oh, you can change many things about their beliefs about the world.

GMJ: How easy is it to do that?

Kahneman: Very easy. I'll give you an example from an experiment. A researcher had someone lurk around a phone booth, posing as a survey researcher. Half the time, he put a quarter in the phone booth. And so half the people who used the phone found a quarter, so they got the telephone call for free. Then, when they came out, the researcher asked them to answer a survey. Among other things, he asked them how happy they were with their lives in general. People who just found a quarter in the phone booth were much likelier to say that they were much happier with their life in general these days than the people who didn't find a quarter.

So even a small event that makes you feel lucky for a just few minutes will make thoughts of happiness much more accessible. If your first thought is a negative one, you are likely to continue to have negative thoughts for a while. You also tend to think about the past in the light of your current mood.

GMJ: So not being able to find a store clerk or getting called by a cranky phone rep can have a negative effect on a customer's behavior? Decisions can be based on perception, instead of reality?

Kahneman: Sometimes, yes. I mean, people should know that if they're in a bad mood, they're going to overestimate the likelihood of failure. People also should know that they're very prone to optimistic biases in judging how likely they are to succeed in different enterprises, and so on. People are wildly optimistic very often. And certain people exaggerate the impact of almost anything that they think about.

I have a "fortune cookie maxim" that I'm very proud of: Nothing in life is quite as important as you think it is while you are thinking about it. So, nothing will ever make you as happy as you think it will. Just thinking about things can make them seem very important.

GMJ: So how should people make reasonable decisions? Especially people like CEOs, who make decisions that affect a lot of people?

Kahneman: There are better and worse ways of making decisions. Probably the worst way is to look at the decision in isolation from everything else. If you are the CEO of a company, there are many categories of decisions that you make frequently. For those, you ought to have a policy. Then just apply the policy in a fairly standard and rigorous way rather than delving into each problem separately.

If you focus too much on each problem separately, you'll get very lost and make bad decisions. But when you get some distance from your problems and look at them as a category, class, or set of problems, you become more reasonable.

GMJ: So getting some context is key to avoiding errors in perception. But how do you know if your decision making isn't just an exercise in risk aversion? Or risk taking?

Kahneman: Well, there are many factors that determine whether people do or do not take risk. It is not correct to say that people avoid risks in general, because most people actually prefer some risks.

What *is* true about people is that they hate losing. They're much more sensitive to what they might lose than to what they might gain. So we say that people are loss-averse, not risk-averse. For example, you ask someone to toss a coin. If the coin shows tails, you lose $20. If it shows heads, you win X amount. And now I ask you, what would X have to be to make that gamble attractive to you? What people tend to say will be somewhere between $40 and $50. So people need to be compensated more than twice as much before a 50/50 gamble becomes attractive. I think that people evaluate gains and losses relative to some reference point and put more weight on the loss, not the gains.

GMJ: How do people figure out that reference point?

Kahneman: It depends on the person and the circumstances, but the anchoring effect is a characteristic error in judgment and decision making. Anchoring is a common effect when you are buying real estate. The asking price is an anchor. It's a number that sticks in your mind, and it's very difficult to get away from it. You don't think of the actual value of the house, you think of the price, then make all your decisions based on that. So recognizing that you're susceptible to anchoring is actually quite a useful thing. A lot of negotiations are about anchors.

GMJ: Speaking of which, explain to me why, when people do home remodeling, they tend to start out with a fairly reasonable budget, then more often than not they go over budget — and quite frequently they go . . .

Kahneman: Way over budget. One reason is that the same expense begins to look smaller in the context of the larger expense. My advice to people has always been that when you're buying an expensive house, buy the furniture at the same time. The amount that you will spend on the furniture will look small relative to the cost of the house. Otherwise, if you buy the house, and then stop, and then start buying the furniture, you'll buy furniture that isn't good enough for your house. That's because you begin to feel poor. So you actually should do everything at once; I think you make better decisions in doing everything at once. I mean, spending a thousand dollars seems like a lot of money, but the difference between $15,000 and $16,000 in remodeling your kitchen — that doesn't seem like a lot of money. So it's the same thousand dollars, but by embedding it in a larger amount, you've made it seem small.

GMJ: So context changes everything.

Kahneman: Everything.

See Related Article
"Are You Happy Now?" (Part 2 of Interview, page 90)

ARE YOU HAPPY NOW?   *Interviewed by Jennifer Robison*

February 10, 2005

In the second of a two-part interview, Nobel Prize winner Daniel Kahneman explains well-being and what it means to business

A *GMJ* Q&A with Princeton Psychology and Public Affairs Professor Daniel Kahneman, winner of the 2002 Nobel Prize in economics

It took a psychologist, Daniel Kahneman, Ph.D., to show economists how wrong they've always been about human decision making. For centuries, economists have based most of their theories on the rational-agent model, which assumes that people make reasonable decisions and do simple cost/benefit analyses on the things they buy. They don't. Dr. Kahneman's research shows that more often than not, decisions are based on perception, context, and faulty reasoning — all of which can be manipulated. For his groundbreaking work, Dr. Kahneman was awarded the Nobel Prize in Economics in 2002.

But now, Dr. Kahneman — the Eugene Higgins Professor of Psychology at Princeton University; a professor of public affairs at the Woodrow Wilson School; and a Gallup Senior Scientist, one of a cadre of leading scientists who lend their expertise to Gallup research — is turning his attention to a whole new realm: the study of well-being. Noting that there's enough to discover to occupy him for the rest of his working life, Dr. Kahneman is studying what makes us happy — and what doesn't.

Dr. Kahneman calls well-being "the ultimate big problem," and he's working with Gallup to develop strategies to understand and measure psychological and physiological well-being. Already, the work has turned up some compelling discoveries, including the fact that though your lips may say *yes* to workplace satisfaction, your prefrontal cortex may say *no* — and the cortex never lies.

This has implications for all humans, but especially the ones who run businesses. In this, the second of a two-part series, Dr. Kahneman discusses matters such as why you shouldn't bother moving your operations to California for the climate and how negative emotions are actually quite rare. He also relates that he's exploring why your French customers never seem satisfied.

GMJ: Though you won the Nobel Prize for economics, one of your major research interests is well-being. How do you measure someone's well-being?

Dr. Kahneman: Well, there are many approaches to the measurement of well-being. The standard ones are to ask people how satisfied they are with their lives. My colleagues and I have been thinking of other ways of measuring well-being, in particular by trying to identify how people spend their time, to what activities they allocate their day, and how they feel about those activities. It's a much more detailed description of people's lives.

But it turns out that there are some physiological indices that show a great deal of promise for the measurement of well-being and emotional states. There is a wonderful gauge of affective emotional state that you measure by the amount of activity in the prefrontal areas of the brain. It turns out that in the human brain, the left prefrontal area is sort of the happy one and the right prefrontal area is the more, well, measured one. By comparing the balance of activity in those two areas, you get a very good idea of people's emotional state. It's true for babies, and it's true for adults — the relative activity of those areas changes when people are in a good mood or in a bad mood.

In my academic research this spring, I will be running a study comparing the well-being of populations in France and in the United States. So by next year, we're going to have fairly extensive measurements in France and in the United States, or at least we hope so. I expect that quite a few people will be interested in the results, including people at Gallup.

GMJ: What do you think you'll find?

Kahneman: Well, we know that the French are very different from the Americans in their satisfaction with life. They're much less satisfied. Americans are pretty high up there, while the French are quite low — the world champions in life satisfaction are actually the Danes. And yet, when you look at the way that the French live, they seem to have pretty good lives. You know, they spend their time in ways that I think many people would envy.

So the question becomes: Where do those differences in life satisfaction come from, and what is their significance? I expect that we'll replicate the standard differences in life satisfaction [ratings], but I expect that we'll find far fewer differences or perhaps no differences at all in the physiological measurements. And we may just find that the French have better lives in the sense that the activities to which they allocate their time may be at least as good, if not better, than the American ones.

GMJ: Is it possible that the French are just more fatalistic when they respond to the questions you ask them?

Kahneman: Well, they're certainly more negative. They're more negative in their responses to many questionnaires, and this is something we're trying to understand. That's a project that I'm doing at Gallup in collaboration with Robert Manchin of Gallup Europe and Norbert Schwarz of the University of Michigan. We are hoping to figure out why the populations of some countries express much higher satisfaction with their life in general — with their health and with different aspects of their lives — so we're beginning a large-scale study of that problem. If we're successful, then it would allow some correction of differences in measures across countries.

It would actually be very useful to have a scale that is calibrated so that multinational companies can compare data across countries. There are cultural attitudes that affect positivity, and there are differences in how people report positivity, and companies need to understand them. You know, in some countries, people appear to be whiners or complainers unless they give very positive responses, while in other countries, people appear rather naïve or stupid if they give very positive responses.

GMJ: Could we use your research here at home? Americans have a lot of trouble understanding the different cultures within our own country — a culture half a mile away may not make sense if you don't belong to it.

Kahneman: Well, that is very interesting. If we were able to develop measures that predict or explain differences across languages or across cultures, then of course we would turn around and try to do the same thing within the United States. But we first have to solve, or sort of make a dent in, the problem across languages and across cultures. But ultimately, certainly the hope would be to apply the same logic to differences within the country.

GMJ: What are the practical implications for business?

Kahneman: It's clear that policymakers and economists are going to be interested in the measurement of well-being primarily as it correlates with health; they also want to know whether researchers can validate subjective responses with physiological indices. It would have a huge effect on workplace health, insurance, productivity, engagement — and other things too, I suspect.

GMJ: You've mentioned that perception and context can greatly influence people's responses, and it isn't difficult to change perception and context — your own or someone else's. How do you work around faulty perception of well-being?

Kahneman: The particular approach to well-being measurement that I've been involved in tries to get around the issue of context by getting people to remember one day in great detail. Specifically, we get people to think about the day they had yesterday from morning to evening, then try to recall what they did and how they felt about it.

GMJ: What is it about well-being or positive psychology that intrigues you?

Kahneman: Oh, this is the ultimate big problem. It's what people are trying to do with their lives; they're trying to achieve some kind of well-being. So it's a very natural thing to be interested in.

My interest in well-being evolved from my interest in decision making — from raising the question of whether people know what they will want in the future and whether the things that people want for themselves will make them happy. And I have doubts about people's ability to predict their future tastes or to make choices that will make them happy in the long run.

There's a lot of randomness in the decisions that people make. I think people are quite often wrong in predicting how they'll feel about the outcome of the decisions they make. They tend to exaggerate the emotional result of almost anything they do. Nothing in life is quite as important as you think it is while you're thinking about it. So just thinking about any change that you want to make in your life tends to make you exaggerate its importance.

GMJ: But we have to make decisions about our future all the time. I was told that the most important decision you'll ever make is whom to marry, because it will influence every aspect of your life. And how can you ever guess how that will turn out?

Kahneman: It's actually tricky. Of course, the main determinant of happiness is not whom you choose to marry but whom you choose to be your parents. A lot is determined by genetics, character, and temperament. Other effects exist, but they're not huge. Temperament and character are the main determinants of happiness.

You know, the standard state for people is "mildly pleasant." Negative emotions are quite rare, and extremely positive emotions are rare. But people are mildly pleased most of the time, they're mildly tired a lot of the time, and they wish they were somewhere else a substantial part of the time — but mostly they're mildly pleased.

GMJ: So if we're mostly wrong when we predict what will make us happy, how come we're most often mildly pleased?

Kahneman: It's called the phenomenon of adaptation. In general, the differences between groups of different circumstances are much smaller than you expect. So, for instance, paraplegics tend to be much less miserable than people expect, and lottery winners are much less happy than people expect. And I think that we have a handle on what is happening there.

What we believe now is that, to a large extent, you change what you pay attention to over time. So, when you're first married or first become a paraplegic or whatever, that is what you think about most often. If you aren't paraplegic and think about what being a paraplegic is like, then you're always miserable while you're thinking about it. But if you *are* a paraplegic, you will gradually start thinking of other things, and the more time you spend thinking of other things, the less miserable you are going to be. That's why you tend to exaggerate the effect of paraplegia if you aren't one and think less about it if you are one.

So your emotional state really has a lot to do with what you're thinking about and what you're paying attention to. Adaptation seems to be, to a substantial extent, a process of reallocating your attention. Many years ago, we did a study in which we asked people if they would be happier if they lived in California. Most people think they would be, and that's because the climate is better in California. And people in California think they're happier than people who live in other places. But when you actually measure it, you don't find it. Non-Californians are just as happy as Californians. In fact, when you live in a place, you don't think about its climate very much. You don't think about any of its characteristics very much. You just go through your day.

GMJ: Do you see positive psychology as a new long-term project for you?

Kahneman: Well, you know, this is certainly going to be my last long-term project. I'm approaching retirement, and there is enough to be done on the study of well-being to keep me working for the rest of my life.

GMJ: It must make you happy.

Kahneman: Yes, it does.

See Related Article
"What Were They Thinking?" (Part 1 of Interview, page 84)

CUSTOMER SATISFACTION IS
THE WRONG MEASURE

by Benson Smith

April 14, 2005

High scores don't necessarily link to sustainable growth. Find out why.

A recent article published by *CRM* magazine reported a surprising decline in e-commerce customer satisfaction scores. The data, drawn from the American Customer Satisfaction Index Annual E-Commerce Report, showed a slump in scores after two years of progressive increases.

E-commerce titans such as eBay, Amazon.com, and Charles Schwab all took substantial hits. Schwab saw a 5.3% reduction in its customer satisfaction scores, while auction leader eBay had a 4.8% reduction, and Amazon.com dropped 4.5 percentage points. This news — which is not the kind of news senior executives like to receive — has significant implications for sales and marketing executives in any industry, even those in old-economy, manufacturing sectors.

You can picture the executive hand-wringing taking place at these e-commerce giants. Few scores are taken as seriously as customer satisfaction indices, and precipitous declines are usually followed by pointed questions such as "How did this happen?" and "What are we going to do about it?" After all, for more than half a century, we have lived in an era in which the "customer is king."

If satisfaction scores are going down, something must be wrong. Isn't the goal of a business to achieve 100% ratings? Shouldn't your company strive for the highest customer satisfaction rating it can get?

No, it shouldn't.

First, let's be clear that the real goal of a publicly traded company is to achieve sustainable growth in income. Stock analysts love companies that are able to grow their income quarter after quarter, year after year — especially when revenue growth is a primary factor driving income growth. Sustainable growth is the most reliable driver of shareholder value.

Intuitively, it's easy to believe that high customer satisfaction scores correlate with sustainable growth. Conversely, significant drops in scores should link to declines in growth. And if two companies are competing in the same marketplace, wouldn't you expect the company with the highest satisfaction score to beat out the other company?

Not necessarily. Customer satisfaction scores do not necessarily link to sustainable growth. So whatever hand-wringing is going on at eBay, Amazon.com, or Charles Schwab may be in vain.

Perplexed?

If you're confused by this, you're not alone. It's almost impossible to believe that a company's future prospects aren't tied in some way to the strength of its customer relationships. Admittedly, not every company or executive believes this or acts this way. P.T. Barnum is rightly credited with many marketing breakthroughs, but he's also credited with saying, "There's a sucker born every minute." And most sources suggest he would have agreed with that.

Not many reputable companies would have the nerve to etch that sentiment into their corporate mission statements (although some might as well). Sure, Barnum's sentiment is uncomfortable, but his success over time was unquestionable. If customer satisfaction scores don't mean much, have companies collectively exaggerated the importance of their customers?

Not at all, according to Gallup Organization researchers William J. McEwen, Ph.D., and John Fleming, Ph.D. The connection that companies have with their customers is extremely important, but traditional customer satisfaction measures aren't an effective way to gauge the strength of that connection.

Backed by Gallup case studies and extensive Gallup research, McEwen and Fleming concluded in their *GMJ* article "Customer Satisfaction Doesn't Count" that companies chasing the coveted prize of high customer satisfaction are "pursuing the wrong goal. That's right. Regardless of how high a company's satisfaction levels may appear to be, satisfying customers without creating an emotional connection with them has no real value. None at all."

Through extensive research, Gallup devised a metric that quantifies the strength of these emotional attachments, or customer engagement. And, as it turns out, customer engagement scores have a very strong relationship with sustainable growth.

McEwen and Fleming cited several case studies that revealed that extremely satisfied customers were just as likely to stop doing business with a bank as were customers who were less satisfied. Furthermore, at a leading supermarket chain, extremely satisfied customers, on average, spent no more than less satisfied customers. In other words, financial outcomes were not affected by customer satisfaction scores.

McEwen and Fleming noticed a difference in financial outcomes only when they isolated customers who were both extremely satisfied with the company *and* emotionally connected to the company with which they were doing business. At the supermarket chain, customers who were both extremely satisfied and emotionally connected visited the chain more often and spent more each month. The pattern was the same at the retail bank: Customers who were extremely satisfied and emotionally engaged were far less likely to leave than customers who were merely satisfied but lacked an emotional connection.

What this means for sales forces

For executives charged with running a sales organization, the implications of this research are enormous. Emotional connections that improve financial outcomes are hard to create on the basis of a product or service alone, no matter how outstanding that product or service is. Products and services are easily duplicated. On the other hand, a sales force can make a significant difference in creating customer engagement — one that is exceedingly difficult for competitors to mimic.

One of the characteristics of engaged customers is that they are much more willing to act as advocates by referring others to your company's product or service. Simply put, engaged customers help companies get other customers.

To understand how this concept works, think about how you use ATMs. For most of us, they have become a routine part of the way we bank; we find them efficient and convenient. When we need cash, we're happy to see one on a nearby corner. But as satisfied as you may be with the service ATMs provide, when is the last time you recommended a particular machine to one of your friends or colleagues? Or recommended your bank, for that matter? ATM users can be perfectly satisfied but not engaged.

In companies where salespeople interact directly with customers, engagement derives from the relationship that develops between customers and the people who take care of them. When Gallup looked at customer engagement scores broken down by sales territory, we found enormous differences in the results achieved by individual salespeople. Sales managers often look at how much a particular rep is selling; few know or understand whether their reps are actually increasing customer engagement each year.

In our continuing evaluation of the factors that help build world-class sales organizations, customer engagement is becoming an increasingly important and reliable measuring stick to evaluate the quality and progress of the sales organization. In fact, almost all of the strategies you use to boost sales must be viewed against that measuring stick.

For example, if you increase the size of your sales force but fail to increase the number of engaged customers, either you haven't adopted the right strategy or you haven't executed it well. Similarly, if you reduce the number of sales managers and end up reducing customer engagement as a consequence, you have actually damaged your prospects for future growth.

Sales managers often have to make tough resource decisions. From time to time, we all find ourselves in the predicament that executives at eBay, Amazon.com, and Charles Schwab now face. They need to be asking questions — not about their declining customer satisfaction scores, but rather about what has been happening to customer engagement. If engagement is rising, they are on the right track. If not, then they really do have something to worry about. In tough competitive markets, no one can afford the mistake of worrying about the wrong measures.

FIXING A MAJOR
BANKING PROBLEM

by Teresa J. Tschida

July 14, 2005

Customer engagement variation in bank branches can drive profits down, customers away, and bank executives nuts. Here's how to eradicate it — and it's the last thing managers would probably consider.

John Richards was not the kind of customer banks love. For a decade, he's had a checking account at a big national bank, call it "A-One," in a Midwestern city — but only because they have a branch next to his office. Richards' certificates of deposit were at one credit union; his car loan was at another. He had a credit card through another bank. And he went to a small, locally owned bank for his mortgage.

When Richards bought a new house, he checked the mortgage rates at A-One only because it was one of the few branches in his new hometown; an online home-loan company was next on his list. But when he walked out of the A-One branch location in his new hometown, Richards suddenly felt like royalty. "I've never been treated so well in my life," Richards says. "The bank *president* helped me get the loan and set me up with an investment advisor who scheduled time to talk to me about when my CDs are due. It used to take me 15 minutes to talk to an A-One *teller* at the last branch."

By the time Richards got the key to his new house, he had eight products with A-One Bank — a mortgage, a line of credit, two checking accounts, two savings accounts, a credit card, and an online banking account. And soon, he will be talking with the investment advisor about those CDs.

Richards is in his mid-thirties — there will be a lot of mortgages, car loans, savings accounts, and investments in his future. Thus, we can suppose that the behavior of a few people at one A-One branch location has ensured the bank of an awful lot of business for decades to come — not to mention the new customers that Richards will steer toward the branch. But how did one small branch make him an engaged customer when another, much larger, branch of the same bank couldn't do it in a decade? Why, after a 10-year relationship, did Richards finally fall in love with A-One Bank?

The conundrum

Banks continue to wrestle with questions like these. A study by Booz Allen Hamilton, for example, found that 79% of European banking customers would rather buy checking and savings account products from a branch than from other sales channels. That's why smart financial institutions work so hard to make their branch locations appealing — by offering a plethora of services, mandating actionable steps for employees, and even going so far as to make the interior decoration identical from location to location. Yet variation in service levels among branch locations can be immense. It's not uncommon for one branch location to *vastly* outsell and outservice a sibling branch only blocks away — while creating engaged customer relationships — seemingly without effort. This drives bank executives crazy.

There is a reason for the variation, of course. Some branch locations are better at customer service than others, and leaders of financial institutions must look past the décor, the training programs, the steps, and the mission statement to find out why. The answer to the bank variation conundrum lies with the people behind the desks and counters — and the answer is not one bit replicable.

No more steps!

A bank branch can reach peak profitability only if it engages customers. To do that, the branch has to find and hire people who have a talent for the job and who actively work to engage customers, then keep them engaged. Relatively speaking, finding the employees may be the easy part. The last part is the hardest — *the key to a successful bank branch is leaving good employees alone.*

Many banking executives look to systemic, actionable steps to create cost-saving efficiencies and face-saving behaviors. They try mightily to make every bank branch the same to alleviate, or perhaps even eliminate, differences that can't be controlled and that can cause problems. But an over-implementation of efficiencies and steps ties bank employees' hands and can make it impossible for them to serve individuals, well, *individually*. And treating each customer the way he or she wants to be treated is how banks create engaged customer relationships.

So how can bank executives learn to back off to develop more profitable branches? How can they eliminate "bad" variation in service to foster healthy individuality? Here are some key actions that executives and managers can take:

- Speak with painstaking clarity about what the customer experience should feel like.

- Be relentlessly consistent in your coaching. Have daily conversations about the customer experience, and celebrate the successes that win customers over.

- Never tire of describing the *outcomes* you want — but let employees figure out how to get there.

- Above all, fight the urge to put in more actionable steps. They create robotic (and unhappy) frontline staff. Robots don't create an environment that grows emotional engagement.

The best people to determine what needs to be done in a bank branch are the people who work there six days a week. The branch manager knows how persnickety Mr. Smith likes to be served as a customer, and she knows which employee on her team helps Mr. Smith best. The frontline staff knows if bilingual tellers need to be added or if paperwork takes time that would be better spent with customers. Freeing bank employees to do what they need to do permits them to focus on growing relationships with customers, which is key to growing the bank's business.

Much of the work of a bank must be done by rote — vault audits, for example — but customer engagement is intensely personal and human. Banks must let the people who know best do their best. That's because backing off — as long as senior managers are clear about the outcomes they want — can produce an astonishing result: competence. As Curt Coffman, coauthor of *First, Break All the Rules* and *Follow This Path*, puts it, "The best way to make a dog crazy is to change the length of its leash every day." The same is true for people. And crazed employees don't run profitable banks.

John Richards is now settled in his new home in his new town. Twice a month, he sees the president of his bank, who encouraged him to join a local club — and was even his sponsor. "I had no idea how much easier a good bank can make your financial life," Richards says.

Clearly, Richards was both a victim and a victor of bank branch variation. With a little less stress on steps and a little more on outcomes — and a lot less stress for the customer — the branch he abandoned might become one he'd go back to.

WHY YOU SHOULD
WELCOME PROBLEMS

by Stefanie Julier

March 9, 2006

If handled effectively, a guest complaint can be the key to increasing engagement

The key to success in the hospitality industry lies in enhancing the guest experience and providing excellent customer service. This phrase — or a variation on it — has been repeated so often that most industry leaders can recite it, verbatim, in their sleep. And this notion is so prevalent — and so powerful — because it's absolutely true.

Too often, though, hotels and restaurants fail to capitalize on a perfect opportunity to enhance the guest experience. It's probably because that opportunity is initially disguised as a problem — and I use that word deliberately. Hotels and restaurants have an unexpected opportunity to engage a guest when he or she has a problem — if it is handled with excellence.

What's the problem here?

Hospitality customers who are most likely to be fully engaged are guests who are delighted by their experience and who feel that the property met or exceeded its brand promise. Guests with problems that aren't resolved to their satisfaction are three times less likely to be fully engaged with the property or brand, according to Gallup research. When guests are extremely satisfied with the problem resolution offered by the property, however, they are about twice as likely to be fully engaged as guests who are less than extremely satisfied.

According to research reported by the online publication *4Managers*, on average, each unhappy customer tells *11 people* about his or her bad experience; 13% tell *up to 20 people* about their unhappy experience. And, for every disappointed customer who complains about a problem when it occurs, another 19 will leave the property without making a complaint.

To hoteliers, the issues themselves may seem totally ordinary: the wrong room type, a lost reservation, noise disturbance, no breakfast table available. To guests, however, problems like these are meaningful enough to ruin a stay, but the majority of guests — 19 out of 20 — may never say a word; they'll just suffer in silence and resolve to avoid that property. This means that for each customer who speaks up about a problem, it's likely that 20 are spreading the word about their dissatisfaction far beyond management's sphere of control. So beware; a low number of customer complaints may not mean a low number of problems.

Thankfully, some guests do complain, which gives management the chance to rectify the problem *and* create a deeply engaged customer. The key is to deal with the guest's problem the right way. The difficulty, however, is that there is no one right way.

Everyone knows how problem resolution works: Take the guest to the side, listen carefully, don't interrupt, be empathetic and sympathetic, apologize, then offer a solution. But do we actually do it? Are we putting ourselves in the guest's position? Do we try to understand exactly what bothers guests? Do we truly care? Most importantly, do we offer the appropriate solution? Examples from the industry suggest that we do not.

Thanks, but no thanks
At a recent hospitality industry conference, an executive of one of the largest hotel chains in the world gave an example of an experience he once had at a hotel. He was traveling on business, and all he wanted was some rest in his room before his next appointment. To his dismay, his room was right next to a construction site. This would be a minor issue for some guests, but to him it wasn't; under the circumstances, sleep was impossible. So he complained at the front desk — and they brought him a fruit basket.

Here's another example, and it happened to me. A restaurant served me a meal that was totally inedible. Even the garnish looked ill. When the waiter eventually came by, I told him my problem — and he offered me a free cup of coffee. I explained that I didn't want coffee, I wanted dinner. The waiter, who gave me the impression that he was taking a huge professional risk, upped the ante and offered me a free dessert.

Both examples show a complete lack of interest in the guest's problems. The hotel exec should have been offered another room. He needed sleep, and a fruit basket wasn't going to solve his problem. If the hotel didn't have a quiet room available, it should have dispatched room service with ear plugs and a soothing cup of hot tea. Better yet, it should have offered to book him in another hotel. That's not as risky as it sounds: Guests will feel that the hotel genuinely cares if it's willing to forgo revenue from that room, and very few customers will opt to move — the hassle is too great.

Similarly, the restaurant that served me inedible food should have offered me another meal or comped the one they had served me (in case I was too disgusted to eat something else). Furthermore, the waiter should have known which menu items were the fastest to prepare, because I was in no mood to wait around for their second try. A free cup of coffee or dessert wasn't going to solve my problem. Hungry people just want dinner.

Resolution

In his book *Married to the Brand*, William J. McEwen writes: "Only about one in seven customer problems are typically handled at excellence, our research reveals. What's more, anything less than excellence appears to be enormously destructive, placing the brand marriage in peril." Because the hospitality industry relies so much on human effort, human error is inevitable, but imperiling customer engagement is not. It is quite possible to put problem-resolution processes in place, and most properties do. But those processes aren't effective unless they are handled with excellence.

The foundation of excellence lies in the standard problem-resolution process: listening, empathizing, apologizing, solving. That's also where, most of the time, the process fails. Staff members may be told the process, but many times they don't do it, or they don't do it the right way. The *right* way to resolve a problem is to tailor the response to what the individual needs; an appeasement offered merely to reduce hostility is not a solution. Real solutions require a certain amount of creativity, which means that customer-facing employees need latitude to make appropriate responses. Immediacy counts. So does attention to detail. But the standard fruit basket should be strictly prohibited, unless the guest's complaint is vitamin deficiency.

Premium customers

It's strange but true: Satisfied customers are no more likely to be loyal to a brand than dissatisfied ones, according to Gallup research — but satisfied customers won't tell 11 people about the rotten experience they had in a restaurant. More importantly, fully engaged customers represent a

23% premium to a business, according to Gallup research, while actively disengaged customers represent a 13% discount. That ought to be reason enough to make problem resolution a serious undertaking in the hospitality industry.

So remember: Whenever a guest has a problem, it's an opportunity to build engagement. That complaining guest might provide you with a clue to a hidden weakness that, if fixed, could prevent 19 other guests from leaving angry (but without reporting a complaint). So perhaps the new catchphrase should be: *The key to success in the hospitality industry lies in enhancing the guest experience, providing excellent customer service — and creating engaged guests by solving problems at excellence.*

See Related Article
"The Constant Customer" (page 61)

To learn more about the levels of customer engagement, see graphic "How Engaged Are Your Customers?" in "Managing the Value of Your Brand" (page 158)

JAMES BOND COMES TO
THE BOARDROOM

by Bill Hoffman

June 8, 2006

How competitive intelligence helps companies anticipate and counter the opposition

During the Cold War, the CIA and the KGB crouched on either side of the Iron Curtain, watching every move the other made. The CIA read everything the Russians let out, debriefed defectors, tracked methods, analyzed motives, scrutinized leaders, and matched the USSR move for move. It was called tradecraft, and it was systematic, rigorous, and — in most cases — highly effective. I can attest to this, because I saw Cold War tradecraft firsthand during my 12 years as a CIA and naval intelligence officer.

Businesses today are developing their own systems of tradecraft for some of the same reasons we did in the CIA: They want to gain a competitive advantage through a better understanding of the competition and the environment in which they operate. In the business world, tradecraft is called "competitive intelligence" (CI), and it is *not* industrial espionage; illegal or unethical actions have serious repercussions. CI is a structured, judicious method of informing business strategy. More importantly, it's an innovation engine that drives better business outcomes.

Making the case for CI

If your company knows nothing more about your competitors than they know about you, or if your offerings are identical to everyone else's in your industry, your business will be unable to differentiate its products, services, or brands. CI offers a framework that helps companies break away from the pack. It gives businesses a means to scan for threats from rival companies, to be optimally configured and properly positioned to confront those threats, and to adapt quickly to changes in the competitive environment. And when it's done well, CI creates significantly more value for businesses than it costs.

A recent Trendsetter Barometer survey from PricewaterhouseCoopers found that CEOs of fast-growth companies who rated CI as being either "very" or "critically" important increased revenues by 14.2 %, versus 11.8% for all others. Merck, the pharmaceutical giant, says its CI efforts saved the company $200 million in 30 months. After I implemented a CI system in a major U.S. financial services company, within 18 months, ROI to the bank was 10 times the cost of implementation, while the revenue impact was in the tens of millions of dollars. In this article, I'll share key insights from what I have learned from my hands-on experience.

The framework

Most businesses already engage in some form of CI: They note the ads of their competitors, read up on them in *The Wall Street Journal*, or check out their rivals' Web sites. Open-source materials like these serve a purpose, but the information gleaned from them rarely reaches the right people at the right time. In reality, many Fortune 500 businesses remain woefully unprepared to understand and counter threats from competitors. High school football teams know more about their rivals than do most companies.

Good CI is vastly more organized and judicious than merely noting competitors' ads and reading the trades. Its basic framework involves determining your company's key intelligence questions, then collecting, analyzing, and disseminating the intelligence. To do this effectively, a company monitors the competition; understands its goals, strategy, and tactics; anticipates its actions and understands the expected impact of those actions; and implements counter strategies. It sounds simple enough, but the components of the framework matter.

Much like our Cold War national defense posture, the CI framework is a strategic triad; its key components are an internal collection system, an external collection system, and a competitor analysis function. The first, the internal collection system, is the most overlooked. It requires human intelligence deployed in the field — in other words, "boots on the ground."

Companies can start developing an internal collection system by interviewing employees who know the competition personally and intimately in some way. CI staff should question former employees of the competition according to legal and ethical standards (not within the first 90 days of employment; don't ask for trade secrets; keep the environment pressure-free). Ask them soft questions, such as *What did you like about working there?*

What didn't you like? Why did you leave? What's the culture like? What are the primary differences between your former and current workplaces?

But "defectors" aren't the only source of intelligence. For example, CI staff can also take field trips to visit competitors' locations (though it's unethical for them to deliberately misrepresent themselves). Trade shows are also an excellent source of information. When employees attend these shows, they should look closely at the competition: What are they offering? How are they marketing it? What response did they get? How many people did they send? In this instance, "boots on the ground" can gather information efficiently and effectively on the products or services your competitors are offering — and on how well they were received.

The second component is the external collection system, which uncovers market and customer intelligence. As mentioned previously, open-source material falls into this category, but again, that's just a small part of the information available for analysis. Comprehensive external collection systems can provide an early warning of changes in competitive conditions. CI staff use a disciplined approach to collect this information, including probing the unmet needs of new and potential clients; analyzing the strategies and messaging tactics used by the competition to acquire new clients; and surveying competitors' customers to identify weaknesses to exploit and risks to mitigate. CI staff should discover what keeps counterpart execs up at night; they should listen closely to what customers say when they switch from a competitor. Essentially, they should know their competitors' customers better than their competitors do.

The third component, competitor analysis function, has several key parts, including value chain analysis (VCA), leadership intelligence, and simulation intelligence.

- **VCA** takes an in-depth look at a competitor's products, services, and processes to identify the linchpins of its competitive advantages (or weaknesses) across the competitor's value chain, from customer acquisition and deepening the customer relationship to retention and fulfillment. For example, a company can use this approach to pinpoint that the source of revenue growth at a key competitor is its new client acquisition strategy; the company then knows where to focus its efforts against that competitor.

- **Leadership intelligence** involves analyzing key competitor staff, including their motivations, decision-making styles and processes, personality and behavior weaknesses to exploit, and strengths to counter. This analysis will help you better understand your competitors' leadership tendencies — and the moves their leadership is likely to make.

- **Simulation intelligence** is a systematic process that uses "what-if" scenario planning and "war games." When conducted jointly with key company decision makers in a workshop environment, this process can uncover unseen opportunities for the company to boost competitive advantages. This requires bold, creative thinking — and it's actually a lot of fun.

Let's say, for example, that your company is rolling out a new product launch. You could build on the knowledge you've gained — from "defectors" during the internal collection process or from external collection sources such as trade shows — to conduct a "war game." By matching your key executive intelligence consumers against the CI unit, you can play out how your leading competitors might respond to the new product launch. You can then use the results to preempt likely competitor attempts to counter your product launch.

Integration

To get results, CI requires tight organization and constant innovation. But even the best intelligence is useless if it doesn't get to the right people in the right way. An effective CI system requires a nerve center or a department of its own, and a small, nimble CI unit is much more valuable than a large, slow-moving one. The bank I mentioned had a CI center staffed with 10 people, and that was all that was needed to support an organization with more than 170,000 employees. A staff of two, or three, or even just one, can be sufficient for smaller organizations, as long as its leader has authority and clearance. In other words, the CI manager must be integrated into the worklife of the company's strategists; he or she must be a partner to the people who make decisions and must be at the center of the CI neural network.

The CI manager must also be visible; the entire company should understand the goals and methods of the CI team. They should also know the process for reporting intelligence, and perhaps be rewarded for doing it. Above all, the CI team should stress ethics; they should promote the importance of the information they contribute to the company and the value they add to the bottom line.

I have noticed that CI units are most successful when they have an in-house champion. The champion doesn't necessarily need to be on the team, but he or she does need the ear of C-level execs. And the best teams are those staffed with good strategic thinkers. The CI manager doesn't need to poach the company's best analysts from other teams, but CI does require creativity and critical thinking.

In addition, because customers and employees are a vital part of effective CI, this process works best in companies that have engaged customers and employees. Though high engagement levels aren't strictly necessary, they do help — engaged employees are more likely to think about competitor intelligence, look for it, recognize it, and forward it to the CI unit. And engaged customers are significantly more willing to discuss what they like about your business and what they dislike about your competitor. Furthermore, talking with engaged customers can help the CI unit identify strategic flaws in your rivals that your company can exploit; it can also help you spot your company's strategic weaknesses so you can take defensive action. When a business has high employee and customer engagement and thorough CI, it has a rare opportunity to see threats from every direction, enabling the company to mount and deploy the appropriate response.

Innovation factory
Good tradecraft builds on itself. When ideas gathered from customer and employee feedback are added to what CI learns from external sources, it can lead to incremental innovations in products and services at the business-unit level. By adding intelligence from competitive analysis to this mix, senior management has the information it needs to "connect the dots" to identify market gaps. Through the intelligence it collects and analyzes, the CI center can become an innovation factory for the company. Robust concept development and prototyping processes start rolling out. These ideas translate into strategies that cross business units and feed project teams, who then take the ideas from development to execution.

These key success factors indicate whether or not a CI unit is functioning at its peak. A top-performing CI unit:

• demonstrates that it creates a unique value — value that would not have existed without the CI function

- leverages unique, primary human source intelligence to build an innovation engine. If all its information is coming from publicly available open sources, the CI unit isn't probing deeply enough.

- incorporates all available information from existing customer and employee engagement work

- focuses on the company's most pressing strategic "points of pain." Its most valuable intelligence is information that can help solve these problems.

- ensures that all its activities are conducted within strict legal and ethical guidelines

Avoiding the pitfalls

I have observed organizations that implemented competitive intelligence units, but — in spite of good intentions and high hopes — their efforts have failed. That's because there are a few common pitfalls that hobble CI before it even gets off the ground. One drawback is putting the CI unit too low in the organizational hierarchy. In most organizations, decisions and strategies are made on the executive level, so the CI unit needs to report to the CEO, the CMO, or the head of strategy/strategic planning. But at the same time, the CI unit needs to provide detailed information at the local level; for instance, if it knows a competitor is launching an offering in a single market, the CI team needs to alert the company's locations in that market in plenty of time to counter the threat.

Another snag comes from a lack of common processes. Too many methods of reporting, analysis, and evaluation are confusing, and employees will soon ignore them — and this can be a serious problem for a team that depends heavily on volunteered information. Further, inadequate governance of legal and ethical norms will doom the CI unit and could possibly invite legal trouble. And finally, the CI team will be perceived as valuable if it is seen to create value. For that reason, inadequate measurement and reporting of its performance will undermine a CI venture, even if the unit is highly successful.

Game on

Competitive intelligence looks, and *is*, complex, rigorous, highly organized, and smart. But it's another thing too: CI is a lot of fun. There's a reason people like reading spy novels and flock to James Bond movies — among other things, they're exciting because the tradecraft is exciting. Pitting your best minds against those of your opponent is invigorating; besting the other guy is the thrill many of us have chased since we joined the business world. That spirit is an important part of the CI toolkit — and it's one that quickly spreads to the rest of the organization. And with engagement like that, how can you lose?

HOW THE RITZ-CARLTON IS
REINVENTING ITSELF

Interviewed by Jennifer Robison

October 12, 2006

A top executive with one of the world's most admired brands tells how Ritz is creating "guests for life"

A *GMJ* Q&A with Simon Cooper, Chief Operating Officer and President of The Ritz-Carlton Hotel Company, L.L.C.

The Ritz-Carlton is one of the best known, most admired brand names in the world, and it has been for decades. Movies have used the Ritz name to connote glamour, elegance, and luxury. The word *Ritz* has even become a part of our language — just about everyone knows what *ritzy* means.

Money can't buy this kind of brand recognition. But brand recognition alone doesn't keep hotel guests coming back. In fact, brand recognition is just the first step in a customer's journey toward engagement with the total experience that is The Ritz-Carlton brand, according to Simon F. Cooper, chief operating officer and president of The Ritz-Carlton Hotel Company, L.L.C. Gallup research shows that emotionally engaged guests spend much more money than loyal guests — and emotionally engaged guests are the customers Cooper is most interested in. But engaging customers is hard work, and it's just as hard for the world's best known luxury brand as it is for any other business.

Cooper, however, is a master of turning a brand promise into customer love. A 30-year veteran of the industry, this hotelier has opened 25 of Ritz-Carlton's 61 locations. And he is spearheading the company's move into resorts, residences, and fractional ownership. There isn't much that Cooper doesn't know about hospitality, including the very real challenges facing The Ritz-Carlton. In this interview, Cooper discusses how Ritz-Carlton's fame can undermine its brand promise, how to train staff to be spontaneous, and why engagement is The Ritz-Carlton's most important commodity — and the only thing its customers can't buy.

GMJ: The Ritz-Carlton is one of the best known brand names ever. What branding problems could your company possibly have?

Simon Cooper: One of our challenges is that Ritz-Carlton is probably more known as a traditional luxury brand because it's the most mature luxury brand in the market. The history of César Ritz is well known, and the expression "ritzy" has certainly been around for a long time.

But that expression probably is tied to the perception that Ritz offers traditional, "chandelier type" luxury, and that's a perception that we're trying to move away from. If Ritz-Carlton as a brand is going to be relevant to our customers in the future, we must balance traditional luxury — or what would have been thought luxurious twenty years ago — with how luxury is executed today, which is quite different. Today, the role of style and design is far greater than it was twenty years ago.

GMJ: How have luxury hotels changed?

Cooper: Twenty years ago, hotels were relatively alike. They were trying to emulate European chateaus, with brocade, crystal, that kind of thing. Today, the role of design and style, and of more contemporary products, has become much more important. I think this reflects changes in what consumers value.

GMJ: Have luxury consumers changed?

Cooper: If you had cast your eye across the lobby of The Ritz-Carlton Boston in 1982, it's likely that most guests would have been mature, formally dressed, and male. Today's guests are much more diverse — younger, more casually elegant, and less formal. There are many more women guests, as well as more families.

GMJ: You've got a lot of competition in the luxury market, and they're all gunning for The Ritz-Carlton. What's your strategy?

Cooper: No matter how outstanding your ladies and gentlemen are, you've got to start with the right product and the right location. In a global portfolio of hotels, the entry stakes are having hotels in the right locations, then having the right product when guests get there. And it takes the right people. You start with where in Moscow your hotel is located, for example, then you animate it to create an absolutely outstanding memory.

GMJ: Speaking of the people, you call your staff "ladies and gentlemen." Why?

Cooper: Because our motto is: "Ladies and gentlemen serving ladies and gentlemen." We chose the motto because we don't want our ladies and gentlemen to think of themselves as servile. Our ladies and gentlemen might not have the wealth, knowledge, or education of our guests, but they do have the same values.

GMJ: Can you tell me what engaged employees do for your brand promise?

Cooper: They're critical to the image and to the execution. When we build a hotel and put in a physical product, that's the initial platform. Everything has to work perfectly, so there is an incredible focus upon functionality — on the product, systems, and food and beverage. It's easy to say we've got great people who can overcome everything — but in truth, they can't overcome *everything*. If things don't happen when guests want them to, then that creates a significant roadblock to creating emotional engagement.

Once the platform is right, then the challenge is animating that platform. At The Ritz-Carlton, ninety percent of the brand image is emotional: It's in how the ladies and gentlemen bring it to life.

As for the value proposition for our guests, they don't even notice there's a platform if everything works. So then the value promise becomes "making their stay memorable." Well, *people* create memories, not things. If we ask guests what color the carpet was in their guest room, they probably won't know. The real value comes from the ladies and gentlemen who bring that hotel to life. Ten percent is the platform, but the rest is people.

GMJ: But you're making a lot of changes to the platform, all over the world. You're changing physical locations and losing some of the employee scripting that Ritz is known for, as well as lots of other behaviors traditional to Ritz-Carlton.

Cooper: Despite the fact that we're the number-one brand, we're making significant changes. That's a tough row to hoe, because we're an organization that's winning accolades left, right, and center — and we have great guest scores, great employee satisfaction scores — nothing but positive results on every single metric. My challenge is to convince our people that we *need* to make all these changes. Now, instead of focusing on process, we're concerning ourselves with outcomes. Though the "scripting" for staff worked so well for so many years, we're focusing on the emotional connections between our ladies and gentlemen and our guests.

Frankly, what was inhibiting us was a mechanical service delivery — some would even call it robotic. It wasn't that our employees didn't mean that it was a pleasure for them to serve you. But if guests heard that same phrase ten times from ten different people, they thought, this must be part of the training — which was true. Now what we want from our ladies and gentlemen is a genuine response that's also spontaneous.

GMJ: But emotional connections depend on uncountable, even subconscious, human interactions. How do you train that?

Cooper: You can't train it at all.

GMJ: So how do you get the outcomes you want when you can't train people how to spark genuine emotional connections? And how do you do it without killing their spontaneity?

Cooper: We try not to kill spontaneity, because spontaneity is what creates the perfect outcome we're looking for. For example, when I'm talking to a group of ladies and gentlemen, especially new employees, about how to open a hotel, I ask them what guests can buy. Then I write down their answers. I write down things such as a room, or food and beverage service, or a spa treatment, and the like. Then I ask, "Now tell me what they *can't* buy." Obviously, guests can't buy things like smiles or relationships or caring service. Then I ask the simple question, "What do you think the guest values?" That's the value proposition — that's how you engage a customer. You engage them emotionally by giving them things they just can't buy anywhere else.

A majority of our guests are well-traveled, wealthy, well-informed, have high expectations, and can buy anything. What they're really looking for are things they can't buy, and many of those things come from spontaneity. So you train your ladies and gentlemen that the most important thing they can do is create a guest for life, and if that means that they must drop what they're doing to help a guest, if that means that they must empathize, they should do it.

We actually compensate our general managers and leaders on customer engagement now, rather than customer loyalty, because we're trying to win the hearts and minds of our guests. And this is good for our business. We have researched what an engaged guest spends versus what a less engaged guests spends, and engaged guests clearly spend more money.

GMJ: Who is your greatest competition?

Cooper: The Four Seasons. From a global competitive point of view, they're the only serious player as we speak. They have about seventeen percent of the distribution, and we have about seventeen percent. Locally, we tend to find the competition is often a great independent hotel, especially in Europe. Often, its advantage is that its sole focus is being a great hotel in a great location. The great hotels in Paris or London are in iconic locations, and economics of scale are not important to them. They're in iconic locations, and they can charge iconic prices.

GMJ: The Ritz-Carlton has hotels all over the world, some in places that may have a very different workplace culture than hotels in the United States or Europe. How do you train people to respond with genuine emotion in, say, Beijing?

Cooper: Even in China, they understand empowerment in our hotel.

GMJ: How do you get to that point?

Cooper: Through encouragement. You can't just script responses, so we encourage the right behaviors through reward and recognition. Now, we only reward through recognition, so we reinforce the actions we're looking for through the kind of stories we tell and the kind of actions we write thank-you cards for. If an employee does something for a guest that is very personal — for example, he leaves work for two hours to take a guest's broken suitcase to someone he knows can fix it, then brings it back in time for the guest's flight — we recognize that. We constantly remind people of the kind of actions that we want to see.

GMJ: Why don't you reward with money?

Cooper: Because we don't think that money sponsors the kind of behavior we're looking for. We believe ladies and gentlemen should be making each guest's stay memorable because they want to do that, not because they get compensated for doing that. At one hotel chain, employees get, like, five bucks if they're mentioned in a comment card. So what do you think happens? "Here's your guest comment card, sir, which I've filled out for you." Also, once you quit paying, people are just stymied.

GMJ: What's the perfect Ritz-Carlton manager like?

Cooper: First off, they aren't managers, they're leaders. The perfect leader is someone who continually balances the constituencies — employees, guests, owners, the brand, the community — that he or she serves. We look for a leader who is personally never satisfied, who is able to continually improve the organization. We look for people who, even with the biggest win or the greatest satisfaction, are happy for fifteen seconds. Then they think, "How do I do it better next time?"

BRAND

BUILDING BRAND
DIFFERENTIATION

by William J. McEwen

June 26, 2000

People are the key

We are often reminded that we are marketing at a time when competing products perform largely at parity levels and when almost any product improvement can be matched by a competitor.

That was not the case some 50 years ago, when packaged goods companies were demonstrating how brands were built and showing the world how profitable businesses could be established and sustained. Brands were differentiated based on product performance (whiter, cleaner, softer, "lemon-fresh"). Product development was a cornerstone of corporate activity, and continual product improvement was an acknowledged (and well-funded) objective for any brand marketer.

However, while companies still invest heavily in research and development and still seek a product performance edge wherever it can be found, it is a marketing maxim that differences in performance now are often minimal at best. It's not merely that many colas taste the same or that many competing pizzas are indistinguishable. Checking accounts are alike. Cellular phone services seem interchangeable. Cars look alike, and — if syndicated customer ratings are to be believed — they perform and satisfy customers to increasingly similar degrees as well.

There is, thus, a critical marketing dilemma that confronts brand managers in this age when products and brands seem interchangeable. How can differentiation — which is the sine qua non of branding — be achieved? How can a brand be made to stand apart from its competitors so that it will be chosen, and chosen again?

Lacking meaningful product performance differences, marketers have turned to other familiar marketing tools as a means to establish unique associations with their brands and to create a unique position relative to competition.

Location, location, location

Retailers, grocers, and bankers, along with gasoline and hospitality marketers, have traditionally emphasized another marketing resource: the "bricks and mortar" solution. Here, brand selection is reinforced by proximity, availability, and ease of access. In other words, products that are conveniently available will — all other things being equal — be chosen most often.

Bricks and mortar is, of course, an expensive solution to the differentiation dilemma. In addition, there are important threats to this marketing solution posed by various direct-marketing alternatives. What could be more convenient than a store on the corner? Possibilities include a catalog on the table, an 800 number, and more recently, a Web site. These alternatives all serve to make physical location advantages rather moot.

The price is right

What other tools are available? Pricing has been another marketing tool often used to establish differentiation. The obvious challenge, however, is how to "own" a real (or perceived) long-term price advantage. Short-term offers, deals, and price promotions can provide a brand with an apparent price advantage and the appearance of differentiation. However, as the acknowledged goal of brand marketing is to build customer loyalty (i.e., not just trial, but repeat business), a short-term advantage or a temporary point of differentiation is simply not sufficient. Sustainable differentiation is required. If the sustainable differentiation is to be based on price, and is to be owned over time, the marketer must occupy the "low-cost provider" position. There can be only one of these in a category. It is an enviable position, no doubt, but only for one competitor — and, given similar production and distribution costs, it simply isn't a reasonable goal for most of the marketers competing today.

Say it with advertising

Where else can marketers turn? The most commonly pursued marketing solution lies in the area of brand communications — advertising and promotions.

At a time when products perform in similar ways, when availability differences are often minimal, and when price differentiation may be only temporary, brand differentiation must be achieved through brand communication — or so the theory goes. After all, there are four Ps in marketing — and, if you cannot differentiate your offerings on **Product, Place**, or **Price**, the astute marketer turns to **Promotions**.

Powerful advertising messages, creatively carving a sustainable and unique position in the minds of a receptive audience. That's the ticket!

Or is it?

In a recent major research and development effort, Gallup surveyed more than 1,600 consumers in each of three service categories that are often cited as examples of product performance parity: checking accounts, long-distance telephone service, and domestic airline travel.

Brands in each of these categories have attempted to create product performance differentiation using strategies ranging from fiber optics to on-time arrival statistics. Many of the competing brands have employed location (branch banking, supermarket banking, and ATMs), pricing (10 cents a minute, no fees), or heavy advertising spending in an attempt to attract and retain customers.

Has it worked?

The customer perspective

To shed light on the impact of these various differentiation tools, Gallup talked to customers in each of these three categories. We obtained information about their current purchasing habits, their brand consideration sets, and their intended brand behaviors (purchase/choice for the next possible use occasion). We asked about a variety of factors that could influence customer decisions to repeat or to switch, and we looked at their perceptions of the leading competitors. These decision-driving factors included ratings of Product, of Price (value), of Place (locational convenience), and of Promotions (advertising). Added to this list (the "four Ps" of marketing) was a fifth P: **People**.

Why "People"? Because Gallup has found that the key to an enduring customer relationship may well be the "customer-facing employees" who provide the products and services and who represent the brand to customers. It is the people, in many service-related categories, who are challenged to fulfill the brand promise and who bridge the gap between brand promise and brand delivery.

What did we learn?

We learned that, in the eyes of customers — and despite the best efforts of marketers — there truly is a great deal of parity. Most customers view several brands, whether they are banks, long-distance telephone services, or airlines, as basically the same.

This perceived parity extends beyond product performance. It's not just that airlines, long-distance telephone services, and banks are all equally reliable. In spite of enormous price competition — or perhaps because of it — customers feel that most airlines feature the same ticket prices, most long-distance providers offer the same deals, and most banks charge the same for their checking services.

Thus, price — as well as product performance — is not what differentiates these brands. So, is price what keeps customers coming back (or keeps them from leaving)?

In most cases, no.

What builds repeat business?

In the **airline** category, price and product were not significant loyalty drivers for customers of any of the six domestic airlines studied. Instead, accessibility and schedule convenience were important. That would be expected, although schedule convenience appears to have only about half the impact as the reinforcing quality of airline ads when it comes to building a brand bond with the customer.

More important than schedule convenience — and as much as three or four times more important than brand advertising — are the people on the ground and in the air who "touch" the customer. Customers who report that an airline's employees stand out are up to 15 times more likely to say they will choose that airline the next time they fly.

When it comes to **long-distance telephone** service, there's a different story. Locational convenience is not an issue; competitors are seen as equally accessible. What drives the decision to continue with a particular carrier? It's not the reliability of the product. Frequently, it is the price/value customers perceive they're getting. Those who believe they are being provided excellent value are two to four times more likely to say they would stay with that same provider.

Again, however, the role of people in this category — in which interaction with employee representatives occurs far less frequently than it does for those climbing onboard airplanes — is dramatic. Customers who feel that the people associated with their long-distance provider are exceptional are from 8 to 12 times more likely to stay with that provider. Thus, when we looked at what motivates customer retention, the company's employees are actually three to four times more important than the perceived value of the service.

It's a similar story in the **banking** world, at least when it comes to checking accounts. Given the perception of price and product parity in this category, neither factor proves to be significant in motivating customers to return. For some banks, locational convenience is a factor. Advertising is an important reinforcer of customer commitment for others.

For all six U.S. banks examined, however, the number one driver of intended loyalty isn't location. It isn't price. It isn't product, and it isn't advertising. It's **people**. Just as in the other categories, customers who feel that a bank's employees stand out are far more likely — as much as 10 to 20 times — to indicate that they would keep their checking account at that bank.

This is consistent — and powerful — evidence that people play a key role in building customer brand loyalty.

Does this mean that product performance doesn't matter? Not at all. Product performance is, however, largely a "dissatisfier." Unreliable performance will drive away customers from a bank, an airline, or a long-distance service. Customers expect highly reliable and dependable service. It does not increase loyalty.

Can outstanding value increase loyalty? Yes. And raising prices can drive customers away. Can increased locational convenience build loyalty? As long as it remains clearly superior to the competitions', it can. Can advertising? Again, yes. Advertising can create an important emotional connection between the service or company and its customers.

Yet, across all brands, in each of these three categories, the most powerful factor in building commitment is none of these. The most powerful marketing tool isn't even thought of as a marketing tool by most companies. It's the people.

Can people be a differentiator in a world of service and product "parity"? They can be, and they are. Moreover, they represent potential brand differentiation on the single most powerful driver of continued customer commitment.

OUTSOURCING THE BRAND
by William J. McEwen

March 4, 2002

How to create consistency in customer contact

A recent announcement by Apple Computer seems at odds with the actions that a company would take to build its business. Apple announced that it would halt sales of its products through Circuit City stores. Instead, Apple will focus its sales efforts on moving product either directly through its Web site or through Apple retail outlets opened during the past year.

On the surface, this might seem strange. Why would Apple choose to abandon a powerful and far-reaching means for distributing its products? Circuit City boasts more than 600 superstore sales outlets in 161 markets. This retailer knows how to move computers and has proven that it can sell products, to the tune of about a billion dollars a month.

Surely Apple would want to capitalize on the customers who regularly visit Circuit City stores, who often are looking for just what Apple wants to sell them. Why walk away from this market?

Apple mentions its own retail outlets, but it currently operates only 27 of them. That's a far cry from the more than 600 stores Circuit City could offer. Apple has just three stores in New York, one in Texas, and none in either Washington or Oregon. Why, at a time when the company is promoting its new iMac and PowerMac G4 products, would they limit their market horizons?

The answer is simple. Apple wants to control customer contact and is willing to trade off "reach" for impact. It would rather reach a smaller number of customers so it can consistently put its best marketing foot forward with each of them. And Apple is acknowledging that it will build its brand and its brand relationships one customer at a time.

People power in brand building

Why remove Apple products from Circuit City? It's not because Circuit City carries multiple brands, and thus a customer entering one of their stores may well confront an HP Pavilion, a Compaq Presario, a Sony VAIO, and a Toshiba Satellite before ever meeting a PowerMac. After all, Procter & Gamble doesn't remove its products from Safeway or Wal-Mart simply because these chains carry multiple brands of the laundry soaps, diapers, toothpastes, and potato chips P&G seeks to promote.

The world of computer marketing is very different. Computer brands don't sell themselves. Nor can Apple count on a clear price advantage to direct customer choice. Computers are more like cars than like toothpaste. They are sold by people, regardless of whether consumers have contact with these people by phone or face-to-face.

In fact, Gallup Organization research offers evidence of just how powerful these people can be when it comes to building an enduring connection between a company and its customers. Sales and service representatives, whether they're selling autos or consumer electronics, have a profound impact on the customer relationship.

This same Gallup research underscores a fundamental need for every brand and the reason why Apple reached its decision. Without a strong base of brand *confidence*, there can be no continuing customer relationship. And what builds customer confidence? Product performance and reliability, for starters. But this research found that the expertise and helpfulness of customer representatives are almost as powerful as product performance. Customers consider these reps an essential part of the brand. These "people" dimensions represent critical components for Apple as it attempts to build connections with customers. Connections cannot be created and sustained through product performance alone.

Keep the focus on the brand

This is the dilemma that has confronted Apple. Should the company continue to capitalize on Circuit City's widespread distribution system? The retailer could provide a steady stream of consumer traffic, but Apple would be attempting to extend its brand connection through people with mixed allegiance to various computer brands and with varying degrees of Apple brand expertise. Should Apple spend money to bring people to Circuit City through a variety of advertising and promotion promises, only to see them build brand connections with Circuit City, rather than Apple?

Apple decided to focus on building Apple-only brand connections with its prospects and customers. That's an expensive solution with considerable risk. Building, staffing, and supporting a retail store network is far more expensive than taking advantage of an existing one.

Apple opted for a solution that the company believes will afford it a far larger share of a much smaller pie.

Apple's brand-building solution is far less like that of the typical packaged goods product marketer or consumer electronics manufacturer and far more akin to how automakers such as Saturn, Acura, Lexus, and Infiniti approach their brand-building challenges. As these companies set out to introduce new vehicle brands, they created entirely new brand-focused and brand-committed dealerships. That's also the route that fashion retailers like The Gap have taken, and it's essentially the same strategy that Ray Kroc employed to build absolute consistency at each customer touchpoint at every McDonald's store.

This is the route of maximum contact control. It's neither the quickest nor the cheapest route to customer relationship management. Yet after weighing the trade-offs between reach and impact, Apple chose to take this new and ambitious direction. If 1984 signaled a time of great change for Apple and its products, 2002 seems every bit as momentous for Apple and its brand relationships.

MAKING MARKET
SEGMENTATION MEANINGFUL   *by William J. McEwen*

February 12, 2004

There are lots of different ways to segment markets. Many of them are useless.

Market segmentation draws on a simple, yet compelling, core premise: Consumers aren't all the same, so they shouldn't be treated identically. Marketers recognized this fundamental fact a very long time ago. Yet the issue remains as relevant today as it was when Wendell Smith talked about it half a century ago. Surprisingly, however, the past 50 years have produced precious little progress in how companies think about, define, and deal with consumer differences.

Consumers certainly differ in any number of ways. For marketers, some differences are important, but many are trivial. Separating the important from the trivial is key, since only the important differences have a direct impact on the effectiveness of a company's marketing programs.

The solution sounds so simple: First, identify the important determinants of consumer response to a company's products or services, then segment consumers into buckets accordingly. But exactly what are these "important determinants"? What should be the basis for segmentation into "buckets"? That's where the battle begins.

Slicing segments for success

As any methodologist would readily affirm, there are vast numbers of ways in which consumers can be divided, grouped, clustered, or classified into segments. These range from simple crosstabulations and correlations to far more complex factor, cluster, and latent-class analyses. Regardless of the method used, however, the logic of segmentation remains essentially the same, and so does the goal: making marketing more effective by identifying a meaningful and manageable number of distinct "people types."

However, in spite of the ready availability of segmentation methodologies and the obvious appeal of — and need for — dividing markets into meaningful groupings, there has been a disconnect between segmentation's compelling promise and its typical performance. Yes, there are cases in which market segmentation has helped focus product development or marketing and communications planning. But there also have been far too many occasions in which segmentation studies have produced hugely disappointing results.

The key consideration isn't *how* to conduct the clustering — but rather, what *basis* should be used for clustering and grouping consumers. Merely defining some number of consumer groupings doesn't ensure that the identified segments will prove to be *useful* in helping to focus a company's marketing efforts. Tossing myriad measures into the statistical hopper and hoping that the computer will somehow discern a meaningful pattern probably won't yield valuable marketing insights. Nor will it show the way to a more effective marketing program. A million monkeys and a million typewriters have yet to produce another *Hamlet*.

The real challenge is to identify *meaningfully distinct* segments of prospects and customers. After all, the goal of segmentation is to make companies smarter and their marketing efforts markedly more productive. With this in mind, consider the multitude of measures that have typically been used for segmenting prospects and customers, including:

- **affective measures:** attitudes, images, and opinions about brands and brand-related activities. Important and useful? Not always, since many seemingly relevant attitudes and images have proven to have little or no direct relationship to what customers actually *do*.

  Consumers who hold a brand in high esteem may nevertheless choose not to purchase it. Satisfied customers may switch allegiances. Brands with a great deal of cognitive or rational appeal turn out to have no emotional appeal. Attitudes, quite simply, are imperfect predictors of the business outcomes for which brand managers are justifiably held accountable.

- **behavioral measures:** current category and brand purchase/usage patterns and experiences; communication and shopping behaviors. Useful? At times. Yet current purchase and shopping habits are often inadequate predictors of *future* behaviors.

  Current behaviors may have been bought (or bribed) at great cost — and with no lasting benefit — to the company. Also, the company's greatest opportunities may not lie with heavy category buyers or users, in spite of the appeal of "fishing where the fish are."

- **classification measures:** geographic and/or demographic characteristics. These are readily measurable, of course. But there are far too many examples of older consumers who behave like younger ones, strugglers who behave like affluent consumers, and near neighbors who nonetheless exhibit completely different shopping and purchasing behaviors. Demography cannot separate great prospects from mediocre ones.

- **general measures:** global life stage and/or lifestyle attitudes, interests, and opinions about life, family, and life requirements. These are tantalizingly interesting, to be sure. Yet the track record for lifestyle segmentation's usefulness is, at best, mixed.

  Segmentation on this basis assumes that the defined groupings are somehow enduring. They are not. Situational variables intervene. Consumers are not the same in all situations. A consumer may well be a "coupon clipper" when it comes to buying laundry detergent and a "sybarite" when it comes to selecting perfume or a bottle of wine.

- **product-category specific measures:** product attributes, benefits, wants, and needs. These most directly pertain to the company's particular brand and product mix, and thus hold great promise of actionability. However, in practice, the focus tends to be on the rational product/service attributes or on rational wants and needs that will supposedly differentiate competing brand users/prospects and help to define targets for each. What's wrong with that? Merely the fact that consumers do not select among alternatives — most of which increasingly offer parity of performance — based on rational considerations. The rational side of human nature reveals only a portion of the true picture, and it can be greatly misleading.

Companies have relied on these various measures, sometimes separately and sometimes in combination, in their attempts to detect the clusters or segments that might exist within the audiences to whom they market. Each of these measures, however, has fallen well short of meeting the overall challenge to be *useful*. They have either proven to be unstable, non-actionable, or irrelevant.

Something is clearly missing.

One major problem is that so many segmentation bases are in fact only minimally related to actual business outcomes. They may appear interesting. They may even appear intriguing. They generate lots of workshop discussions. But in many cases, they are also largely irrelevant. They result in segments that either can't be reproduced, can't be addressed, or have no marketing viability. Thus, they are of no help to a company seeking to improve its marketing planning and performance.

The net result is that far too many applications of segmentation, as Clayton M. Christensen and Michael E. Raynor note in *The Innovator's Solution*, result in marketers designing "me too" promises and products that merely mimic the features and attributes offered by their competitors. And, we might add, they also result in "me too" marketing that targets the exact same audience "buckets" with the exact same appeals. Thus, instead of stimulating *differentiation* in product performance or brand communications, the result has been quite the opposite.

Segments that matter

What's missing from the extensive list of alternative segmentation bases is this: something that can generate the crucial marketing insights that simple geographic, demographic, or behavioral segmentation schemes lack, something that truly reveals key *insights* about consumers.

Too many approaches reveal only superficial information. Too many create the misleading impression that companies know their customers simply because they have applied human names or psychographic labels to consumers — clusters that may be neither enduringly real nor meaningfully distinct. Naming is not the same as understanding.

What has been missing from each of the available approaches is a deep understanding of the ways in which consumers form *lasting* connections with the brands they buy and use. Scientists at Gallup, however, have been probing the nature of these relationships through extensive exploration into "customer engagement" and the bonds that are forged between companies and consumers.

These Gallup investigations have revealed a simple truth that sheds important light on the ways in which companies can identify and act upon truly *meaningful* customer segments. The connections, and the potential for connections, that exist between consumers and branded products or services are, at their core, *emotional.* More to the point, these emotional connections represent a powerful new way to segment consumers — one that offers companies a more complete view of their challenges and opportunities.

- Emotional connections are *meaningful.* Gallup researchers have shown that these connections are bellwether business performance indicators, directly related to key business outcomes ranging from share of wallet and purchase frequency to customer retention and profitability. Customers who are fully engaged with their current brands represent assets that are far more valuable than those who are less engaged. Prospects high in "engagement potential" for a brand are far more likely to form a lasting relationship with that brand. In short, engagement matters.

- Emotional connections are *actionable.* Gallup has shown that the key marketing drivers (product, promotion, process, price, place, and people) of these emotional connections can be reliably identified and, more to the point, they can be enhanced by marketing actions.

- Emotional connections help define the extent to which alternative consumer segments are *viable,* because these connections reveal the extent to which *lasting* consumer relationships are being built. Heaviness of use does not necessarily indicate the strength of the customer relationship, nor is it a useful tool for targeting desirable prospects. Heavy users may switch brands, and they may do so regularly. Emotionally engaged users do not.

Impressive credentials, to be sure. But why would consumer segmentation that is based on a brand's evident degree of "emotional connectedness" be a better solution for guiding a company's marketing efforts?

Of course, it could be interesting for a brand manager to know that there is a large group of consumers who are 35-49 years of age and earn in excess of $75,000 a year. It might also be interesting to know that they have written a letter to their state senator, shop for clothing at least once a month, associate a particular store with having a wide variety of current fashions, say they try to keep up with the latest fashions, and reportedly choose their clothing based on how well they feel the clothes are made. But is it really *useful* to know this? In truth, not one of these measures reflects the extent to which these consumers have formed any sort of emotional bond with a store.

How much *more* useful would it be to know the extent to which these consumers have an emotional connection with a particular store — but not with its major competitors? Only emotional connectedness represents the existence — or the lack — of a meaningful bond between the brand and the consumer. And yet that brand connection represents the company's most important asset.

Segmentation based on measures that reveal the *true* strength and health of a company's consumer relationships provides companies with the crucial insights that have been missing from their previous segmentation efforts. Whether measures of emotional engagement are focused on current customers, as measured by customer engagement, or on non-user prospects, as measured by engagement potential, they provide the basis for market segmentation that can at last meet the management challenge.

How important is an emotional connection? Nobel laureate Daniel Kahneman contends that emotions have a basic and elemental role in all decision making. Marketers who fail to include the essential ingredient of emotional connectedness in their segmentation efforts will find the resulting consumer portrait incomplete or even misleading. Without a fundamental focus on what it takes to create enduring consumer relationships, the promise and power of segmentation will remain unfulfilled.

See Related Article
"Building Brand Differentiation" (page 125)
"What Were They Thinking?" (page 84)

CAN ADVERTISING STILL CONTRIBUTE?

by William J. McEwen

July 8, 2004

New studies contend that advertising has lost its punch. But perhaps it's just lost its way.

On the heels of what seems to be a never-ending series of attacks on advertising, two new studies purport to reveal more evidence of its diminishing impact.

For several years, respected industry leaders have been assailing advertisers and their agencies for lack of performance. Some experts, such as Sergio Zyman, former advertising head at Coca-Cola, claim that ad agencies have abandoned their basic responsibility to sell the brands they're paid to advertise. Others, including noted author Al Ries, have gone even further, contending that advertising's business-building capabilities now pale in comparison to the "buzz" public relations can generate.

Adding fuel to this fire are two recently released studies. The first, by Yankelovich Partners, maintains that the effectiveness of ad campaigns has been declining markedly. It cites as evidence the apparent growth in consumers' negative perceptions of advertising. According to Yankelovich, about 6 in 10 U.S. consumers report that they now feel more negatively about advertising than they used to. Furthermore, they claim to "avoid buying products that overwhelm them with advertising and marketing."

The second study, recently released by Deutsche Bank, is based on a more wide-ranging analysis of sales and marketing spending data. It concludes that TV advertising delivers, in most cases, a negligible return on investment (ROI) for mature packaged goods brands. According to the Deutsche Bank data, only 3 of 18 major brands competing in established product categories (ranging from beer to detergent and from snacks to toothpaste) could demonstrate financial returns that exceeded the company's investments. In the other 15 cases, the companies were simply spending more money than they were making.

No bang for the buck

Reports such as these have caused consternation among advertisers and the agencies they've enlisted to create and deliver sales-building and business-enhancing messages. Wall Street analysts and company boards are increasingly expecting and demanding accountability for marketing expenditures. If, as the Deutsche Bank data contend, major advertisers such as Coca-Cola, Heinz, and Colgate are realizing no tangible business benefits from their expenditures, then ad money will likely be reallocated to other, higher return uses.

The dilemma, of course, is to identify what those alternatives might be. According to the Deutsche Bank report, the solution is *not* an increase in trade-promotion spending, as this tactic also falls short when it comes to ROI. So where are companies to turn? What are these studies telling today's brand marketers?

Perhaps, as some have suggested, the solution is simply "better advertising." The argument is that the money is squandered — not because all advertising is wasteful, but because too many companies have been lured into creating ad campaigns that just don't work. Either marketers are employing the wrong media mix (for example, relying on expensive and inefficient TV commercials), or they're relying on the wrong selling strategies (such as creating messages that have little or no potential impact).

Does a company's advertising just need to "work harder"? Or is the real problem that today's advertisers are heading in the wrong direction, and as a result, are making no apparent progress toward meeting their ROI challenge? It appears that far too many companies operate under an incomplete or erroneous model of how advertising can best contribute to building a healthier brand. Consequently, they fail to hold their ads — and their ad agencies — accountable for the end results they should be delivering.

Consider the Yankelovich study, which apparently equates "liking" advertising with its *impact*. The study suggests that if people say they're feeling increasingly negative toward advertising, then that means that advertising has increasingly less impact. This argument would imply that the solution for enhancing the return on advertising expenditures would be to make the ads more entertaining and fun to watch, hear, or read.

But should that be the goal? Is advertising's real purpose to entertain — or to sell? As experts from David Ogilvy to Sergio Zyman have pointed out, advertising's objective is not to be "fun to watch." Entertaining consumers is *not* the reason companies invest billions of dollars in ads.

Customer acquisition or customer retention?

What *should* advertising's goal be? What are the appropriate objectives for today's marketers to pursue? These are the questions that marketers must answer as they rethink their targets and reexamine their strategies.

Some time ago, companies began shifting their emphasis from customer acquisition to customer retention. That's because myriad published studies have emphasized what has now become a management mantra: *It costs a lot less to keep a customer than it does to acquire a new one.*

Yet the goals that many companies set for their advertising have remained essentially the same as they were decades ago, when brands were being launched and the aim was to attract new customers. What are these stated objectives? What do today's marketers demand of their ad agencies? They want agencies to build brand and advertising awareness, increase consumers' positive attitudes toward identifiable purchase motivators, and boost the number of customers who state a positive intention to buy the brand.

But these measures all derive from a time past, when packaged goods companies were defining what marketing was all about (the "Four Ps" of product, place, promotion, and price) and focusing on building brand share for frequently purchased, low-involvement consumer products. And they were pursuing these goals through advertising that was designed and executed to increase the brand's profile and make it more "top of mind."

But those outcomes are not the hallmarks of increased customer *retention*. Rather, they are indicators of the potential for customer *acquisition*. As several Gallup Organization studies have pointed out, the health of a company's customer relationships is reflected in the nature and depth of the emotional connections that have been forged between the brand and the customer. Brand *awareness* is an insensitive and even inappropriate indicator of the strength of a company's customer relationships. *Customer engagement* — the degree to which there exists a strong cadre of "fully engaged" customers who are wholeheartedly and passionately connected to a brand — is a far better measure. Furthermore, it is much more closely aligned with the brand marketing goals of most companies.

If a company's stated goal is to strengthen its bonds with consumers to generate the financial returns that fully engaged relationships yield, then the company's advertising must align with this aim. But in most cases, advertising is not in alignment with this goal. Advertising today, as in decades past, is seldom designed to reinforce purchase decisions that have already been made and thus ensure that they will be made again. Rather, advertising is envisioned and assessed as an acquisition tool. It's assumed to be most powerfully and appropriately used to invite new consumers into the company fold.

However, that may be exactly why the Deutsche Bank study has concluded that advertising typically doesn't work for mature brands in mature categories.

What should the role of advertising be for brands such as Coke and Heinz? Should their ads focus on increasing the awareness of these already-familiar names? Or should they seek to deepen and extend brand relationships by enhancing the engagement of their current customers?

The problem with attacking the issue of advertising that reportedly doesn't work is that too many companies are still defining what works according to an outmoded customer acquisition model. They are looking at what it takes to generate trial, and that's a mistake. In a world that's now strongly focused on customer *retention*, advertising must be designed, crafted, and held accountable for its ability to enhance the customer relationship, not just initiate it.

This means that company marketers — at least those who are marketing established brands — must rethink not just what they're spending, but what they're doing, what they're saying, and how they're monitoring their progress.

Unless advertisers and their agencies reexamine where they're heading and reconsider what they're striving to achieve, marketers will continue to read bleak and dreary reports about advertising's lack of impact and effectiveness. Ad expenditures, already clearly in jeopardy, will decline. And the real promise and potential of advertising will, sadly, continue to be left unrealized.

See Related Article
"The Constant Customer" (page 61)

GETTING EMOTIONAL
ABOUT BRANDS

by William J. McEwen

September 9, 2004

Marketers realize that emotions are important. But they're not quite sure why — or what to do about it.

It should come as no surprise that humans are emotional creatures. Even a casual glimpse into the nation's driveways, liquor cabinets, and cosmetics shelves reveals that consumers make buying decisions based in part on their feelings and emotions about particular brands. And marketers have long recognized the fact that emotions play a key role when consumers are talking about — or purchasing — products in categories as disparate as those represented by brands like Mercedes, Kodak, and Louis Vuitton.

Although none of this seems all that newsworthy, marketers appear to be rediscovering the power of human emotions, as evidenced by a raft of books and articles now in bookstores and on marketers' desks. Perhaps you've already read *Passion Branding, Emotional Branding, The Culting of Brands,* or *Lovemarks.* Or you may have noticed that the *Journal of Advertising Research* recently devoted an entire issue to studies of "Emotion in Advertising."

Suddenly, it seems that the new marketing millennium is all about emotions. And whatever has sparked this resurgence of interest, it's apparently contagious.

Emotional connections: links that last

Why all the interest? In part, it's because of the intensified focus on customer retention. To reap the enhanced financial benefits that can result from customer loyalty, marketers have enthusiastically pursued strategies intended to keep customers coming back. In fact, marketers want to move beyond customer "retention," which is merely a behavior, to generating customer "commitment," "delight," and even "evangelism" — all of which represent enduring psychological bonds that link a customer to a company.

In their books and articles, brand consultants have talked about consumer emotions and emotional connections. They've written about the passionately strong bonds that companies as varied as Harley-Davidson, Krispy Kreme, eBay, Starbucks, and Virgin have cultivated with their consumers. There are fascinating stories of brands that have intense customer loyalty that is the stuff of legend. They describe the sort of loyalty that, as marketers, we all covet.

But what about the marketer who is challenged to sell checking accounts rather than motorcycles? What about the brand managers who are tasked with pitching canned peaches, software, or home mortgages? Is there any hope for them? Or should they change jobs and join a company that sells, say, expensive watches, seeking a brand or product where a rich array of human emotions can come into play?

Many of the writers who focus on the brand new world of emotions have overlooked the mundane, favoring the highly visible "badge" brands that operate in "emotional" categories. Much of their writing and analysis seems to imply that emotions are something that your brand or product either inspires or it doesn't. Sports cars and perfume are emotional, while office supplies and household cleaners are not.

Whether or not its brand or product is viewed as "emotional," a company faces a major dilemma when it seeks to better understand how consumers connect with its brands. Emotions are treated as something that can be sensed but that otherwise defy scientific measurement. For example, Coca-Cola has "it" — but we're never quite sure what "it" is. And too often, when measures of emotions are proposed or provided, they are complex and difficult to administer. They rely on strategies that are not always easy to replicate, like nonverbal photo sorts or deep psychological projective probing. More to the point, while these measures may correlate with consumers' stated intentions, they may fail to provide the sort of evidence that is demanded in the boardroom: How well do they link to actual, hard-number financial outcomes?

Psychologists have been studying human emotions for some time, and they've identified a number of them, ranging from "anger" to "disgust" and from "envy" to "love." But what are the emotions that a brand marketer should seek to embrace? What is the *value* of an emotional association? How on earth can a CEO tell when an emotional connection is present or when it's growing or intensifying — and above all, why should he or she care?

In short, despite the interesting stories and intriguing case histories, all the books on emotional branding really haven't given much guidance to brand managers.

Cracking the emotional code

As mentioned in several *Gallup Management Journal* articles, Gallup has dug deeply into the nature of emotional relationships and how they can be reliably assessed and effectively managed. Gallup scientists have examined the role that emotions play in consumer decisions, and they have documented the impact of those emotions on a wide variety of hard-number business outcomes.

The following conclusions emerged from the findings of an extensive global R&D effort, along with the results of a number of company applications:

- Emotional connections are not only the province of certain "emotional" categories or brands. Consumers are emotional about checking accounts and discount merchandise, not just about soft drinks and expensive fountain pens. Bank of America and Wal-Mart create emotional connections just as surely as JetBlue and iPod do. They do it in different ways — depending far more on their people than on their products — but the result is the same.

- Gallup surveys have shown that 11% of U.S. car owners are passionate about the car they own, but 13% are passionate about the place where they bank, and 12% are passionate about the mass merchant retailers where they shop. People aren't either "emotional" or "unemotional." Consumers are typically highly emotional about some brands and products while completely indifferent and "unattached" to others. Business customers are as emotional about their B2B purchases as car buyers, clothing shoppers, and resort visitors are about their selections.

- Consumers' emotional connections have a specific — and fairly simple — structure, regardless of the nature of the particular emotions involved. As revealed by Gallup's customer engagement metric, the structure begins at the foundation of the customer relationship with Confidence, then proceeds through Integrity to Pride to — at the pinnacle of the relationship — Passion about the service, product, or brand.

LEVELS OF CUSTOMER ENGAGEMENT

Through an extensive research and development program, Gallup has developed a set of rating scales that efficiently and reliably measure four critically important emotional states. Together, these states represent the strength of the emotional connection existing between a customer and a brand: **Confidence** in the brand's promise, belief in its **Integrity**, **Pride** in being a customer, and **Passion** for the brand. Analysis of responses to the individual items in this set of measures has revealed that customers develop emotional attachment to a brand in a cumulative way, with **Confidence** as the foundation of a brand relationship and **Passion** as the pinnacle. Here are definitions of the four components:

CONFIDENCE reflects the belief that the company can be trusted, always and everywhere, to keep the promises that it makes.

INTEGRITY reflects the belief that the company will always treat its customers fairly and can always be counted on to stand behind its products and resolve any problems that might occur.

PRIDE reflects the degree to which consumers feel appreciated by the company and proud of their personal association with the brand.

PASSION reflects the belief that the brand is essentially irreplaceable and represents a seemingly perfect fit with the customer's personal needs.

- Emotional connections are not merely warm and fuzzy, nor are they simply interesting to contemplate and debate. They have powerful financial consequences, ranging from share-of-wallet to frequency and amount of repeat business. "Fully engaged" retail customers spend more and return more frequently than those who are disengaged. Retailers that have taken action to enhance their customer engagement by capitalizing on the engagement-building skills of their own customer-facing employees have seen double-digit increases in both sales and profit per square foot. Gallup has seen these results not just in the United States, but around the globe — and we've seen them for banks, auto dealers, hardware stores, and business services marketers. Emotional connections are universally important, and managing those emotional bonds pays off handsomely.

- Some companies are very good at creating emotional connections with their customers. Most, however, are not. Companies that are successful at creating emotional connections benefit from stronger results, not only in cash flow and profit, but in market share.

- Emotional connections aren't static. They ebb and flow, and the results can affect a company's long-term business success. Emotional connections can be measured. They can be enhanced. And they can be managed. It's not easy, but it's demonstrably possible.

Thus, brand "passion" is not simply a topic that provides for interesting reading. And brand passion is not an atypical emotional response — something reserved only for atypical brands operating in atypical marketing environments. Emotional brand connections are, for any company that plans and hopes to compete, a business imperative.

See Related Article
"The Constant Customer" (page 61)

WHAT'S YOUR
COMPANY'S PURPOSE?

Interviewed by Jennifer Robison

December 8, 2005

The creator of ads for Wal-Mart, Southwest Airlines, and the U.S. Air Force tells why a business' purpose should be sacred and what to do if its leadership gets off track

A *GMJ* Q&A with Roy Spence, president of advertising agency GSD&M

In 1971, six friends graduated from the University of Texas at Austin and realized that they had better get jobs. One of them had sold ads for the college paper, and all of them had enjoyed making multimedia projects for the college. They didn't want to leave each other or Austin, so the group decided to start an advertising company — GSD&M (a combination of their initials, of course). "We were naïve; we didn't know anything about advertising," says Roy Spence, GSD&M's president. "We were mavericks, not renegades. Renegades know the rules and break them by design. Mavericks don't really know the rules — they just go their own way."

GSD&M lost their first client, a jeans store, because they ran the wrong size ad. But things improved for the mavericks. Thirty-four years later, four of those friends are still together and still making ads. But now their agency is 650 employees strong and is creating campaigns for organizations such as Wal-Mart, Southwest Airlines, BMW, the U.S. Air Force, Chili's restaurants, and a host of other organizations whose slogans you know by heart. And GSD&M is billing $1.5 billion dollars a year.

Over the years, Spence has had a hand in the development of some of the world's greatest businesses. (He's so invested in them that he reflexively uses the word "we" when he speaks of his clients.) A close friend of Bill and Hillary Clinton, Spence has also observed decades of politics from the vantage point of the leaders and the led. And his ongoing education in advertising and human nature has taught him a thing or two as well. In this interview, the "Reverend Roy" — as many of his friends and employees refer to him — discusses some of what he's learned: how a sense of purpose can sustain a business, why values connect with customers but morals don't, and how advertising can have value in a fractured media world.

GMJ: You've been running the same company for 34 years, since the month you graduated from college. What's the most important thing you've learned?

Roy Spence: We represented a bunch of little retail stores because nobody else would hire us, and what we didn't know at the time — I didn't anyway — was that these guys had borrowed the money to pay for the advertising. So if we didn't help them create sales, we wouldn't get paid. And they lost a lot of money. So we learned in Year One that we're not in the advertising business at all — we're in the business to build our clients' business. People talk about ROI and return on ideas, but at the core of our company — not because we knew it, we just lucked into it — is the belief that if we don't create sustainable branding and ideas that help our clients drive their business, we don't get paid. That first great lesson has been at the heart of our company from the start.

GMJ: No good advertising company creates the same ad for every client, but yours are strikingly different. Kohler print ads are done by famous artists, while Wal-Mart's ads look homemade.

Spence: Right. Our philosophy is simple. We don't have one creative style, because every brand — its purpose, its values, its products — is different. We do what we call reflective branding: We reflect the values and purpose of an organization within our work. I mean, everybody basically knows how to sell stuff — "This is a product, and it has 25% more lemon," or whatever — but we believe that the deepest river that you can dive into is values and purpose. So we seek to reflect a company's values and personality within our work, because it strikes a more authentic chord both inside the company and among consumers. By the way, much of our advertising serves as role modeling for the people who work at that company.

GMJ: Why? How do you do role modeling in a commercial?

Spence: Well, from a consumer's point of view, employee behavior has to match the brand promise. If it doesn't, the company is destined to over-promise and under-deliver. So we inculcate cultures in our advertising. We role model the culture, we celebrate the culture and values of that brand, and we use our advertising to motivate and build pride among the associates and employees of our brands.

This is especially important in service industries, because what so many business leaders don't understand is that their people may be the tiebreaker. No one knows or cares who made their Snickers bar, but for non-packaged goods, the image depends on the people.

One of the things Herb Kelleher [the founder of Southwest Airlines] said was, "They may be able to match our fares, they may be able to match our frequency, but they can never match our people." So our ads [for Southwest] promote freedom of the skies for consumers, but they also promote freedom for employees. They're free to have fun, free to make decisions, free to be themselves. And Southwest's employees are proud of the commercials — we know because we survey them. We know, and they know, that they are also the audience for the ads.

Our ads for the U.S. Air Force have three audiences. They're meant to recruit airmen and airwomen, of course, but they're also intended to reflect the Air Force to every American. The third audience is the people who are already in the Air Force, because retention is a huge issue.

We always factor [culture] into service brands. These ads have a branding message to the public, but they also have an encoded message about the culture for employees. We recognize that ads can make people proud or embarrassed of the places they work. We'd rather go with proud.

GMJ: Tell me about your relationship with Jim Collins [author of Good to Great: Why Some Companies Make the Leap . . . and Others Don't *and coauthor with Jerry I. Porras of* Built to Last: Successful Habits of Visionary Companies].

Spence: Well, GSD&M was celebrating our 25th anniversary, and I didn't know if we wanted to do this anymore. The truth of the matter is, I don't know of any company today that has the same four partners after 34 years. So I was thinking about it when I read a review of *Built to Last* in *USA Today*. I went out and bought the book, and as soon as I finished, I got on the phone and called Jim. I called him because I didn't know how to pronounce the other guy's name, that's the truth. I said, "You don't know me, and I don't know you, but I'll fly you to Austin, Texas, because I want to hire you to consult with us on how we can build our company to last." Then, when Collins did *Good to Great*, we were an unpaid consultant with him. So that's how we got to purpose-based branding.

He inspired me to dig deeper than values and go to purpose. I think purpose trumps everything.

GMJ: What do you mean by purpose-based branding?

Spence: I've studied the whole issue of cultures because I was up close and personal with two of the remarkable cultures of the 20th century: Southwest Airlines and Wal-Mart — underdogs, you know, that ended up being top dogs. And of course our company has a very unique culture too, and we relish it, and we live by it. So I gave these cultures a lot of thought. Then, in the late 1980s, I wrote an op-ed piece saying that I believe that because of the acceleration of technology, consumers will make a purchase decision based not just on what you sell, but on what you stand for. I'm not talking about morals — morals are arguments that no one wins. But values are great connectors.

Now, a couple years before that, what led me to this idea was that Southwest was facing a lot of competition and getting a lot of flak. You know, we were cheap, and we were no-frills. They attacked us for being a cattle car and for all the things that Herb Kelleher did to keep costs down so that Southwest could spend the money on safety and airplanes and people — which, in the end, are all that people really care about. So we took a close look at Southwest Airlines, and we saw that the business model was to keep fares low so we could give more people the chance to go and see and do things that they never dreamed of. And we looked at that model from our branding strategy and said we're not in the airline business, we're in the freedom business. We are in the business of democratizing the skies.

At that moment, we knew that being in a higher-calling business long term is a clearer and more compelling place to be — not only in the minds of the consumers, but also in the hearts of the employees. At Southwest Airlines, every decision we make, we have to decide if it enhances people's freedom to fly or curtails it. And that realization led to a lot of wins, because people want to be in a business that's not just an operational business.

GMJ: But what exactly do you mean by "purpose"?

Spence: Purpose is a definitive statement of the difference you're trying to make.

GMJ: In the world?

Spence: In the world or in the marketplace. A definitive statement. That's the stake in the ground about why you exist, and it will never change. People get confused between purpose, mission statements, and vision. "Mission" is basically how you execute your purpose, and vision is a statement of how you see the world after you've done your purpose and mission.

But purpose is the deepest river: You start with "What difference are you trying to make?" Your tactics will change, your ads will change, your mission might too, but your purpose never will. You build on all of that, and do it every day — not on Saturdays or Sundays or during sales. Every company that's survived and gone into the "thrive mode" has a purpose or had one. Sometimes you've got to dig down because leaders will change purposes and, I'll tell you something, that's when companies get in deep trouble. You start looking for love in all the wrong places.

GMJ: Give me an example.

Spence: When Sam [Walton] started going into urban areas, Sears, Roebuck and Co. was the dominant company, and Kmart was number two. Wal-Mart was a distant, distant third. Now, Sears was always known for "You can bring anything back." People abused that policy, but it was at the core of their trust machine. You could always trust Sears not to take advantage of you, and you could return anything, satisfaction guaranteed. So, just as Wal-Mart was about to launch into the urban areas, Sears gave up that policy. Some CEO, some bean counter, decided that policy was costing too much money. And that day, Sam Walton put a sign on every single store that said "satisfaction guaranteed."

GMJ: What should a company do when it starts to lose its way or realizes it's strayed from its purpose?

Spence: A purpose-based leader and company will 'fess up when they mess up. You don't want to mess up often, but when you mess up, if you 'fess up, people will give you another chance.

I think there are a couple of ways that you can reignite the purpose. First, go back and find your purpose and be authentic. Second, 'fess up — especially with your own people, because if you lose their belief, consumers won't believe you either — and admit there were some things you did wrong. And third, slowly but surely, work to re-earn trust by performing your purpose on a daily basis.

But it's hard. You've got to be very careful of the word "tweak," as in "I'm going to tweak our model." You can do radical things with your products and your ads, but don't tweak your purpose. If you don't know what your core purpose is, then you'll change strategies every year, you'll bring in new chief marketing officers all the time, and it will cost you. If you start messing with your purpose, you better be really, really ready to go through a *total* reinvent, not a *kind of* reinvent.

GMJ: Can you name a company that totally lost its purpose and came back?

Spence: [Long pause] No, I can't. Like Enron. The purpose of Enron was to be the best in the world at gas and power pipelines; they had the best and brightest people in the world, and they were awesome. I mean the company was great; the culture was great. Then they decided to get greedy. There are so many examples of companies that started out with great purpose, but at some point, they lost their way and never recovered. I don't know of too many companies that lost their purpose, or changed their purpose, or corrupted their purpose, and came back.

GMJ: How can a company catch itself in time and find its purpose again? And what does GSD&M do to help?

Spence: We always tell people that every company in the "thrive" stage has always had a core purpose. We start by going back and looking at it. We hire cultural anthropologists on our staff to go back to the original charters of companies, to look at the original business plans, and to interview the fan base and the old-timers who were in the business of preserving the core. To last, organizations have to preserve the core *and* stimulate progress, as Collins says. So many organizations that have lost their way said, "Let's stimulate progress, and to hell with the core." Others get stuck in the mud, saying, "This new thing, well, that's against our core." Really, it's not against the core; they're just producing the same old crap they produced before. The core is not about what they produce; it's about what they stand for. We go back in there and start putting language and leadership to their purpose.

GMJ: A lot of companies are beginning to question the value of advertising in a fractured media world. What do you tell them?

Spence: I tell them they're exactly right. And I tell them there's a big difference between marketing and advertising. Marketing is how you drive your business, your channel of distribution, your point of sale, your packaging, your PR — that's why they call them chief marketing officers and not chief advertising officers.

Advertising is a toolbox. We love this space right now *because* it's in constant turmoil. People who say advertising is dead don't know what they're talking about. It might get to be like it used to be, knocking on doors, except we're knocking by way of the Internet. There could be a great fulfilling of the circle where advertising goes back to — and I know it's overhyped and overused — one-on-one marketing.

That's what's so great. If you're fleet of foot and you're curious, if you're always looking at ways to make sales, not make ads, this is a great time to be an advertising company.

UNLEASH YOUR BRAND
AMBASSADORS

by William J. McEwen

April 13, 2006

A pharmaceutical giant awakens to the untapped brand-building power of its people. Will other companies (and industries) follow?

A decision earlier in the year by GlaxoSmithKline appears to have taken the advertising industry by storm. Confronted by negative public images of the pharmaceutical industry, Glaxo has enlisted its 8,000 U.S. sales representatives to act as "public relations ambassadors." The company hopes that the reps' collective efforts will help to counteract these negative images and burnish the image of the industry generally — and of Glaxo-SmithKline in particular.

The decision was considered noteworthy by *Advertising Age* because this sort of image-polishing effort has typically taken the form of a high-profile corporate advertising campaign. Companies and industry groups have traditionally turned to public relations firms and advertising agencies when seeking to confront negative images. They've relied on professional communicators to get the job done through memorable ads and integrated communications campaigns. That's how oil companies, beer marketers, and tobacco producers have tackled the problem in the past.

So why has Glaxo taken a much-less-traveled road? Perhaps it's because the company has determined that what could be the most powerful communications weapon at their disposal — their people — will prove more credible than a 30-second commercial. What's more, enlisting Glaxo's employees as ambassadors might well add something that Gallup scientists have found to be crucially important when it comes to creating positive emotional bonds: the ability to personally *connect* with an audience.

Some observers have questioned the wisdom of this effort. There's concern that the army of Glaxo reps won't all speak with one voice. An ad campaign, in contrast, offers the company the promise of total message control. In the words of one senior marketer at another drug company,

"I'm not sure I want eight thousand people on the ground given that level of responsibility."

Living the brand

Clearly there's the risk of multiple, even conflicting, communications. And it's hardly likely that all 8,000 sales reps will prove equally adept at delivering this new, "non-sales" image message. After all, sales reps are chosen because they can sell, not for their ability to deliver an industry PR image message.

In order to arm their troops with what Glaxo deems to be the requisite nuggets of supporting information, the company has created a short training module. Through this training, the company aims to reinforce sales rep credibility and equip the reps to respond to the sometimes thorny questions they may encounter. However, a 50-minute learning session, no matter how well designed, may not be enough to turn a sales pro into an industry spokesperson. So it's entirely possible that the net results of this sales force PR campaign may fall short of company expectations and requirements.

Nevertheless, the upside potential clearly remains. The 8,000 Glaxo reps are, indeed, living the brand — and in this case, they're living the industry as well. Regardless of whether the reps consistently deliver the same scripted message, this effort does add a human face to what is frequently an anonymous and fuzzy industry image. And a human face on the messenger raises the potential for a personal connection, the kind of connection a TV ad may struggle in vain to accomplish.

But there's a larger issue at play here as well, and it's a vitally important one. Some ad agency pros may register surprise at the Glaxo initiative, in part because they believe that real impact can best be achieved through centralized message design and delivery.

But Glaxo's sales reps — like the employees of every other company around the globe — already represent the brand and the industry to their friends, families, and communities. Regardless of whether companies acknowledge this fact, or whether they intentionally manage, equip, and empower their front-line employees to act as brand messengers, that's exactly what they are.

People represent the company's brand promise in ways that are both memorable and meaningful — and they always have. As our research has shown, a company's brand representatives — who may be tellers at a bank, checkout clerks in a supermarket, or sales reps calling on customers — are in many cases the most important determinants of the strength and health of a company's customer relationships. They are the often-overlooked but always-crucial "fifth P" that must be added to the old customer relationship-building mantra of "Product, Place, Promotion, and Price."

If a company is worried about its brand or industry image, why should it focus on its human touchpoints?

Imagine that Colgate took great pains to get the product exactly right, but ignored the package. So some packages were attractive, bright, and clean, while others were scruffy and uninviting, impossible to open, with labels and instructions that were unreadable. Or imagine that Nikon had produced a new camera, but each camera was different. Some were a pleasure to use and took wonderfully clear photos that you wanted to share with friends, while others were impossible to decipher and took fuzzy photos that made you want to warn your friends not to repeat your unhappy purchase.

Obviously, Colgate and Nikon wouldn't let this happen. These companies spend time and money to ensure that their packages and products are consistent. That's because their marketing departments know that the package and the product represent their brand. They speak volumes to customers about the company's brand promise.

Well, if there are people interacting with your customers on your behalf, they are every bit as important as your packaging or your product. Glaxo is simply embracing that marketing reality, and they certainly should not be alone in doing so. It's time to begin recognizing and leveraging the brand-enhancing power of that "fifth P."

MANAGING THE VALUE
OF YOUR BRAND

by William J. McEwen

October 12, 2006

Companies that seek to enhance their brand value must first understand where it comes from

Business leaders and financial analysts are in apparent agreement: Brands represent valuable corporate assets that are well worth protecting. Brand assets can be bought and sold, and they sometimes come with an impressively hefty price tag. Brands can be worth billions.

Last year, Nanjing Automobile Group spent about $90 million to buy the rights to the MG brand. Lenovo bought IBM's PC unit in a deal worth $1.75 billion, and Procter & Gamble purchased Gillette and its stable of brands for more than $50 billion. Lenovo and P&G didn't shell out all that money simply to acquire manufacturing and distribution capabilities. They spent it to buy established brand names like ThinkPad, Braun, Oral-B, and Duracell.

What's a brand worth? One way to figure this out is to put a brand up for sale and see what price it will fetch. That's what Ford is reportedly investigating with the Aston Martin brand it owns.

But there are other ways. Each year, *BusinessWeek* reports the "best global brands" ranking compiled by Interbrand. Another ranking, compiled by the researchers at WPP's Millward Brown lists what it contends are the 100 "most powerful brands."

These two firms differ in how they assign values to brands, and the amounts they report often diverge. For example, Interbrand maintains that Coca-Cola, its top-rated brand, is worth about $67 billion. Millward Brown, however, contends that Coca-Cola is only number 3 on its list and places a much lower price on the brand ($41.4 billion). As another example, Millward Brown suggests that the Google brand ($37.4 billion) is worth about three times what Interbrand ($12.4 billion) reports. Regardless of the method that might be used to ascribe a value to a brand, however, there is general agreement that these big brands are worth a lot of money.

While it's certainly interesting to read that the Coca-Cola brand would fetch many billions of dollars, the reported brand values raise some fundamental questions. Just how does a brand like Coca-Cola come to be worth that much? And exactly what does a company's management need to do to *increase* the value of its brand assets? After all, a billion dollars of brand "worth" doesn't just happen.

Interbrand values brands by looking at the revenue stream associated with a brand's current and projected business performance, subtracting the role of certain intangibles (such as patents) and the costs of business operations. What's left over is, essentially, what the brand contributes to the company's earnings. Millward Brown, in contrast, looks at a brand's reported earnings and intangibles, but combines this with the results of surveys that assess consumers' images of the brands versus their competition.

Consider the source
But where does the "revenue stream" come from? Which are the brand images that truly matter? And which "intangible" investments generate a direct financial return? After all, if companies seek to manage their brand value, they must understand where this value originates. They need to know more than the destination (for example, a billion dollars of brand worth) — they also need to understand what it takes to *reach* that destination.

Conceptually, it's quite simple. A brand is worth nothing if people aren't willing to pay for it. There's no revenue stream. So the key component in this brand-value equation must be the consumer.

But consumers aren't all the same, and they can't be valued equally. The broad world of consumers who might be surveyed consists of some who are already customers of the brand, some who are prospective customers, and some who are neither buyers nor prospects.

These groups of consumers are very different, and it's a mistake to lump them all together. They don't think alike or act alike. They experience the brand in different ways. And they contribute in different ways to the brand's overall value.

In the world of automobiles, for example, Interbrand reports that the BMW brand is worth $19.6 billion. But the thoughts, feelings, and experiences of a BMW owner are quite different — and contribute more directly to the value of the BMW brand — than the thoughts, feelings, and experiences of someone who owns a Mercedes or a Lexus. And in turn, the thoughts and feelings of BMW owners and prospects matter much more than those of the center-city dweller who neither wants nor needs to own a car.

For the moment, let's remove those who simply aren't viable prospects from the equation. That leaves the BMW owners and non-owner prospects, and these represent very different brand constituencies for BMW. Each presents a unique set of marketing and management challenges. And, while each contributes to BMW's reported overall brand value, they contribute disproportionately. Owners bring tangible worth to the brand via their checkbooks. Non-owners bring worth to the brand only to the extent that they are viable prospects for future ownership.

An extensive body of Gallup research has documented that the real value of an *existing customer* varies according to that customer's level of engagement with the brand.

"Fully engaged" car owners are more likely to repurchase the brand and recommend it. They are also more willing to pay a price premium in spite of the price incentives offered by competing brands. More to the point, companies can identify the factors that build customer engagement; then they can manage those factors to increase engagement. That's one way BMW's brand value can be enhanced and not just measured.

BMW's current owners are only part of its total brand equity — although they're critically important, because only customers spend money. There is a second important contributor to BMW's total brand value, and it's manifested in BMW's ability to *connect* with its target car-buyer *prospects*. These prospects are the consumers who are qualified and open to buying in the category but who are not yet BMW owners. The ability to connect with these prospects represents the future vitality and positive momentum of the brand.

Connect and engage

Healthy brands must retain their customers, but they also need to attract new ones. Even the strongest looking brands will eventually wither if they fail to entice new customers into the fold. Customers, even the fully engaged ones, don't live forever.

HOW ENGAGED ARE YOUR CUSTOMERS?

FULLY ENGAGED customers are strongly emotionally attached, and they're attitudinally loyal. They'll go out of their way to locate a favored product or service, and they won't accept substitutes. True brand ambassadors, they are your most valuable and profitable customers.

ENGAGED customers are emotionally attached, but they're not strongly loyal. They do like your product or service, but they can be tempted to switch by a more convenient, more attractive, or lower-priced offer.

NOT ENGAGED customers have a "take it or leave it" attitude toward your product or service. They're disconnected emotionally and are attitudinally neutral toward your brand and what you're selling.

ACTIVELY DISENGAGED customers are completely detached from your company and its products and services. They will readily switch or — if switching is difficult or impossible — may become virulently antagonistic toward your company or brand. Either way, they're always eager to tell others exactly how they feel.

Thus, an important portion of BMW's brand value derives from the company's ability to connect with its non-customer prospects. These connections begin with powerful brand promises — promises that are credibly and compellingly delivered in a way that prospects can readily say, "I can just see myself sitting behind that wheel." These are the connections that can turn a prospect into a customer.

Connecting with prospects reflects the power of a brand's promises — and the company's ability to clearly communicate those promises. Engaging customers, in contrast, reflects the company's ability to consistently *keep* those brand promises. Making and keeping promises are both essential. But they are not the same thing, and they shouldn't be measured — and they can't be managed — in the same way.

Making promises and enticing new prospects is where BMW's advertising, public relations, and promotional efforts come to the fore. *Keeping* promises and engaging BMW owners, however, involves far more than marketing communications. Customer engagement — or disengagement — is the result of the BMW ownership experience. This experience includes the vehicles and how they perform over time, but it also encompasses the company's processes and policies, as well as everyone at BMW and its dealerships who helps support the ownership experience.

Any company — whether it's Coca-Cola, Google, or BMW — that wants to understand and measurably boost its brand value must take meaningful action on two fronts. It must:

- increase its ability to *connect* with prospects
- build its capability and commitment to *engage* its customers

Brand value requires both — and so does brand value measurement.

Regardless of the methods used to put a price tag on a company's brand assets, managing those assets requires painstaking attention to the needs and feelings of the consumers who are responsible for the rise and fall of those billion-dollar brand valuations. Brand assets aren't owned by the company or by the firms that assign a dollar value to those assets. They're owned by the consumer. Listen to them, and learn.

See Related Article
"The Constant Customer" (page 61)

STRETCHING THE BRAND
UNTIL IT BREAKS?

by William J. McEwen

January 11, 2007

Marketers, beware: Extending your brand offerings may bring big profits — but also big trouble

As companies around the globe search for ways to grow, they aggressively explore new markets and new products. Whether it's Wal-Mart opening stores in China, General Motors developing electric vehicles, or United initiating flights to Kuwait, it's evident that businesses are driven to expand their scope.

New markets promise the potential for additional sales volume and evergreater income. And since investment analysts demand evidence of a company's continuing growth prospects, new market volume speaks directly to the apparent value and vitality of the company.

But growth can be expensive. New product launches and market development activities require investment. Many companies look to enter new markets while relying on the existing brand franchises they've created, hoping to reap the returns that expansion can offer while leveraging their already considerable investment in brand building. It's more efficient — and far simpler — to make use of an established brand name and its supporting materials, which can include logos, store signage, and packaging as well as employee uniforms and consumer communications.

When designing new-product and market-expansion outreach programs, companies typically assess their brand's appeal among the new market segments they hope to attract. And to enhance their appeal to these new segments, they may tweak their brand promise and add attributes to their product or service offerings.

For example, to attract a new, environmentally conscious audience, an automaker might include a more fuel-efficient hybrid engine. A fashion retailer might add hot colors and hip styles and adjust its sizing to entice a teen audience. And to interest fast-food customers in India, a restaurant might add masala spices to its fried potatoes.

However, as a company's brand promise is adjusted or expanded and its product offerings are changed to accommodate new needs, it must address a vitally important matter: What should the company do about its *current* customers? After all, their loyalty and passion built the brand to the point where it could afford to reach into new territories.

Dance with the one who brought you

Companies can redefine their brand promise and seek to expand their markets. But if they ignore their current customers, they do so at their own peril. Companies may be essentially abandoning their existing customers while failing in their efforts to attract new ones.

Consider the dilemma faced by St. John Knits, a venerable West Coast marketer known for traditional knit fashions for women. As described in a story that appeared in the *Los Angeles Times*, St. John trumpeted its new collection at its annual fashion show in August. Its loyalists were there, proudly wearing their classic St. John suits. Instead of updated versions of the classic suits they expected to see, they were treated to new ads featuring Angelina Jolie and the company's newest array of "clingy, plunging cocktail dresses" with a much less forgiving fit. As one disappointed loyalist stated, "I wish I was skinny." In the words of another, "They didn't want us anymore. Isn't that awful?"

These two customers aren't the only ones expressing disappointment. Sales have reportedly suffered. And as a result, St. John has shifted its emphasis back to the familiar styles that made the company a long-term success. In the words of a senior designer at the company: "The new direction was too far from what our customer relies on." Lesson learned.

Other companies are learning the very same lesson. An article in *The Detroit News* reported that Saks Fifth Avenue is returning to its classic roots and its core customer base after chasing younger customers with styles that didn't attract them and that seemed to turn off its older, loyal customers. However, many lessons are learned only after the fact, making them quite expensive — particularly when the merchandise is considerably pricier than a new suit.

Staying true to the brand

In the automotive world, Volkswagen proudly announced the arrival of what was proclaimed by its then-chairman as "the best car in the world." The VW Phaeton, by all accounts a very fine car, was a rather resounding flop in the United States. Only 1,433 Phaetons were sold in 2004, followed by dismal sales of 820 in 2005; the Phaeton reportedly has been withdrawn from the American market.

The Phaeton may well be a superb car, but it also comes with a premium price tag of about $70,000 and, more to the point, a large VW emblem on the grille. And unlike the launch of Toyota's Lexus brand, the Phaeton was sold and serviced by VW dealers, in VW showrooms. That's not necessarily a $70,000 brand experience. What's more, while vainly pursuing customers who remained more attracted to the BMW 7-series or the Lexus LS, VW was diverting its precious resources — and the attention of its dealers — away from the Jettas, Rabbits, Beetles, and GTIs for which VW was known and loved.

St. John, Saks, and VW have something in common, and it's enormously important. In the eyes of their customers, they are well-defined brands. And the brand, for any company, represents a *promise*.

A brand tells your prospects and customers who you are, what you stand for, and what makes you different from competing brands. And, in pronouncing who you *are*, the brand also affirms who you are *not*. That basic fact must be kept in mind whenever companies set out to embrace an expanded consumer universe.

A brand that heads off in new directions may be sending unintended messages to its current customers. It may be telling them that the company isn't particularly excited by, or proud of, what it now offers — or who it now does business with. But brand relationships, like marriages, require evidence of mutual commitment.

That brings us to a critical question: When a brand is redefined, what does it now stand for? A brand that attempts to mean all things to all people — or new things to new people — may wind up meaning nothing to anyone. Is a VW a sensible, small, fuel-sipping car or a large, leather-seated, gas-guzzling luxury vehicle? Or is it none of the above?

Brand meanings aren't infinitely elastic. Like the value of the brand itself, those meanings aren't defined in the company's boardroom. Their home is in the hearts and minds of the brand's customers.

A clearly defined brand makes a statement to the world — and this world also includes the people who work for the company. For companies like St. John, Saks, or VW, the brand serves as a compass, aiding those who design the products and those who support and serve the brand's customers. The brand promise informs and guides the delivery of the brand experience.

This does *not* mean that marketers should abandon their existing brands in the aggressive pursuit of new markets. Growth is, after all, one hallmark of a great company. And there are companies that have managed to extend their brands — but they've always done it while remaining true to what the brand really stands for.

Ivory soap has always meant "pure and gentle," even as it extended its product line into liquid hand soaps. Virgin maintained its focus on youthful and slightly irreverent fun as it moved from a record label to an airline. And Tiffany retained its characteristic blue packages and air of sophisticated elegance when it expanded from Fifth Avenue to the Ginza and beyond.

But smart companies know when the brand meaning gets stretched too far. Thus, when Toyota sought to attract upscale buyers with a new luxury auto offering, it did so by creating Lexus, a totally new brand entity that would promise a distinct brand ownership experience. In much the same way, Hilton reinforces the intended differentiation of brand experiences in a family that ranges from Hampton Inn to The Waldorf-Astoria. And Yum! Brands uses Taco Bell to sell tacos and Pizza Hut to sell pizza; it doesn't attempt to sell both through a single brand.

Clearly, companies must pay close attention to the real owners of the brand — their customers. And that means that management must understand the deep emotional bonds that have been created with those customers. When new directions represent a strong fit with the core message the brand conveys — as Kellogg's Special K fits with weight-watching and Starbucks fits with coffeemakers and classic CDs — the growth opportunities are impressive. However, success isn't inevitable, and mistakes are all too common, even among the great and powerful. In many ways, VW's Phaeton isn't all that different from New Coke. Strong brands build strong bonds, to be sure. But those bonds, like the brands themselves, are well-defined. They can be stretched too far. And they can be broken.

DID ADVERTISERS LOSE
THE SUPER BOWL?

by William J. McEwen

February 8, 2007

Companies should expect a lot more from $2.6 million than a smile from the viewers and a temporary bump in brand awareness

On February 4, 90 million Americans were glued to their TV sets watching this year's great battle. But the contest that attracted a good many of these viewers wasn't the on-field tussle between the triumphant Indianapolis Colts and the Chicago Bears; nor was it the strategic toe-to-toe contest that pitted Tony Dungy against Lovie Smith. That's because the game was, for many of these TV watchers, a relatively minor sidelight. It wasn't about Peyton Manning's offense outmaneuvering Brian Urlacher's defense. And no, it wasn't about whether Prince was a better halftime choice than the Rolling Stones.

For many of those watching Super Bowl XLI, the most riveting clash was between the companies that were each paying about $2.6 million to rent America's collective eyeballs for 30 seconds. In fact, The Gallup Poll noted that a third of those who were planning to watch the Super Bowl expected to be entertained more by the commercials than by the game. As in prior years, the Super Bowl excitement didn't just stem from running backs colliding with 300-pound defensive tackles. Rather, it was highlighted by the war between Coke and FedEx, Snickers and Sierra Mist, Chevy and Doritos — and between Go Daddy and the network censors.

This fight has nothing to do with which of these advertisers did the best job presenting its brand message and its wares. Instead, the debate centers on which commercial was the most entertaining. It's all about amusing and impressing the viewers — not to mention the advertising columnists — with an emphasis far more on kindling belly laughs than on motivating purchases.

It seems that the ultimate TV commercial isn't one that causes Americans to change how they think, feel, or behave toward a brand. Rather, it's a TV spot that can cause a hush over a barroom crowd or one that successfully pulls Americans away from their nachos for a full 30 seconds.

And so, as in Super Bowls past, leading marketers have turned to attention-getting celebrities, amusing animals, impressive special effects, catchy music, innovative animation, and breathtaking scenery — and, of course, funny vignettes. They were spending millions in pursuit of stopping power, but that's not the same as *selling* power.

There's nothing wrong with entertaining an audience; Hollywood is built on it. But entertainment isn't the return that most company stockholders expect from a $2.6 million investment that's allegedly earmarked for brand building. Entertainment can enhance a compelling brand message, but it's not a *substitute* for one. As former Coca-Cola marketing leader Sergio Zyman stated, "Advertising that only entertains doesn't work."

Entertaining without connecting

The business-building and brand-enhancing impact of these expensive Super Bowl messages can certainly be called into question. While many observers point to the brand-enhancing brilliance of Apple's famed "1984" Super Bowl XVIII launch of the Macintosh, there are precious few of these success stories.

Lots of ad messages aired during Super Bowl XLI, but it's not clear how many of them managed to do the job they were hired to do: credibly and compellingly *connect* with the viewers. Viewers may remember the celebrity, marvel at the visuals, or chuckle at the story. But how many can remember the name of the sponsoring brand? And how many feel any sort of personal connection with the message? And so, the average viewer may well have been chortling at the Sierra Mist commercial while happily guzzling a can of Coke, or chuckling at a Doritos ad while contentedly polishing off another plate of store-brand tortilla chips — and genuinely puzzling over what a "Go Daddy" is or why on earth he might want one.

Of course, Super Bowl XLI is merely the latest and most vivid reminder of the need to enhance the brand, not just amuse the audience. Rex Briggs and Greg Stuart recently compiled an impressive amount of research in reaching their conclusion that 35%-40% of advertising is simply wasted money, achieving essentially nothing of substance. Given the emphasis on grabbing attention in a cluttered ad environment, it's likely that at least that much of Super Bowl XLI's advertising was wasted money — and it was wasted at $2.6 million a pop. Maybe that's one reason why Unilever and Procter & Gamble, two of the world's largest and most respected advertisers, decided not to advertise in this year's Super Bowl. But while P&G waited on the sidelines, Garmin, Izod, and Salesgenie.com jumped right in to take their place.

Interestingly, in 2007, the battle to entertain and amaze viewers moved into new arenas with new contenders. This year, the contest was waged by more than just ad agencies; it was also waged by consumers who were asked to submit their ideas regarding what it takes to woo an audience. It stands to reason. It's all part of a new emphasis on "consumer-generated content," and some marketers are apparently convinced that what works for YouTube must also work for Chevy, Doritos, and even the NFL. After all, maybe a breakthrough entertainment idea lies just around the corner — even though it's unlikely that it's also a breakthrough *selling* idea.

So, if marketers aren't seeking to create credible and compelling brand messages that connect with the viewers, why not let anyone give it a whack? If marketers aren't trying to sell anything, they might as well just give everyone a shot at using their camcorders to create a message that's vivid or outlandish enough to interrupt viewers on their way to the kitchen.

The Super Bowl, however, is about winning on the field, and not just about entertaining the fans. That's why Tony Dungy and Lovie Smith didn't let the fans design and call the plays. Team owners demand a return on their investment, which is one reason for the merry-go-round of coaching changes that is part of each new season. "Just win, baby."

Brand owners should be just as demanding as football team owners, but it's not clear that they are — at least when Super Bowl time rolls around. Perhaps some of them are confusing fun with work. And yet, company shareholders and brand stewards should require no less of a Super Bowl commercial than what they should require of any brand message they transmit.

Celebrities, catchy jingles, special effects, and funny stories aren't part of the requirements for an ad; they only make sense when they serve to support advertising's *real* job. It must be *credible*. It must be *compelling*. It must be capable of *connecting* with the brand's target audience. And it must yield a meaningful return, especially when it costs $2.6 million.

See Related Article
"Can Advertising Still Contribute?" (page 139)

LEADERSHIP

MANAGING DURING
A CRISIS

by Mick Zangari and Benson Smith

September 24, 2001

How great managers lead employees during turbulent, fearful times

The next few weeks and months may be the most challenging time in any manager's career. Returning to "normal" will be easier said than done, as all of us try to cope with the horrific events of September 11 in our own way. For some, just trying to think about business at a time of tragic loss will seem inappropriate, while others will need to immerse themselves in work.

Although Gallup has been studying managers and employees since the 1960s, it's difficult to find an event that compares to the terrorist attacks on September 11. Nevertheless, we have observed many companies navigating through their own crises. Companies that have done the best at managing difficult situations have used these strategies: They continually evaluated the circumstances they faced as result of a rapidly changing landscape, and they engaged their employees by sticking to fundamentals of "great management."

Evaluate your situation

One of the reasons returning to "normal" may be difficult is because we may not know what "normal" is. Everyday life has changed dramatically and will never be quite the same. Certain industries will see a potentially devastating impact. The airline and travel industries already appear to be in this group, and many other industries may feel a short-term impact as decision making slows. There will be a ripple effect throughout the economy as businesses with customers among the affected industries experience the impact of change.

Other industries will find themselves pushed to meet new customer demand. Governments and businesses are likely to spend more on security and surveillance, but other industries also will see an uptick in spending. If Americans are reluctant to take back to the air or they postpone their travel plans, what will they spend those dollars on instead? What will be the ripple effects of any changes in spending habits?

At this point, no one knows the answers to any of these questions. Often the experts guess wrong, and circumstances turn out to be very different from what we anticipate. The best companies, when faced with a crisis, continue to examine the situations they face until they have a clear picture of what "normal" means. In the interim, keeping your employees engaged is critical.

Engaging employees during adversity

Setting clear expectations is important under any circumstances, but it's even more so in a crisis. People who deal with crowd evacuations, for example, find it necessary to repeat simple and obvious instructions over and over again. Phrases like "Keep moving" or "Don't stop" are essential elements of an evacuation process. Why is this so? Aren't these things obvious?

In times of confusion and uncertainty, people require crystal-clear expectations of what they need to do. No matter how carefully you set expectations for your employees before September 11, no doubt they have changed. Your annual budgets may no longer make sense. Your daily patterns may be interrupted, or your customers may need special help, reassurance, and assistance.

Redefining expectations in response to a crisis is absolutely essential. This takes work and thought. And sometimes, we as managers dodge this responsibility with watered-down expectations. Don't tell employees, "Do the best you can." A crisis is no time for vagueness. Meaningful expectations, though, cannot be set without employee input.

Seek opinions

We know from our research that an employee's connection to an organization is linked to his or her sense that "my opinions seem to count." As you try to understand a rapidly changing landscape and set new expectations, listen carefully to feedback from your employees.

While one of our client companies was going though a crisis, Peter M., a senior executive, made this observation: "More than ever before, we needed the information our workforce provided us. They were visiting with our customers and suppliers every day. We relied on them to tell us what was going on and to help us develop the right strategies."

Kathy C. worked for a company that took a very different approach when its industry was in trouble. "We kept getting memos from the home office that told us, 'Everything is okay. It's business as usual.' I wondered, 'Who are they trying to kid?' Everything was far from okay, and I was reminded of that on every customer call I made."

As you reshape your company's plans, you need to include your workforce in the information-gathering process and ask for their suggestions on what the best recovery strategies might be.

Use mission to unite your workforce

Your company's mission also can sustain employee engagement. We all work for many reasons, and a paycheck is just one of them. During a time of crisis, those "other reasons" assume paramount importance. We rally around the countries, causes, and companies we believe in.

In difficult circumstances, we can show our employees that our company's mission statement is not merely empty words. Instead, it embodies values that are important — ones we can fall back on when times are tough.

On September 11, U.S. citizens experienced an attack on our economy and our way of life, much more so than on our military strength. An important and vital response to this attack is to rebuild our economy. A short-term military action won't accomplish this. The process of rebuilding the economy will happen company by company, job by job, and person by person. Great managers can find a way to harness each person's overwhelming desire to help by showing them how their job contributes to the rebuilding process.

Show employees that you care

Harnessing that energy takes more than a sense of shared values. It takes a relationship. Our research clearly shows that people don't work for companies — they work for people. They work for their supervisor or their manager. They work for you.

All of us, in some way, have been touched by recent events. All us have a unique way to cope with our feelings and to put events in perspective. Great managers understand this, and they resist the temptation to rush their employees through this process. A manager who sends mixed messages —

who tells his employees, "You are important to me," but whose actions say, "I am much too busy to bother with you right now" — will lose credibility with his employees.

A time of crisis is a time to build relationships. It can be a time to show what you and your company really stand for. And it can be a time to tap into values that are more important to us than the numbers on our paycheck.

Clarity, not complexity

If all this seems simple — it is. Difficult challenges do not usually require complicated solutions, but rather straightforward ones.

Our role as managers and leaders is to minimize confusion, not add to it. No situation is so bad that it cannot be made worse by overreaction. Take stock of your situation, but understand that it may change dramatically in a few short weeks and months.

Set clear expectations. No battlefield commander says, "Do the best you can." Instead, he says, "Take that hill," or "Knock out that bunker." Be clear. Be specific.

Don't pretend things are normal if they are not. Give your employees good information about what's happening, and ask them what they're hearing from customers or suppliers. They are often your best source of information, and they need to express their observations and opinions.

Finally, use this opportunity to show what your company mission is all about. You will build relationships that will endure long after the crisis has passed.

LEADERSHIP IS A
PROCESS, NOT A ROLE

Interviewed by Jennifer Robison

January 8, 2004

**Why great leadership demands self-awareness, self-regulation —
and sometimes, self-sacrifice**

A *GMJ* Q&A with Bruce Avolio

Sometimes leaders are glorified; sometimes they're reviled. Often, they're simply taken for granted. Whatever the case, leaders clearly play a vital role in the success or failure of every organization — not to mention every city, state, and country.

So how come most fast-food workers get more direct and ongoing training in their fields than do many top business and political leaders? The fact is, there's a dearth of authentic personal-development programs for the very people who make or break organizations — and even societies.

This is the situation the University of Nebraska-Lincoln Gallup Leadership Institute set out to rectify. This research institute, housed within the College of Business Administration, offers masters and doctoral programs focusing on authentic strengths-based leadership development.

The program's director, Dr. Bruce Avolio, the Donald O. and Shirley Clifton Chair in Leadership, has studied leadership in dozens of countries, and his research and consulting includes work with seven militaries around the globe. Dr. Avolio has written more than 80 articles and five books on leadership, including *Full Leadership Development: Building the Vital Forces in Organizations* and *Made/Born: Leadership Development in Balance,* which will be published by Lawrence Erlbaum Associates in 2004. He is also a Gallup Senior Scientist — one of a group of leading researchers who share their expertise with Gallup.

Dr. Avolio's insights shed light on some enduring truths of leadership, including why leaders have to be trustworthy to produce sustainable performance and why all leaders, ultimately, have to know themselves to lead and grow their followers and their organizations to full potential.

GMJ: Why the focus on leadership development? What is there to be learned?

Dr. Avolio: The field of leadership development is probably the most under-researched in all studies of leadership. Yet, it's probably one of the most crucial factors in sustaining organizational success. So in our institute, we wanted to research how best to develop leaders, particularly those who were authentic leaders, based on a strengths-based philosophy. There's a lot of work that needs to be done to help people learn to leverage their talents to be more effective leaders.

GMJ: What's your vision for leadership development?

Avolio: To me, leadership is not a role, it's a process involving how an individual or a group influences others toward a particular goal or objective. Leadership development occurs across one's life span. Some people qualify that process — and what it means — by adding words like *inspiring* leadership or *directive* leadership. I look at it as a social-influence process. Many leadership development programs don't come close to what life does to produce outstanding leaders. So one of the most important elements of our work on leadership development is the focus we take on sustaining the development experience over an extended period of time, keeping in mind our impact points on performance.

The University of Nebraska-Lincoln Gallup Leadership Institute (UNL GLI) enables leaders to go out, apply what they learned, and learn how to do things better — with our extended support — even when they're "officially" through with our program. We track our leadership students over time and support them — exactly when they need it, we hope — to help them get through challenges they haven't confronted before. In the MBA program [that the UNL GLI offers in partnership with Gallup], we instituted a coaching process that continues three years *after* graduation. We do this because once leaders accumulate this knowledge, then go out and try it, we find they generally need support to get through their initial challenges to be successful.

GMJ: Not to be facetious, but none of my college professors offered to be there three years later to help me with post-graduate challenges.

Avolio: It's like telling someone, "Here, read this computer manual. Now put the manual down. In about six months, come back and show us what you just learned to do with the computer." It's absurd — and yet that's what people expect leaders to do. That's why we offer this kind of ongoing support.

GMJ: Can anybody learn to be a leader?

Avolio: Yes, but in very different levels of capacity, and I think that goes against the grain of what most people think. There are moments when people with the needed strengths will emerge, and that can vary tremendously depending on the nature of the context.

I think there is an enormous range of opportunities for people to lead, not the least of which is self-leadership. You establish your own guide point and think, *This is what I'd like to accomplish in my world, in my slice of humanity.* But there is an enormous self-fulfilling prophecy that people come to believe: If they're told they're not born to lead, then why bother putting energy into it? It keeps some really good people from having an impact in terms of leadership. I'd rather err in the direction that more — rather than fewer — people can lead.

GMJ: Tell me about your emphasis on self-awareness. You don't hear a lot about that in business administration programs.

Avolio: We're increasingly focusing on self-awareness and what it constitutes. As people go through life, their experiences change who they are if they have any sense of themselves. Some people close themselves off from life; they stop developing themselves. We're trying to include self-awareness as part of the life span development process. We believe you really release people when you help them identify what their talents and strengths are. It gives them a sense of clarity about themselves that allows them to explore in greater depth what they can be and to self-regulate. It provides a tremendous level of focus.

For instance, if I learn what my talents are, my new focus will be on how to leverage them — and perhaps I won't worry so much about the things that I've kind of stumbled through. At the same time, I look to other people and think about how I can help them leverage their strengths with mine. It's all part of the process of developing self-awareness.

In our leadership program, I hope we put people through more positive growth experiences rather than major negative life events that are often seen in the popular literature to cause someone to become "a better leader." A while back, I had three executives together, and they were waxing enthusiastically about the kind of leaders they had been — right before they had their stress-related quadruple bypass heart surgeries. Afterward, they miraculously became more open to developing themselves and their leadership. I think leadership development should be easier than open-heart surgery.

GMJ: What are the talents of highly successful leaders?

Avolio: In the long run, I can't imagine a leader who would last without an orientation toward the future or the capacity to leverage it in others. That's a crucial one. However, leaders who plan for the future without a strong sense of belief or responsibility are, I think, potentially dangerous people.

It's wonderful to have a leader with Empathy talent, but there have been many great leaders without it. Hopefully, they surround themselves with people who have Empathy, so that others feel like their needs are considered and taken care of. I think Ideation is an important talent theme, but it is more important in certain leadership roles than others. In industries that turn over ideas every couple of years, such as nanotechnology and biotech and life sciences, it's extremely important that leaders in those positions are fertile with ideas.

GMJ: What about Command?

Avolio: Some people would argue that Command talents are important, and in the leadership literature, talent in this theme has been called "dominance." And clearly, leaders tend to be more dominant or command-oriented in general. I think we're moving into a time of purer leadership, where Command probably won't be as important to the kind of organizations that we're going to be creating. In fact, "command" will be shared to a much greater extent.

GMJ: Does that have anything to do with the influx of women into higher echelons of business? Or do women simply have to be dominating to get results?

Avolio: I think women have to be more dominant in this particular period of time. Very few people at Hewlett-Packard would say that [Chairman and CEO] Carly Fiorina doesn't have Command. But I do think that the numbers of women in very senior positions throughout industry and government are changing ideas in this country — and eventually globally.

GMJ: What's an example of that?

Avolio: I vaguely remember Eisenhower when I was growing up, I remember Kennedy somewhat, and I remember Johnson very vividly. But I never remember any of them crying. And yet it seems like our president can cry now, and it's okay. Earlier, tears would have been perceived as a tremendous weakness, whereas right now it seems so much more acceptable. And I think what's happened is that more women have entered into these very senior positions, allowing us to all be more in touch with our basic emotions. And leadership itself has changed. You might say that leaders have become more androgynous — they can be understanding, and they can also be very tough.

GMJ: Every day, you hear about some new and horrible business scandal. It seems as if the robber barons have given up on the public and have started robbing their own businesses. These leaders are terrible examples of self-interest, yet leaders have to have a certain amount of self-interest to perform, don't they?

Avolio: Well, at the very base, self-interest is about survival. But in a world where survival isn't the only issue, leaders must make decisions that aren't necessarily based just on self-interest. And sometimes leaders must ask people to ignore what's best for themselves — that's one of the fundamental challenges that every leader at every level has to face. But they also have to take into consideration the impact that will have on those people. These are the trade-offs that leaders make all the time, and those who aren't even at the level of enlightened self-interest will have much greater difficulty taking their organizations to the next level to sustain verifiable growth and performance.

GMJ: It sounds like leaders have to make painful choices, sacrifices.

Avolio: Leadership requires strengths-based leaders who build a sense of identification with the mission in their people and who realize that sometimes, leaders must sacrifice and allow others to push the mission forward. That's a huge challenge. It's a real sacrifice. But to me, that's what leadership is about. Leaders make choices and sacrifices to focus on something they want to accomplish. Thinking about great successes, it often took a huge sacrifice to create a great accomplishment.

GMJ: How does the idea of their legacy affect leaders?

Avolio: A key element of leadership is how leaders frame things. Dictators frame things to control people: "I'm going to control you because that's the only way I can accomplish my desires." But the kind of leader people *want* to follow frames the world differently, in a way that leverages others' potential. These leaders understand that they can't control things beyond their life limits. If they want to have an impact, then they're going to have to change some of the things they do. They understand that if they don't have people's trust, if they only control the direction their followers are going, they have no chance at building a sustainable legacy. Basically, once they're gone, their followers will knock down their statues and move on.

GMJ: Do you have to trust your leader to perform? Or is it enough to trust the mission?

Avolio: Well, leadership without trust is a false sense of influence. Trust is at the center of what influential leadership is about. Identification with a leader is a profound part of trust that in turn creates trust in the mission. Throughout history, leaders have had followers who have identified with them so much, they've been willing to give up their lives for the cause or mission. Those feelings of trust and identification are universal — whether it's a soldier, a nurse in a hospital, or an employee for the railroad. If people truly believe in the organization and identify with its leadership, they'll work as hard as it takes to do what needs to be done. That's an awesome form of control — and it comes from the inside out.

THE SEVEN DEMANDS
OF LEADERSHIP

by Barry Conchie

May 13, 2004

What separates great leaders from all the rest?

Who wants to follow someone who's going nowhere? Or someone who's unreliable or untrustworthy? Organizations wrestle with these questions and many others as they confront the elusive challenge of defining effective leadership.

Most people are certain that leadership is about direction, about giving people a sense of purpose that inspires and motivates them to commit and achieve. Leadership is also about a relationship between people — leaders and followers — that is built on firm ground; enduring values build trust. Few would disagree with these views.

Not everyone, however, offers the same answer to this question: What's the best way to develop talented leaders to achieve sustained high performance? Indeed, Gallup Organization researchers have long been intrigued with this question. Having studied leadership talent for more than 40 years, Gallup set out to discover the demands that leaders must meet to be successful. We also wanted to uncover the developmental framework that would enhance leadership performance.

Our research confirmed the importance of two rather obvious demands — visioning and maximizing values. What was surprising was the presence of five other important demands that are essential to the development of all great leaders.

The research

First, a few words about how we arrived at these demands. Our study drew from a wide cross section of leaders who had a proven track record of success; we had evidence that they all delivered the goods. They were measurably the best when compared to others in similar roles. Their performance could be tracked to significant improvements to the bottom line. They enjoyed the endorsement of their bosses, peers, and direct reports. And they sustained high performance, often through adverse times.

For our initial leadership-development research, we identified and studied 100 leaders. They were drawn from general management, human resources, marketing, sales, manufacturing, research and development, and finance. They represented distinct levels of hierarchy, from managers to directors to vice presidents and senior executives. They had all faced significant demands that built and developed their leadership talent. Indeed, it was in researching this group that we uncovered the seven key demands that every leader must meet to achieve high performance.

We then expanded our study to include an additional 5,019 leaders from a wide range of industries and sectors, including education, healthcare, the military, government, finance, insurance, and retail. Our analysis directly linked those leaders who developed their talents by encountering the seven demands to significant improvements in their overall leadership performance. Their companies achieved specific business outcomes such as financial growth, customer and employee engagement, employee retention, and safety. Our continued tracking of more than 40,000 leaders continues to affirm these findings.

The demands

It's no great surprise that *visioning* is one of the seven demands. Successful leaders are able to look out, across, and beyond the organization. They have a talent for seeing and creating the future. They use highly visual language that paints pictures of the future for those they lead. As a result, they seem to attain bigger goals because they create a collective mindset that propels people to help them make their vision a reality.

These leaders also recognize that through visioning, they showcase their *values* and core beliefs. By highlighting what is important about work, great leaders make clear what is important to them in life. They clarify how their own values — particularly a concern for people — relate to their work. They also communicate a sense of personal integrity and a commitment to act based on their values.

As a result, employees know where they stand with these leaders. Their values — consistent and unchanging through time — operate like a buoy anchored in the ocean, holding firm against the elements while indicating the way.

By galvanizing people with a clear vision and strong values, the leaders we studied were able to challenge their teams to achieve significant work goals. In fact, those leaders themselves had been assigned significant *challenging experiences* at key points in their careers while being given the freedom to determine how they would achieve outcomes.

Confronting challenges produces beneficial effects for leaders. It accelerates their learning curve, stretches their capacity for high performance, and broadens their horizons about what is possible for an organization to achieve. As one of the leaders we studied said, "Our company had experienced three cycles of negative revenue growth, but I knew that our next cycle would give us the opportunity to turn in our best figures ever. Everyone thought I was crazy, but we did it, then did it again."

But great leaders aren't simply hard charging and highly driven. They also understand the importance of personal relationships. Indeed, the leaders we studied consistently had a close relationship either with their manager or someone in the best position to advise them. This is often someone from outside their organization who serves as their *mentor*. These mentoring relationships are not the product of formal company-wide mentoring programs — not that these aren't helpful. Instead, these informal, yet successful, mentoring relationships enable each individual leader's needs and differences to be taken into account.

Inspired by their positive experiences with mentors, the leaders we studied have become intentional mentors themselves. They selectively pick one, two, or three highly talented individuals and invest greatly in their growth and development over a significant period of time. They see the success of these "mentees" as a reflection of their own success. These leaders practice a form of succession planning that cultivates the next generation of leaders.

Beyond close one-to-one relationships, leaders also create rapport at many levels across their organization and beyond. They know the benefits of *building a wide constituency*. One leader said, "My work forces me to have a relationship with certain people. I just think about those I don't yet work with and figure out who might be useful to know. I nearly always find that relationships built this way bring dividends." These leaders understand networks and the importance of networking.

In all their relationships, effective leaders enlighten others because they can *make sense of experience*. They also learn from their mistakes and their successes, and — as they seek out a range of experts across their wide constituency — they ask questions and listen.

What's more, these leaders are able to deal with the complexity of business life and help those around them make sense of it. They do this by keeping things simple and making information accessible. This way, these leaders help individuals understand what's going on so that they are better able to achieve success. As one leader put it, "There's so much happening that affects our work. I make sure, at each meeting, that we understand all the important factors and ensure that the next steps are clearly laid out."

The most revealing discovery was that effective leaders have an acute sense of their own strengths and weaknesses. They *know who they are* — and who they are *not*. They don't try to be all things to all people. Their personalities and behaviors are indistinguishable between work and home. They are genuine. It is this absence of pretense that helps them connect to others so well.

Organizations are struggling to build and grow their leadership capacity. Our research suggests that talented leaders require the very best development experiences to realize their potential. And for this potential to be converted into sustained, high organizational performance, these experiences must be framed around the seven key demands of leadership.

SHAPING LEADERSHIP DEVELOPMENT: KEY QUESTIONS

VISIONING

- Who contributes to, controls, or communicates the "big picture"?
- Are leaders encouraged to "paint pictures" of the future?
- What opportunities do leaders have to talk about and shape the future?

MAXIMIZING VALUES

- How do corporate values align with individual values?
- Are leaders encouraged to lead with their values?
- Are leaders asked to describe the values that are important to them?

CHALLENGING EXPERIENCE

- Are leaders free to think outside of conventional approaches?
- How much latitude are leaders afforded in decision making?
- Are leaders given significant responsibilities with wide-ranging delegation?

MENTORING

- Is value attached to mentoring outside of the organization?
- Are leaders expected to accelerate highly talented individuals through the organization to their optimum levels of performance?

BUILDING A CONSTITUENCY

- Are leaders expected to grow networks beyond their immediate work relationships?
- Does your organization promote the growth of networks through measuring their business impact?

MAKING SENSE OF EXPERIENCE

- Are leaders able to meet with peers to share understanding and learning of new issues?
- Is there a clear leadership focus on "lean" communication?

KNOWING SELF

- Is every leader clear about his or her strengths and weaknesses?
- Does your organization sponsor individualism in leadership through role models?

THE IMPACT OF POSITIVE
LEADERSHIP

by Tom Rath

May 13, 2004

How seemingly small interactions can dramatically boost your team's productivity

This could be a typical morning in the life of one of your star employees:

Suzie walks into the office at 8:00 a.m. The affable receptionist greets her with a smile, calls her by the name she prefers ("Suzie," not "Susan"), and strikes up some small talk. **Suzie's Positive-to-Negative Ratio: Positive 1, Negative 0.**

As Suzie rounds the corner, she notices that the elevator door is beginning to close. So she speeds up, knowing there is usually a wait for the elevator first thing in the morning. It looks like she will miss the elevator, but at the last moment, an arm shoots out and stops the door from closing. As the door reopens, Suzie thanks the unknown woman who held the elevator for her. **Suzie's Ratio: Positive 2, Negative 0.**

A few minutes later, Suzie settles in at her desk and starts to read her e-mail. One of the first messages is from her least favorite coworker, Greg. Even before opening the message, she knows what to expect: relentless complaining. As if on cue, Greg's note starts with a one-liner about how bad traffic was coming in to work. Then he breaks into a tirade about having to "pick up the slack" for the rest of the team. "Yeah right," Suzie mutters to herself. She knows that Greg's constant negativity is the real drag on her workgroup's productivity. And reading his note is a lousy way to start her day. **Suzie's Ratio: Positive 2, Negative 1.**

Instead of venting her frustration to others, Suzie decides to grab a cup of coffee and settle down. In the break room, she sees Amy, one of her closest friends. Amy smiles and immediately tells Suzie that she "loves the new shoes." They end up chatting for about 10 minutes, and Suzie feels much better. **Suzie's Ratio: Positive 3, Negative 1.**

Suzie loses track of time while she happily chats with Amy. But then she discovers that she's running late for her 8:30 meeting. As Suzie rushes down the hall to the conference room, she feels guilty. She is rarely, if ever, late to meetings. Suzie finally makes it to the conference room — about seven minutes behind schedule, according to her wristwatch.

Meanwhile, you — Suzie's boss — are sitting in the conference room, along with five other people who report to you. Everyone else had arrived on time and was ready to go by 8:30. By the time Suzie walks in, your patience is running thin.

The first thing Suzie does — before even taking her seat — is to apologize to the group for wasting their time. Then you decide to kick off the meeting by saying, "Well, now we can get started, albeit ten minutes behind schedule." This jab hits Suzie like a brick. She already felt guilty and had apologized to everyone. Your comment only exacerbated her bad feelings. **Suzie's Ratio: Positive 3, Negative 2.**

In the span of just over 30 minutes, Suzie, your best performer, had three interactions that were positive and two that were negative. Put another way, her positive-to-negative ratio, or PNR, was 3:2.

Sound good? Well, it's not good enough for her — nor for anyone else you lead. And beware, manager: Unless you are actively working, today and every day, to make sure Suzie has more positive interactions, you may soon have a disengaged employee on your hands — or worse, you could lose one of your best people.

"The magic ratio"

Over the past decade, scientists have explored the impact of positive-to-negative interaction ratios in our work and personal life. And they have found that this ratio can be used to predict — with remarkable accuracy — everything from workplace performance to divorce. This work began with noted psychologist John Gottman's exploration of positive-to-negative ratios in marriages. Using a 5:1 ratio, which Gottman dubbed "the magic ratio," he and his colleagues predicted whether 700 newlywed couples would stay together or divorce by scoring their positive and negative interactions in one 15-minute conversation between each husband and wife. Ten years later, the follow-up revealed that they had predicted divorce with 94% accuracy.

So what is the optimal positive-to-negative ratio in organizations? A recent study by psychologist Barbara Fredrickson and mathematician Marcial Losada found that work teams with a PNR greater than 3:1 were significantly more productive than workgroups that did not reach this ratio. Positive emotions, however, need to be grounded in reality: Their research also uncovered an upper limit for positive-to-negative ratios of 13:1. When workgroups exceed that PNR, things are likely to worsen; completely blind optimism can be counterproductive — and downright annoying — in some cases.

But managers shouldn't worry about breaking the upper limit. The levels of positive emotions in most organizations are woefully inadequate and leave substantial room for improvement.

Consider the effect your comments had when Suzie walked in late. Had you simply told her "It's OK" — or maybe even offered a few encouraging words — her PNR would have been a healthy 4:1. (She is a top producer who's never late — you could have cut her some slack.) And instead of sitting through the meeting feeling guilty and disengaged, Suzie might have added a few more ideas to the discussion. Perhaps she would have inspired or praised someone else — thereby passing her positive energy along to others. Had you decided to handle Suzie's tardiness differently, it could have had a ripple effect.

When leaders display positive emotions, others take note — and take action. Positive leaders don't sit back and wait for things to get better on their own. Instead, as they walk around the office, make calls, or write e-mails, they are always trying to catch excellence in action. When they spot a job well done, they call attention to what is right. This in turn raises the entire organization's PNR and its productivity.

Ken, the CEO of a large organization, calls positive emotion his secret weapon as a leader. As Ken travels around the globe, he stops by his company's local offices. And he doesn't visit to spy on his employees or check in with top brass. Instead, his goal is to energize every employee in each office.

Before arriving at a location, Ken recalls the successes and achievements he has heard over the past few months involving people in that office. As soon as he arrives, Ken casually visits with these individuals and congratulates them. He may offer kudos to an employee who recently got married or had a child, or praise someone who delivered stellar customer service. His favorite line is: "I've been hearing a lot of good talk behind your back."

Ken just loves to "watch the energy move through the network" once he sets it in motion. He realizes that he can light up an entire office building with a few brief — but very energizing — conversations. As a result of this approach, thousands look to him for motivation and guidance.

What positive leaders accomplish

Indeed, the litmus test of a positive leader is the *esprit de corps* he creates with his troops. Positive leaders deliberately increase the flow of positive emotions within their organization. They choose to do this not just because it is a "nice" thing to do for the sake of improving morale, but because it leads to a measurable increase in performance. Studies show that organizational leaders who share positive emotions have workgroups with:

- a more positive mood
- enhanced job satisfaction
- greater engagement
- improved performance

What differentiates positive leaders from the rest? Instead of being concerned with what they can *get out of* their employees, positive leaders search for opportunities to *invest in* everyone who works for them. They view each interaction with another person as an opportunity to increase his or her positive emotions.

COACHING:
NO MORE MR. NICE GUY

by Barry Conchie

April 14, 2005

The most effective executive coaches offer blunt advice — and focus relentlessly on the numbers

To understand a big problem with executive coaching, let's start by replaying a recent conversation between a management consultant and an executive coach:

Consultant: "What does executive coaching involve?"

Executive Coach: "I get to work one-on-one with senior-level executives in different organizations."

Consultant: "Yes, but what do you actually do?"

Executive Coach: "I get paid to coach them, to sort of help them. It's difficult to describe."

Consultant: "What kind of coaching do you do?"

Executive Coach: "I try to help leaders discover themselves, to encourage them, to make them feel better about their work, to keep their spirits up. They have a tough job, and I just try to make it a little easier for them."

Consultant: "How do you know you're making a difference?"

Executive Coach: "Well, the leaders I work with say that they feel better when I help them, and they keep asking me back."

Consultant: "No, I meant, are you able to measure the difference you are making? Do major numbers shift as a result of your work? What scores do you track?"

Executive Coach: "Look, my work is far too important to reduce to numbers. I help leaders grow. If they want numbers, they should ask an accountant!"

Sadly, in the growing field of executive coaching, exchanges like this are common. A cadre of well-intentioned coaches peddles their wares in a "feel-good" market that caters to the upper echelons of corporate America. Coaches like these are able to make a healthy living by providing a "solution" to a perceived gap between senior managers' development needs and their businesses' needs. They work closely with leaders and develop strong, long-lasting relationships that endure. The problem is, the results just might not make a difference for the leaders' businesses.

My own extensive experience of working with top executives reveals that coaching that focuses on business performance is key to improvement in executive performance. The contrast between a "feel-good" approach and one that is candid, objective, and incisive, is stark. As executives search to address their vulnerabilities by seeking out an independent voice, feel-good feedback can give them a nice emotional boost, but the results may leave them wondering whether it was worth it. For some, feeling good becomes synonymous with feeling *comfortable*.

Understand the business strategy

What sets performance coaching apart from feel-good coaching? What should leaders consider before embarking on what could be either a lifelong business-building relationship or an expensive journey toward mediocrity?

First, a productive performance coaching relationship shouldn't start with an analysis of the individual leader. Instead, it should begin with an evaluation of the leader's business goals and responsibilities. Coaches must possess more than business or market savvy. They also must grasp the specific short-term and medium-term business issues that the executive faces.

The best executive performance coaches start a coaching relationship with a careful analysis of the company's business strategy. Then, they help leaders get specific and real in translating big ideas to ground-level activity. Step-by-step, they work with executives to understand and develop the measures and numbers that must be achieved to attain significant performance outcomes.

A real-life example illustrates how this process should work. In mid-2004, an executive took over a global product development team for a multinational manufacturer. Upon assuming this new role, he said that the last thing he needed was to have his head filled with big ideas.

"I have goals to meet, and I just need help with three things," he said. "First, our overall product market is declining. I have to source and then develop new product to achieve 5% growth targets in 2005. Second, this team costs too much for its current productivity. I have to cut headcount and increase per-person productivity by at least 12%. Third, this team operates in silos, and we are missing too many cross-selling opportunities. I have goals to expand our product ratios in our top five markets from 5:1 to 3:1 by the end of the fiscal year." For this executive, improving ratios means equalizing the balance of sales between two products through better cross-selling, while continuing to grow overall revenue.

Once his leadership performance coach understood the executive's business goals, the coach could use that knowledge to push and guide him toward meeting them. In this example, deftly deploying and managing personnel would be key to his success. His coach asked questions like: Who is best to position where? Who has the talent to succeed? What do you need to communicate, and when?

The best performance coaches help leaders connect the future to the present by breaking down the steps that lead toward success. Then, they help leaders think through the implications of their decisions and actions. Coaches should help leaders anticipate and strategize by presenting alternatives, taking the contrary view, articulating the strongest points of resistance, and connecting the leader with external experiences and insights.

Know the leader's strengths and weaknesses

Once the performance coach has a firm grasp of the business and where it's going, the next step is to understand the strengths and weaknesses of the leader and the teams with which she works. What does she do best? What innate talents can she leverage? What blind spots might prevent success?

For example, the product development executive above was not cut out to be a slick communicator. He continually stumbled to recover from a stream of inept and ill-timed messages. He tended to over-elaborate information about upcoming meetings; when he finally sent information, it arrived too late for team members to be able to fully consider options. His poor communications threatened to undermine his efforts to meet his team's goals.

To help him overcome this problem, the performance coach had to provide clear analysis of the problem and how it could be solved. After an analysis of team strengths, the coach recommended that the executive delegate the task of handling team communications to a team member who had the most natural talent in this area.

Without insights from his performance coach, this leader would not have reached this decision on his own; in fact, he did not want to let go of the communication responsibilities. Ultimately, his coach persuaded him to make the change by focusing on the desired outcome.

"This team won't reach 12% per-person productivity growth if you keep sending unclear messages immediately before important meetings," the coach said bluntly. "You're better at setting the goals and dealing with customers; get someone else to do the communication."

It turned out to be a smart move because it liberated the leader to focus his efforts on product diversification — an area in which he excels. In fact, a turnaround in cross-selling growth occurred after the leader delegated his communication responsibilities. Currently, with four months still remaining in his company's fiscal year, the team's product ratios are at 3:1 or better in its top five markets, with growing revenues. His team's employee engagement levels have also increased.

Challenge every assumption

Executive performance coaches who focus more on how leaders feel than on how effectively they perform rarely step into uncomfortable territory. But challenging fundamental assumptions is essential if leaders are to confront obstacles and achieve professional and business growth. Knowing what buttons to push and when requires good judgment — but the best leadership performance coaches attack areas of mediocrity first. They challenge leaders who want to creep toward goals through incremental gain. They recognize that excellence rarely results when leaders spend too much time doing things they don't do well.

Effective leadership performance coaches drive improvement by challenging leaders to expand their scope of what is possible for the organization to achieve. They might do this by bringing in case studies and benchmarks to help the leader learn and grow. But more often, they start by challenging any assumption — like the assumption that a 12% growth in per-person productivity is sufficient.

A great executive coach isn't a "Dr. Feelgood." Rather, he or she delivers incisive analysis and brutally honest, detached advice and feedback. Effective coaches — the kind that really want to help leaders and businesses grow — use an array of tools and objective assessments to inform their advice. They operate close to the edge of executive tolerance, knowing how far and to what extent to push for change. And they measure their success not by how good they make executives feel, but by how far each leader moves the numbers.

GOOD TO GREAT?
OR LOUSY TO GOOD?

by Jim Clifton

June 9, 2005

Lousy companies sell 100% on price. Great companies pursue organic growth.

My phone rings, and it's the division president of a large telephone company. She offers to replace our current Gallup long-distance lines for a quick 10% savings. This means a lot of money to us. And the telephone lines we need in the United States and around the world are a commodity. They all seem to work well and sound fine, regardless of the long-distance carrier we use. As we are a business with serious employee owners, it seems an easy decision to dump our longtime partner for one offering a significantly lower price.

I call our top managers in the IT department, Phil and Phil, and they say they will study it. They soon get back to me with their recommendation to stay with our current technology partner — Partner A. Phil and Phil are super-competent technology leaders at our company, and I was sure that they would have a great explanation.

Phil and Phil described in detail the innovations that Partner A has brought to the table over the past few years, including a deal-saving technology breakthrough that helped us rescue one of our best accounts, a large and demanding retailer. They felt that Partner A brought more to the table than just global lines. This partner helped us win, save, and grow accounts.

Phil and Phil reported that Partner A knew our industry as well as or better than our own people. They also informed me that Partner A was re-engineering our global teleconferencing to VOIP and building a new state-of-the-art interviewing system throughout the 25 European Union states that would quickly make us the technology leader in our field in the EU. And they are in the middle of helping us compete to win a complex project in Brussels.

Higher margin business from current customers

If you've ever wondered what, exactly, is meant by the financial term "organic growth," there is no better example than this story. Organic growth occurs when an organization like Partner A creates more transactions with its current customer base and with continuously growing margins. Organic growth first occurs by retaining current customers, then by increasing transactions with them. Whether your company has 100 customers or several million, organic growth occurs when you increase the amount of sales with your current customer base.

Many executives think that an organic growth strategy is the opposite of an acquisition strategy. They are not opposite as much as they are extremely different, and they require extremely different approaches and cultures to execute them successfully.

Let's go back to the story about Partner A for a moment. Partner A has developed a "fully engaged" relationship with our company. Fully engaged customer relationships like these embody four distinguishing characteristics:

1. Fully engaged customers *renew*. You keep them.

2. Fully engaged customers *buy more often*. You have more transactions per customer per year.

3. Fully engaged customers *create positive conversations* in your organization and in the market. They create leads.

4. Most importantly, fully engaged customers will *pay a higher margin*. Put a better way, they value their total partnership with your organization rather than just its price.

Partner A perfectly executed an organic growth strategy. An organic growth strategy succeeds when companies maximize relationships with current customers. This is very different — and much more powerful — than losing existing customers based on price, then replacing them with new customers based on price.

What Wall Street is missing

Financial analysts often miss this crucial point: Lousy companies can churn through customers and still show sales growth through replacement. But accounting reports won't reveal their huge customer turnover. This cycle — losing customers based on price, then getting new customers based on price — is what I call "riding the razorblade," and it has been the unspoken strategy of most companies over the past 20 years.

Company leaders talk a good game about growth at state-of-the-company speeches. But then they go right back to their offices and continue okaying new contract lows to hold customers or win replacement business. They do this largely because Wall Street has not really caught on to the deep implications of organic growth and how to spot it, even though it remains the best single metric to predict sustainable growth, sustainable profit, and share growth. If someone said to me, "In your 30 years of studying customer data, what is the indicator or single metric that is the key to buying or selling stock?" My answer would be, "Same-customer sales."

Wall Street analysts deserve credit for closely studying same-store sales in retail. But even there, financial analysts can't be sure if they are seeing improved sales with fully engaged customers or through tricky marketing and merchandising that compensates for customer defections — in other words, through what is actually a replacement strategy. It's impossible to see if a company is achieving true organic growth.

The key to organic growth is how your organization performs one customer at a time. And here are the million-dollar questions: Are you developing fully engaged relationships with every single customer? Is your company a partner with every customer, or are you just a vendor? Consider your answers carefully, because the sum total of these relationships is your stock price.

Organic growth is revealed by figuring out how many of your customers have an "advice" relationship with your organization versus how many have a "price" relationship. The ratio of advice to price is key to your company's future. The higher the ratio, the better — and as this ratio moves, so does sales growth. This ratio is your company's best predictor of whether it is creating sustainable growth — or riding the razorblade.

When it comes to managing customer relationships, many Fortune 1000 companies' offenses come in the form of extremely well-run marketing sales and merchandising practices. And practices such as Six Sigma, lean management, and enterprise relationship management have all been brilliantly used to create leak-proof defenses. But none of these strategies or tactics will help your business go from "good to great," as the popular book says, or even from "lousy to good." What these approaches are missing is the magic of sustainable stock increase through a sustainable customer strategy. That is exactly why companies need a genuine organic growth strategy — one that is about moving from price to advice.

The challenge of extreme competition

Now, it's crucial to note that advice-versus-price relationships are present in *all* businesses, organizations, and professions. Advice-versus-price exists in hair salons just as it does in major technology or medical or government sales. Whether the business is dance lessons, pharmaceuticals, new and used cars, jet shares, real estate, hotels, hospitality, churches, suits and dresses, or delis, advice-versus-price relationships matter to some degree in every business in which transactions matter.

Regardless of its industry, the worst thing that can happen to your business is for 100% of your customers to base their relationships 100% on price. When this happens, your leadership needs to go from "lousy to good" in a hurry. Yes, price matters, but in a great organization, price should account for no more than 30% of your relationship with any customer; the other 70% should be based on your advice and ideas.

The obstacle that prevents leadership from moving from a price to an advice relationship is extreme competition, and it is everywhere. Not long ago, many markets had a handful of competitors per industry, all of which conveniently shared the market, and all were profitable. In those days, third place wasn't that far from first. These "convenient monopolies" represented the state of national competitiveness.

An easy example is the old network television industry, where NBC, CBS, and ABC ruled. Being number one was about the same as being number three. All three printed money for 20 years. Network news and big-city network affiliates made a staggering 50% pre-tax profit. Ad slots were always sold out.

Imagine a conversation from those days between Joe, an advertiser, and a network TV salesperson at the 21 Club over martinis and cigarettes. "I'm sorry, Joe, but we're sold out until January, but I can get you some spots on *Gunsmoke*. By the way, the new rate card will be in effect in January, and prices are going up fifteen percent." Joe takes the deal.

Today, many prices have dropped to unimaginable lows. Twenty-five years ago, Gallup paid 30 cents per minute for phone calls. Gallup now pays only 3 cents per minute. Phil and Phil say it will someday go to zero. If someone had said this 25 years ago, during constant rate increases, no one would have believed it. The thought that prices would stop increasing and would actually drop to 3 cents, let alone to nothing, was not something anyone could have imagined.

And if you look at what has happened in Detroit — where all three car companies used to enjoy a well-defined and rich convenient monopoly — automakers now give away the cars at the cost of labor and steel and attempt to make money on the loans. So now in Detroit, the cars are the "free toasters" to entice you to take the loan. Nobody saw that coming. This is what happens when you bet your organization's future on price.

Advice relationships

It's pretty clear that companies must re-order their priorities or they will go broke. Many are going broke now. They must find an alternative to price slashing, and the solution is to create value based on *relationships.*

Now, you might say, "Tell me how relationships can solve this problem." First, let's drill down to make relationships more actionable; let's define an "advice" relationship. In an advice relationship, someone brings you a new idea, teaches you something she has learned about your industry, or offers you a new way to save money or a new process to streamline operations. She might have a sales lead for you; she might connect you with a valuable new partner.

At the core of this kind of relationship lies a tangible business value, like Partner A demonstrated with Phil and Phil. You must know the customer and his business very well and have a passion for it. Above all, the engine driving the relationship must be your *imagination.* An organic growth strategy demands extraordinary creativity and imagination from the people who interact with customers.

Many consulting firms refer to the highest level of relationship as that of a "trusted advisor." That relationship works in almost any industry. It is not only true for McKinsey, Ernst & Young, and Gallup; it is also true for the wholesale meat salesman.

Doing a great job

Here's a story that illustrates my point. I recently walked to my local bookstore in Georgetown to get the *U.S. News & World Report: America's Best Colleges 2005.* This is a major bookstore, with three stories of books, escalators, a big music department, and a Starbucks coffee shop. I looked all over the store and couldn't find the college report. The staff person I checked with was on the phone to a friend and was ever-so-slightly put off that she was interrupted. "If it wasn't where you looked, we don't have it," she said, then went back to her call. Suddenly, it felt like everyone in the store was unhelpful.

As chance would have it, just as I was getting on the escalator, a real young, super-skinny, 15-year-old-looking kid with a bookstore ID tag asked, "Is there something I can help you find?"

He didn't have the greatest personality in the retail world, and he didn't pretend to. He didn't say, "It's great to have you here." He said, "Can I help you find something?" He not only got wound up helping me find my college guide, but he also found a book that was more precisely what I wanted — a book specifically about law schools. He was grinning because he not only found what I was looking for, but he helped me discover that there was another book that better met my needs.

Then he asked, "Is there anything else I can help you find?" I asked if he was familiar with the book *The United States of Europe*. He said he was, and it was excellent. I told him that I don't like to read hard academic books. He guaranteed me that this wasn't. In the end, I bought two books I didn't intend to buy, and we looked at some others I will soon consider getting as well.

My trip to the bookstore is a perfect example of organic growth. Three outcomes were possible when I walked in the store. The bookstore staff could do a "good" job and sell me exactly what I came for. They could do a "lousy" job and sell me nothing. Or they could do a "great" job by discovering what I really wanted, which was information about law schools, and advising me to buy something I really wanted, something I didn't even know was available — then following up by asking what else I needed and recommending another great idea.

I left the store enthusiastic and feeling victorious about my new books. My clerk was genuinely enthused because I had taken his advice, and we became acquaintances. I will always seek him out on future shopping trips.

One million moments of truth each day

These three potential outcomes not only illustrate the concept of organic growth, but also a phenomenon Gallup calls the "emotional economy."

For this bookstore, the difference between making $0, $10, or $50 from a customer doesn't lie with its merchandising, its ad agency, or its Six Sigma restocking or shipping techniques; it lies with the sales associate who senses an unmet emotional need and fulfills it. Within the concept of the emotional economy lies the potential economic impact of millions of missed transactions — or millions of transactions fulfilled — every day.

As an example, let's say this large bookstore chain has about 1,000 stores, and each day, 1 million prospects walk into them. So every day, there are 1 million moments of truth — 1 million opportunities to provide service that's lousy or good or great.

To dollarize this, let's say the range per transaction is $0 to $50. If 1 million customers were treated like I was by the first clerk, this bookstore chain would go flat broke. They couldn't drop their prices low enough to make sales. If their service was good, they might survive on $10 per transaction. But if the service was great every time, the difference would be $40 on every transaction (the difference between a $10 sale and a $50 sale).

It may not seem like much at first glance, but $40 by 1 million customers is 40 million extra sales dollars every day. Over a year, it adds up to $14 billion, which would triple this chain's current sales and boost their profit 5 to 8 times.

FROM LOUSY TO GOOD TO GREAT AT THE BOOKSTORE

At the core of every advice-based relationship, there is a tangible business value. For this bookseller, the difference between lousy and good service in one transaction is $10, while the difference between good and great service is $40.

SERVICE LEVEL	RESULT	SALES VALUE
Lousy	Fail to take the order and sell nothing to a sure prospect.	$0
Good	Take an order, and sell the customer exactly what he asks for.	$10
Great	Advise the customer to purchase not just what he asks for, but what he really needs.	$50

This may seem like a crazy scenario, but it shows how enormous a company's untapped emotional economy can be. The amounts left on the table are huge, especially when a company's customer service is only lousy or good. If this bookstore could improve just 10% of its 1 million daily customer interactions from good to great, it would easily double its market capitalization.

From good to great through organic growth

Many people have asked me, inspired by the popular book, of course, "How can my company go from good to great?" My answer is, "Create organic growth by maximizing the emotional economy that exists within your current customer base."

Gallup provides consulting services of various kinds to 100 of the Fortune 500 companies. Only five of these companies are clearly in the great category. I define a "great" company as one that understands the emotional economy and has a clear strategy to increase organic growth.

Gallup's research shows that, on average, only 20% of the customers of business-to-consumer organizations are fully engaged; only 12 % of the customers of business-to-business organizations are fully engaged.

What Wall Street and even the best CFOs still miss is that in business-to-business companies, lousy, good, or great management occurs about one to two years before it shows up as earnings; it shows up more quickly in retail. Basically, earnings are a one- to two-year trailing indicator of customer performance. And a company's success in managing its emotional economy is never included in formulas that calculate future earnings. When you maximize this economy, it is called "organic growth."

Right now, there is enormous variation in how companies serve and engage their customers. In the case of the retail bookstore, customer service that ranges from lousy to great means $0 to $50 to this company, 1 million times per day. In the case of Partner A, a successful relationship with Phil and Phil means retaining a growing account.

One more story: I sometimes interview our clients' customers personally to get a feel for their emotional economy. During a discussion with the CIO of a large U.S. grocery chain, I asked how he would rate Tech Firm A on a 1-to-5 scale. He said, "A 1, because they do nothing but deliver cheap technology and equipment." I asked who their best supplier of technology was, and he said Tech Firm B. Get this: He said that he would give Tech Firm B his highest marks because rather than just sell him products, "They teach me how to sell more groceries." This CIO spends about 10 times more with Tech firm B than with Tech firm A.

For most companies, whether they're going from "good to great" or "lousy to good," there is more cash laying on the table here than through any other leadership approach. The newly discovered emotional economy that lies within customer interactions is bigger than what W. Edwards Deming found when he first started looking at defects and variation 60 years ago. Remember, Deming discovered that 50% of all U.S. manufacturing costs came from redoing product. The range Gallup finds in customer service performance is as big as or bigger than the defect ranges Deming found in "lousy-to-great" manufacturing.

First steps to institutionalizing organic growth

So how can companies institutionalize organic growth? How do leaders get a large organization deeply focused on a very different customer service strategy, one based more on advice than price? Here are some suggestions:

1. *Measure customer service at the local level, or your employees won't take it seriously.* You must use a short, powerful questionnaire with near-perfect question items that can accurately predict whether an account is in trouble or will grow. Gallup has done this for 20 years, and we've found that separating "engaged accounts" from "accounts that are in trouble" is an easy way to predict future buying behavior. Then hold managers and workgroups accountable for their customer performance. Very few companies have succeeded in measuring and managing customer service at the local level, but it's the only way to get everyone focused on customer service. Use this audit as your engine for change.

2. *Make it 100% about money.* First, use your customer service metric to calculate the existing range of performance throughout the company. Just as with Six Sigma, you will find extreme variation in performance from workgroup to workgroup. Use advanced statistical and economic modeling to show where your company and its divisions could be if they were maximizing organic growth opportunities. Then extrapolate organic growth from the divisions all the way to the company's total market capitalization.

3. Change compensation and review programs to reflect leader, manager, and employee performance on this highly predictable indicator of organic growth. Identify teams with fully engaged customers. Make them heroes. Tell everyone in the company their best practices.

4. Create a Web site that enables managers to scan "state-of-the-customer" data by division, region, and client teams. This can become sort of like a global weather map, something that managers check regularly, like stock prices or baseball scores.

5. Create an organic growth leadership camp. Replace your current leadership development program with one focused 100% on organic growth. Use this program to teach your managers, salespeople, and key employees how to earn "5s" rather than "1s" from their clients. Help them understand what makes your customer relationships grow and what makes them wither away. Teach them that a price-based relationship fails to create organic growth and that an advice-based relationship is 30% price and 70% advice. Give certifications — like the Black Belt in Six Sigma — to those who master the new approach. These certifications will become the talk of the company because your leaders will learn that there is more money to be made in growing your current customer relationships than in any other growth strategy.

DISCOVERING HOW YOUR FUTURE
LEADERS THINK   *by Barry Conchie with Jerry Hadd*

November 10, 2005

The key questions your organization's coaches should ask every developing leader

D
o you want to get the best performance from your organization's future leaders? Then start asking them direct questions that, when answered, will help shape and define the type of leaders they will become.

Great teachers and coaches have always known that the deepest learning results from asking thought-provoking, probing questions. These questions cause people to think, and the sharpest questions can have tremendous influence on how executives formulate strategy.

Furthermore, probing questions demand a response. They focus the mind on the most important aspects of a problem. They spark thinking and learning that affect outcomes.

Many forms of leadership coaching attempt to teach future leaders "about" leadership. But relatively little coaching encourages leaders to concentrate on activities that will reliably improve their capacity to lead. So what are the questions your organization's coaches or mentors should ask every developing leader? What are the questions that most promote leadership growth?

Gallup has been researching top-performing leaders for more than 40 years. One crucial discovery has been that top performance is strongly correlated to seven main leadership activities or "demands." Those demands are: visioning, maximizing values, challenging experience, mentoring, building a constituency, making sense of experience, and knowing self.

Focusing each leader's growth on the seven demands can accelerate leadership development. Below, we outline the seven demands and suggest probing questions for developing leaders in these key areas.

Visioning

The best leaders talk often about the future and how it will be better than the present. Their forward-looking approach engages and excites their audience and elicits commitment.

Questions about visioning:

- Can you articulate the long-term direction of your organization?
- With whom have you recently discussed your views about the long-term future direction of your organization?
- Did this discussion positively affect and motivate your audience?
- Who will be in your next audience? What will you say to them?

Maximizing Values

Great leaders live their values, and this fact is usually revealed in the predictability of their behavior. Those leaders also clearly and passionately articulate how their organization compares to its competitors.

Questions about maximizing values:

- For any situation or issue you face, how accurately could each of your team members predict your behavior or response?
- Why is your organization so much more important to current and potential customers than any other organization?

Challenging Experience

Leaders constantly raise the bar for themselves and others. Top-performing leaders seek out and welcome new challenges — they don't avoid them.

Sometimes setting high standards requires having difficult conversations with others. The best leaders have those conversations early. While challenging employees, leaders never lose sight of performance, whether the time frame is short, medium, or long term.

Questions about challenging experience:

- How have you stretched performance goals for your organization, division, or team recently? Why did you do this? What results do you expect?
- What are the three main performance goals on your agenda?

- Have you made someone uncomfortable and someone else excited about his or her performance over the past week? What did you say, and why did you say it? What result did this have? When and how will you follow up?

- What challenge have you accepted while others struggled or failed? Why will you be successful?

Mentoring

Great leaders selectively mentor talented associates toward top performance. These leaders understand how to focus their mentees' attention on the right areas for optimal performance gains. Leaders understand what these people can achieve and position them in areas where their talents can become true strengths.

Questions about mentoring:

- Who are the top and bottom performers on your team? What will you cover as you spend with them this month? How will you know if your mentoring has been effective?

- What is the current performance ranking of your direct reports? How has this changed over the last quarter? Why has it changed?

- What will be your key coaching points for your meetings with your top three performers?

- What are the strengths and weaknesses of your direct reports? How has this influenced how you position these team members?

Building a Constituency

The most effective leaders are constantly building their network and growing their constituency. This is not superficial; instead, it comes from a genuine desire to know and be known. These leaders not only help others, but they also build relationships that enable them to call on help when needed.

Questions about building a constituency:

- Over the last month, how have you intentionally grown your constituency? Who have you targeted?

- How much bigger and stronger is your constituency now compared to last year? How do you know that? What actions did you take to strengthen your constituency? What further actions do you propose to take?

- What have you done to grow the visibility of your high-potential team members?

- How has your constituency helped you over the past month? What recognition did you give them for their help?

Making Sense of Experience

At a time of increasing business complexity, great leaders understand the need for simplicity. It is easy to look smart by communicating complex pieces of information. Leaders strive to make information understandable and accessible to as many people as possible.

Questions about making sense of experience:

- Recently, how did you take a complex issue and simplify it so that others understood it?

- What three points provide the clearest explanation of the current financial performance of your organization, division, or team?

- Do all of your direct reports clearly understand the difference between excellent, good, and unacceptable performance? How do you describe these differences? How do you know they understand?

Knowing Self

Effective leaders are transparent in how they present themselves to others. They don't come to work pretending to be someone else. They are aware of their strengths and weaknesses and don't assume that they know everything. They don't try to do everything, either; they build partnerships that complement their capabilities.

Questions about knowing self:

- What do you do better than just about anyone else you know?

- What tasks or activities drain your energy and, as a result, cause you to disengage?

- What new discoveries have you made about yourself?

- How have you intentionally applied your talents to increase your performance?

- Who are your complementary partners, and how do they help boost your performance?

- How does your performance rank alongside your peers? How do you feel about this?

Asking developing leaders these questions provides a starting point for discussions about their leadership growth. Although there will be many things that leaders need to do, these questions help leaders understand their role — and the actions they can take that will matter most to the future of the organization. The questions are role defining, and all leaders should be able to answer them.

See Related Article
"The Seven Demands of Leadership" (page 183)

START FINDING TOMORROW'S LEADERS NOW

by Vandana Allman and Barry Conchie with Jerry Hadd

February 9, 2006

The keys to discovering who will take your organization to the next level

The hot topic at water coolers these days is: "Who's retiring now? And who's taking their place?"

That's not a surprise. In 2006, the oldest of the baby boomers will turn 60, which will mean big changes in the workplace. According to the U.S. Department of Labor, baby boomers will reach the traditional retirement age of 65 between 2011 and 2029, and "their retirements will dramatically affect the workforce of the future."

Even though this a reality, too many executive teams are neglecting to have thoughtful discussions about their leadership pipelines. The question they should be asking is: *Who is capable of guiding our organization into the future?*

Forward-thinking organizations know that they need leaders and a leadership succession plan that deliver results. Most succession plans are devised with good intentions, but few have the right criteria and measurements in place to deliver those results.

As you think about your organization's succession plan, keep these points in mind:

- What experience and skill factors are essential to your future?
- How will you assess the talents of potential leaders?
- How can you best assess the performance of emerging leaders?

Skills and experience. A candidate's skills, knowledge, and experience must be considered and weighted appropriately. For example, to lead the financial function in an international company, a candidate's immersion in and expertise about exchange rates — and his or her appreciation of cultural nuances — could be very important.

Talent. An effective leadership succession plan starts with fundamentals, beginning with a talent review. Who has leadership potential in your organization? And how do you identify those people? Identifying leadership potential requires a way to predict how effectively a candidate will perform in a leadership role. The accuracy of that prediction depends on a variety of factors and sources of evidence, not just whether an employee has demonstrated leadership capability in his or her present role.

Current performance. What are the key performance outcomes for the candidate's current role? How well is he or she meeting them? Reviewing current performance provides insights into his or her potential performance in a leadership role. It is difficult to imagine promoting poor performers into leadership positions.

Integrating measures of a candidate's current performance with an accurate prediction of leadership potential is crucial to an effective talent identification process. In the following sections, we'll discuss how to evaluate current performance and explore how to assess a candidate's potential for leadership success.

Evaluating current performance

The first step in the talent identification process is determining what metrics to use to plot current performance. What are the key performance outcomes for the role? In other words, what actions or responsibilities are non-negotiables, and which ones are merely "nice to have"?

Most performance measurement systems lack simplicity and clarity or are too heavily weighted toward subjective factors. Performance measurement typically falls into one of these categories:

- **Poor metrics.** Some organizations use metrics that measure the wrong things or measure the right things ineffectively. Systems like these can actually encourage behaviors that run counter to the organization's goals or values.

- **Too many metrics.** Other organizations use a numbers-happy potpourri of metrics. In systems like these, employees are often confused about expectations and have a hard time knowing what's important in their roles. They end up chasing after multiple metrics and are never quite sure whether they are doing the work that matters most. In this situation, few employees are able to perform their jobs well, let alone at excellence.

- **No metrics.** Sometimes, there's no measurement at all.

Examples of skewed measurement systems abound. In one call center Gallup studied, customer service reps (CSRs) weren't rated on how well they solved customers' problems; instead, they were rated on their ability to adhere to rules, such as taking breaks at the appropriate times. So, to get good evaluations, CSRs at this company take their breaks on time, but they often end up transferring customers to a different CSR, who then must start the problem-solving process all over again. Is it any wonder their customers are unhappy? In another company, sales executives were held accountable for 13 different metrics that measured everything from revenue and profit to counting cold calls. Another company had such strong employee relationships that the very idea of talking about performance and metrics was considered sacrilegious because it disrupted team harmony.

To plot performance consistently and accurately, organizations must:

- **Identify quantifiable measures** that drive performance. This is not always easy. It requires organizations to avoid subjective assessments or irrelevant measures.

- If multiple performance measures are used for a specific role, **combine these measures into a single rating** that reflects the relative significance each measure has on business growth.

- **Calibrate performance measures** to a common and comparable scale so they can be accurately compared on the Succession Planning Grid. This may mean accounting for factors such as differences in location or market opportunity.

- **Hold line managers accountable** for exporting talent internally. Great managers have a knack for identifying, growing, and moving talent within an organization. This helps expand the organization's performance capacity while preserving a workgroup's ability to achieve top performance. "Hoarding talent" does not aid leadership development or sustained growth.

Assessing leadership potential

Determining how to spot leadership potential can be challenging. When assessing possible leaders, executives often rely heavily on gut instinct and personal judgment, which have profound limitations. Part of the problem is that the existing crop of leaders generally has a pretty good picture of what it currently takes to be successful in their roles. It seems logical to them that they should be able to spot "rising stars" who are deserving of future advancement. But our experience suggests that they are not consistently good at it.

Well-meaning executives may go so far as to observe and evaluate leadership roles to determine the behavioral characteristics that are necessary for success in the role. Then a scoring process is used to assess these characteristics. There is tremendous value in clearly articulating leadership competence this way; it sends a strong message that the organization values leadership and knows what it takes to perform at excellence in a leadership role.

Unfortunately, this kind of assessment also has serious limitations. It's not easy for organizations to maintain objectivity and consistency about what is being assessed. They will have to be particularly vigilant to prevent unintended biases from influencing their assessments. This challenge is evidenced by the observation that many leadership teams lack diversity, whether it be in age, gender, race, or disability.

Using a validated, predictive assessment that is grounded in research is a far more effective way to assess a person's potential for success in a leadership role. Given that an organization's future rests on its ability to identify and develop leaders, using a validated predictive assessment is essential.

The Gallup Leadership Assessment is a good example of one such tool. Built on research conducted across industries and in numerous organizations throughout the world, this tool measures innate leadership talent and assesses aspiring leaders' talents in relationship to those they are seeking to succeed. It provides an objective measure that can help companies achieve diversity and avoid adverse hiring impact. It can also provide a benchmark of existing leadership strengths within a company or executive team, as well as assess potential leaders in light of those strengths.

How does a measure like this work in practice? Let's say, for example, that Gallup is asked to measure a potential leader's fit with Company A's existing executive leadership team. First, Gallup would question the leadership team members using the executive leadership assessment, measuring leadership ability in four crucial dimensions. (This assessment also provides a more complex analysis within each of these dimensions; this in-depth analysis has been omitted for the purposes of this article.) The four dimensions are:

- *Direction* measures future focus and strategic capability. It assesses "big picture" aptitude and breadth of thinking.

- *Drive* measures primary motivation and influence. It assesses what motivates leaders and how they enlist support and commitment.

- *Relationship* measures a complex range of talents. It assesses the importance of close relationships, whether a person has natural networking abilities, whether he or she "reads" people well, and whether the person gets close in a coaching role.

- *Management* evaluates management and operational ability. It assesses operational thinking, organized thinking, and natural capacity to thrive on complexity. It also assesses a person's goal orientation.

The result is a report detailing scores for Company A's chief executive officer, chief financial officer, chief operating officer, and five other executive team members, as shown in the graphic "Executive Team Leadership Report."

As the graphic shows, the individual team members show strong scores in different leadership dimensions. Generally speaking, though, this team is a highly driven, hard-charging group that is operationally astute. You can imagine them rolling up their sleeves and throwing themselves at every challenge they face — and for the most part, they'll overcome their challenges.

Although it's likely that they work well together, most of the executives on this team show lower scores on the Relationship component; work is what brings them together. They also show lower scores on Direction. This suggests that the team will function well when work provides a clear direction, though they may not adapt easily to change. Thanks to their Drive and Management talents, this team may be expert at squeezing costs out of an operation, but they may be less adept at anticipating new market trends or exploiting new strategic opportunities.

If you look at the profile of the CEO, it's clear who is providing the executive team's Direction. This is a high-performing group, but it's less certain whether they will remain so once the CEO moves on. A smart team builder, this CEO has surrounded herself with people who complement her. However, does she fully appreciate her own contributions to the executive team or what it will take to match those contributions once she moves on?

EXECUTIVE TEAM LEADERSHIP REPORT

The members of this executive team show strong scores in different leadership dimensions. This hard-charging team shows higher scores in the **Drive** and **Management** dimensions; together, they will overcome almost any operational challenge. But they show lower scores on the **Direction** and **Relationship** dimensions. They rely heavily on their CEO's intense **Direction** to harness their energy and focus it on the right targets. If the current CEO were to leave the team, they would need to replace her with a successor with equal or greater **Direction** to help ensure their future success.

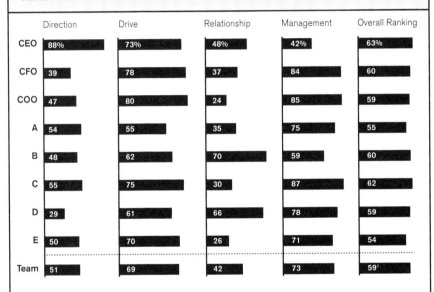

	Direction	Drive	Relationship	Management	Overall Ranking
CEO	88%	73%	48%	42%	63%
CFO	39	78	37	84	60
COO	47	80	24	85	59
A	54	55	35	75	55
B	48	62	70	59	60
C	55	75	30	87	62
D	29	61	66	78	59
E	50	70	26	71	54
Team	51	69	42	73	59[1]

Note: [1]The benchmark for this team is 59%.
Source: Gallup

Company A's profiles reveal two leadership challenges. First, this team needs to seek long-term successors who can sustain leadership capacity as current executives retire. And it's imperative that they seek a leader with a vision for the future when they're recruiting a new CEO.

Second, each new person who joins the executive leadership team needs to have as much leadership talent — or more — than the person he or she is replacing. For organizations to grow, top leadership needs to commit to hiring successors whose objectively assessed leadership talent strengthens, not weakens, the organization's leadership capacity.

Pulling the picture together

For every key leadership role in an organization, potential leaders should be evaluated against a succession matrix using objective measures of performance and leadership talent. This approach will provide a more complete picture of those who have the potential to be successful, as shown in the Sample Succession Planning Grid.

Organizations should invest the most time and energy developing the high-potential group. Using the Succession Planning Grid can also help organizations identify emerging leaders who may need additional experiences, skills, and knowledge to convert their potential into results. When organizations adopt this approach for their leadership or executive teams, they can effectively manage their succession planning needs.

Board members and customers are counting on companies to be diligent in succession planning in leadership roles. Choosing a poor leader can tarnish a company's brand promise both internally and externally. So every company has the responsibility to be a disciplined "talent scout" — to use a rigorous, validated process to spot rising stars — and to foster and advance that talent.

SAMPLE SUCCESSION PLANNING GRID

This sample grid shows how organizations can use the succession planning process to spot emerging leaders and groom them for future leadership roles. Candidates C, G, and I show the most potential for leadership success; the organization should immediately invest in their development. Candidates B, F, and J show high potential for success but need additional support or training to boost their performance in their current roles. Candidates A and D, in contrast, shine in their present jobs; these strong performers can make their best contributions to the organization by remaining in their current roles. And candidates E and H, who have low leadership potential, are also struggling in their present jobs; the organization should consider moving them to a position that better fits their skills, abilities, and talents.

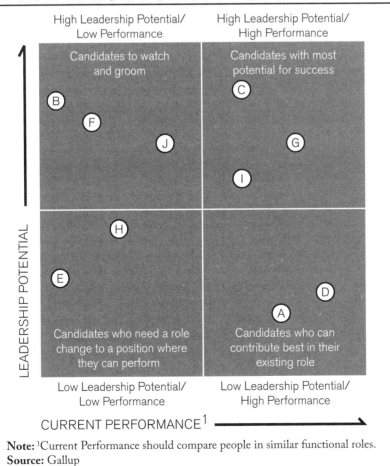

Note: [1]Current Performance should compare people in similar functional roles.
Source: Gallup

HOW ANN TAYLOR INVESTS IN TALENT

by Wei-Li Chong

November 9, 2006

The key is measuring how education and leadership development programs improve business performance

At a talent-management conference that I recently attended, executives from many industries discussed their best practices in workplace learning and development. These execs were from organizations regarded as leaders in this area, so I was amazed at how the attendees listened in envy as the speakers compared curricula, state-of-the-art learning centers, and overall spending on learning. I was amazed because it was unclear to me whether that investment had paid off.

So I asked the speakers, "How has the investment in learning affected your business results?" Responses varied from driving retention to improving employee morale. But in the end, it was clear that the learning strategies were more of a "nice to have" element of their organization rather than a "need to have" requirement. I left the conference disappointed at the lack of focus on, or regard for, how learning practices had measurably improved performance results in these organizations.

At Ann Taylor, we've taken a different approach. Our learning and development strategy is aligned with our overall business strategy. What's more, our measurement shows a clear relationship between our talent investment and bottom-line business performance.

A better way

Near the end of 2004, I had the opportunity to meet with Kay Krill, who at the time was the president of Ann Taylor brands. We discussed the issues affecting our workforce and how we could get better solutions from the human resources department. We knew, for example, that Ann Taylor had invested tens of millions of dollars over several years in sales training that yielded no significant improvement in sales productivity. Furthermore, our best leadership talent pipelines were external. We needed a way to develop an internal source of leaders who would be ready to meet the growth demands of our business.

"We need to find a better way" was Kay's challenge. The first step toward a solution was to consolidate our training departments into a function that we called Organizational Effectiveness (OE). Rather than simply deploying training sessions, OE was responsible for developing and measuring the effectiveness of our performance management and talent investment strategies for the corporate office and stores. The OE team was staffed from within. Most staff members had been with Ann Taylor for 10 years or more and had a proven performance record; we felt that business acumen was more important for OE than familiarity with employee training concepts.

With the right players in place, we started to develop our core philosophy and strategy for measuring our impact. Our talent strategy was based on this simple notion: Leveraging each individual's greatest talents can have a profound impact on performance.

This became the foundation of our talent investment philosophy. We moved away from competency-based models — we felt we would gain more impact with an individualized approach — and shifted to a focus on talent. We chose the Clifton StrengthsFinder — an online assessment that reveals individuals' top talent themes, such as Achiever, Strategic, and Relator — as our tool for discovering talent. And we created Ann Taylor University to help employees learn how to use their talents to drive business outcomes, with all learning branded as "Taylored to Your Growth."

Once the basic philosophy was established, our next step was to find the linkage between business impact and every talent investment concept we proposed. Finding the linkage — or lack of one — provided an effective way to allocate resources based on where our investment would yield the best return. Using this method, we decided to focus on our best talent at the store-manager and district-manager levels — which was where we found the most direct correlation to sales productivity.

A program is born

The Ann Taylor Stores division, which operated more than 350 stores in 2005 with net sales of $873.9 million, was an ideal pilot group for our investment strategy. The division already had a talent assessment process in place in which leaders discussed their teams' performance and potential with relative objectivity. This process identified 11 store managers and district managers with the potential to accelerate the performance of their stores or districts — and with the potential to grow into leadership roles at Ann Taylor.

We started with a basic hypothesis: We would invest in these managers' development for 12 months, then compare their business results against other managers who did not receive the same in-depth learning.

This program — the Accelerated Leadership Program, or ALP — included two key learning experiences. The first, the Clifton StrengthsFinder, was designed to help these managers develop an intense awareness and understanding of their talents. Managers also studied the Seven Demands of Leadership: visioning, maximizing values, challenging experience, mentoring, building a constituency, making sense of experience, and knowing self. Gallup arrived at these demands by studying a wide cross section of effective leaders who excelled at running the financial side of a business and at leading and motivating employees; they were also highly regarded by their peers and their direct reports.

This approach made the program philosophically simple but individually complex, as training was specific to each manager. The curriculum was developed to provide a clear learning sequence through:

- **quarterly classes:** The phased approach started with self-discovery, then showed managers how to lead a business growth strategy and maximize performance, and ended with insights into "putting it all together." We discussed specific demands of leadership in each phase.

- **analysis of business scenarios linked to learning objectives:** Every activity was designed to challenge participants to articulate the factors that were driving results in their business and to develop methods to increase productivity among their direct reports.

- **leadership accountability exercises:** "Owning" results was crucial to build participants' understanding of their own values, of the role values play in determining priorities in their business, and in how others perceive them.

- **individual performance coaching linked to learning growth and business objectives:** Managers were paired with performance coaches to help them increase their understanding of their talents and how to use those talents to measurably increase performance.

Selection and attendance were the "price of entry" to the program, and graduation was not guaranteed. Because participants' results would be compared to the rest of the division, their ability to accelerate and sustain those results was key — not only to their graduation, but also to the overall success of the program.

The results

The performance of the ALP participants was measured against a key metric called Return on Visit (ROV) that measures how store traffic is converted into sales. This is a clear indicator of store productivity and one that store leaders at all levels — including store managers, district managers, regional vice presidents, and the director of stores — can significantly influence.

The chart "Converting Learning Into Sales" shows how the ALP participants' results compared to those of other managers in the Ann Taylor Stores division. As you can see, the ALP participants were underperforming prior to the launch compared to the rest of the division. After the launch, the participants not only outpaced the rest of the division, they also sustained their performance through the remainder of the year. In fact, if the rest of the division performed at the same level as the ALP group, we estimate that the division would achieve up to a $33.5 million increase in net sales.

The ALP participants have become increasingly valuable to Ann Taylor. Aside from their outstanding profit performance, they are filling crucial roles in our organization. One store manager has been promoted to district manager and is now leading one of the division's top five districts as measured by volume. A district manager who was promoted to regional vice president in the Ann Taylor LOFT division is currently seeing tremendous growth in her business results. Finally, the regional vice president who sponsored the ALP pilot *and* participated in it was most recently promoted to senior vice president, director of stores for the Ann Taylor Stores division.

CONVERTING LEARNING INTO SALES

To measure the effectiveness of Ann Taylor's Accelerated Leadership Program (ALP), the company tracked participants' performance against a key store productivity metric, Return on Visit (ROV). ALP participants were underperforming compared to the rest of the Ann Taylor Stores (ATS) division at the start of the program, but after a year of intensive learning experiences, they outpaced the rest of the division. The company estimates that if the rest of the division managers performed at the same level as the ALP group, the division would achieve up to a $33.5 million increase in net sales.

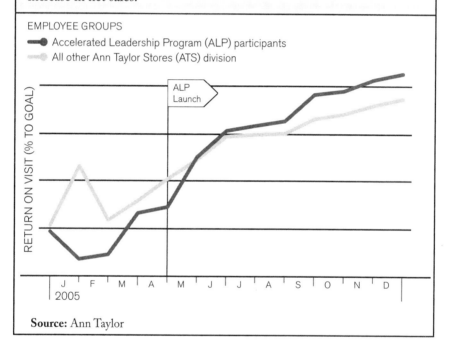

EMPLOYEE GROUPS
- ━● Accelerated Leadership Program (ALP) participants
- ━● All other Ann Taylor Stores (ATS) division

ALP Launch

RETURN ON VISIT (% TO GOAL)

J 2005 F M A M J J A S O N D

Source: Ann Taylor

The future of education at Ann Taylor

In 2005, Kay Krill became president and chief executive officer of Ann Taylor Stores Corporation. Since that time, she has outlined her vision for the organization, which includes a significant focus on investing in and leveraging our talent.

Why? Because we're now certain that focusing on talent will drive business results and ensure a pipeline of internal talent to meet the continued growth needs of our business. We've started a new class of ALP participants that includes more than 20 of our field leaders across all three divisions — Ann

Taylor Stores, Ann Taylor LOFT, and Ann Taylor Factory. We've launched Ann Taylor University to garner the Accelerated Leadership Program's results in our global corporate offices and in all store locations.

We will continue to take an analytical approach to our learning programs and investment strategies by first diagnosing the potential impact on our business, then determining how we would measure our results. In the end, we have found a "better way" — using education in the workplace to achieve business growth *and* measure success.

See Related Article
"The Seven Demands of Leadership" (page 183)

PERFORMANCE

OPTIMIZE

by John H. Fleming and James K. Harter

December 15, 2001

Be good at many things, rather than best at one. Your company's profits depend on it.

In his famous essay "The Hedgehog and the Fox," the philosopher Sir Isaiah Berlin identifies two types of thinkers: the fox, cunning and resourceful, knows many things; and the hedgehog, diligent and persevering, knows one big thing.

Berlin's formula might also be used to distinguish styles of management. Many companies focus on "one big thing," the financial performance that is every business' ultimate goal. They start with an idea of how to make the company grow, then work from the top down to get the job done. Staring straight at the balance sheet, managers decide whether to build stores or factories, crank up marketing outlays, or cut costs and people.

That approach can succeed, assuming the vision is brilliant and the execution flawless. The business world has always had a few charismatic chief executives whose companies seem to prosper on the strength of sheer will alone. But for most businesses, grand plans have a tendency to unravel somewhere down the chain of command, often when front-line managers and workers fail to meet customers' expectations.

That's the problem with the hedgehog's singular vision and the benefit of the fox's wide-ranging view. The first tends to ignore the importance of human relationships in business, while the latter celebrates them. And it's the quality of those millions of one-on-one interactions — between boss and employee and employee and customer — that often separate businesses that thrive from those that founder.

For years, Gallup has plumbed the human depths of business. Our researchers have learned how to measure customer loyalty and employee "engagement," a nuanced gauge of job satisfaction, tracing a direct path from those human interactions to the bottom line. When customers are passionate about a brand, we have shown, they tend to try its new products and spread the word to their friends. And employees who like their jobs and feel appreciated are likely to stick around and improve their companies as they improve themselves. Paying attention to these many local human interactions helps businesses of every stripe meet that one big objective — higher revenues and earnings — more surely than focusing on financials alone. Gallup has even coined a term for the process of achieving this most desirable blend: optimization.

Our research on employee engagement, based on feedback from more than 1.5 million workers, was groundbreaking in demonstrating the supreme importance of human interactions to the bottom line. For employees to feel engaged, they must know what's expected of them, have the resources to do their jobs, and get encouragement from bosses. They also need to feel that they have opportunities to grow and that their opinions and ideas are taken seriously. What's particularly encouraging about this research is that all of the factors that affect worker engagement are things that front-line managers can influence.

Businesses whose workers score high on Gallup's Q^{12} scale — so called because of the 12 items (questions) employees respond to that measure engagement — outdistance competitors across the board. Companies with highly engaged employees have less worker turnover, stronger customer loyalty, and higher sales and profit margins than do those with workers who feel less of a connection to the business.

Our research on customer loyalty also has important lessons for managers with their eye on the bottom line. The research combines two separate measures — rational commitment and emotional attachment to a brand — to get at the heart of customer loyalty. And it shows that proper understanding of these components can make virtually any brand capable of winning the undying devotion of consumers. Because it's more profitable to keep established customers happy than to recruit new ones, companies that use this research to guide marketing and sales strategies stand to benefit from a steady flow of capital into their coffers.

These findings are certainly compelling — after all, they give companies the tools to improve the myriad human relationships that underlie financial success. But it wasn't until managers began asking for ways to identify their top-performing business units that these two tributaries of Gallup research, customer loyalty and employee engagement, flowed into a new river of possibilities: optimization.

Our researchers began asking whether companies with satisfied workers also were companies with throngs of loyal customers and vice versa. When the two lists didn't match — some of the best places to work turned out to be less-than-perfect places to shop, or the other way around — we decided to dig deeper. That's when researchers found that business units that are above the median on both employee engagement and customer loyalty often outperform those scoring highest on just one or the other.

Consider how things played out at one national clothing retailer: A Gallup study showed that the company's stores that strived to satisfy customers *and* employees had significantly better profit margins than stores that focused on just one objective or the other. Like most retailers, performance at this chain is measured by something called a conversion rate, which is the percentage of customers who actually buy something. Stores that scored in the top in terms of both customer satisfaction and employee engagement had much higher conversion rates than stores that scored in the bottom on both measures. That translated into millions of dollars more in annual profits for the top-scoring stores.

Shown these results, the manager of one low-scoring store in the study made strategic changes. Ordinarily, a manager might ask a retail employee to check stock, clean up dressing rooms, or work at the register. That system does little to encourage employee engagement, nor does it put a priority on enhancing a customer's experience in the store. So the manager decided to give workers the freedom to respond to customer needs on their own. When store clerks noticed that the dressing rooms were filling up, for example, several clerks immediately moved to the registers, anticipating that customers who were trying on clothes were about to make purchases. This pleased customers, because they didn't have to wait in long lines to pay, and it made employees happy because they felt as if they were making a difference.

At another retailer, Saks Fifth Avenue, managers are in fact being trained to heed both customer loyalty and employee engagement, also with compelling financial results. Saks stores that score in the top half on both measures earn an average of $21 more per square foot, before interest and taxes, than other stores. With an average size of 103,000 square feet, optimized stores earn almost $2.2 million more each year than stores that are below average on one or both measures. That amounts to $34.6 million more in annual earnings for optimized locations.

With so much to be gained financially, it makes sense to find ways to engage employees and customers. When employees know what makes customers passionate about a brand, and when managers allow workers to seek out solutions to customers' concerns, employees and customers benefit. Or, as Jay Redman, vice president of service selling and training for Saks, puts it: "Highly engaged associates deliver highly engaged customers."

Companies that pay attention to the quality of the human relationships at the core of their businesses stand to reap substantial profits. And the more factors they improve, the bigger the gains. So, for instance, business units that have above-median employee engagement — that is, a store, department, or division that scores in the top 50% of a company's units on that measure — will have a 38% higher success rate, as measured by sales and earnings, than those that score below the median. Similarly, business units boasting better than median customer loyalty improve their chance of success by 50%, and an above-median rate for employee retention means a 70% increase in the success rate. But a unit that ranks in the top half on all three measures is a whopping 94% more successful than a store or department in the bottom half.

Such findings reinforce the concept put forth in 1996 by Robert S. Kaplan and David P. Norton in their book *The Balanced Scorecard: Translating Strategy Into Action*. The authors demonstrate that the best way to understand corporate performance is through a variety of factors, including human ones, rather than strictly financial data. This approach allows managers to mobilize workers in a way that channels their unique abilities in pursuit of the company's goals.

It is a powerful idea, one that has gained momentum in recent years. Our contribution has been to start with the outcome — the hedgehog's one big thing, whether it be productivity or profits — and to work backward, fox-like, to find the best balance of human factors that contribute to that outcome.

In his essay, Berlin describes the fox's thought process as "moving on many levels, seizing upon the essence of a vast variety of experiences and objects." That's a pretty good description of the human forces that companies must harness in pursuit of their financial goals. The lessons of our optimization research provide a map to get from here to there, to approach each relationship with a plan for making the most of a company's resources.

Or, in other words: If you're a fox about the small things, the hedgehog's big thing will take care of itself.

THE SOURCE OF FUTURE GROWTH   *by Glenn Phelps*

June 12, 2003

It's your people, not your processes. But you won't tap employees' potential if you manage them like machines.

For much of the past 30 years, creating corporate value was a lot easier than it is today. The mistakes most companies made in product quality were often so obvious that the value of fixing them was readily apparent.

For instance, it doesn't take powerful metrics to spot the quality problem if your car breaks down almost every time you drive it — and to estimate the comparable market value of a car that doesn't. Thank goodness for quality improvement efforts; it's good to have a car that starts with the first turn of the key every morning.

Likewise, corporations are finally reaping the benefits of automating processes. Computers make it easier to count money, design products, produce documents, manage inventory, and countless other business tasks. The benefits are improved accuracy and, more importantly, increased efficiency.

Consumers and businesses have benefited from the trend toward *faster, better, cheaper.* But compared to the giant improvements companies made when quality and reengineering efforts began, gains in competitive advantage via those methods are now incremental. When quality nears perfection and efficiency efforts have picked all the low-hanging fruit, what's next? For researchers at Gallup, the answer is clear: Improvements in employee performance will provide the next big opportunity for corporate growth.

Quality initiatives for humans

Employee job performance is the one key aspect of business performance in which there has been little appreciable improvement in management techniques since World War II. Think about it. If companies were effectively managing employee performance, consumers contacting any corporate call center would receive consistently high levels of service. Unfortunately, that's not the consumer experience.

Examining job performance data employee by employee reveals a truth that may be unknown to management but that is painfully obvious to customers and coworkers: Too many workers are lousy at their jobs. And poor performance isn't limited to employees who interact with customers. Objective data from virtually any job type that Gallup has studied show tremendous variations in performance. While some employees are great at their jobs, many others aren't carrying their weight. This wide variation in performance is exactly the phenomenon that quality initiatives removed from product manufacturing through improved processes. The question is, why don't businesses implement similar initiatives to improve employee performance? And if they do, why aren't they effective?

Three possible reasons come to mind:

- Managers can't see differences in individual performance because of poor measurement.

- Managers don't realize how an employee's poor performance affects the bottom line — again, because of poor measurement.

- Managers think they have processes and procedures in place that sustain the highest practical levels of performance.

This last — and most common — reason is the most intriguing. How could managers think that every reasonable action has been taken to improve employee performance? Frequently, it reflects a misapplied quality or reengineering concept — get the steps in the process right, and quality or efficiency will automatically improve. While that approach works in linear systems where machines are responsible for production, it doesn't help improve human performance.

Different people, different motivators

People are notoriously nonlinear. So squeezing every employee through the same set of process ringers rarely extracts the desired improvement.

One of the fundamental problems of using a process-oriented management philosophy to control people is that too many variables affect employee performance. It's impossible for managers to identify all of them. Therefore, the effort to manage via a process that covers every misstep an employee might take is futile, although there are process manuals that try. Even if managers could somehow discover every relevant variable and describe a process that controlled every possible step in a task, their efforts would be wasted simply because each employee is different and will react differently to the tasks they face. For example, some people reach optimal performance when motivated by financial rewards, while others are coaxed to the highest levels of performance by individual recognition.

So what can an organization do? Write a process manual for each employee? That's the right idea (individualization), but it's serving the wrong management philosophy (process control).

Companies should heed Will Rogers' sage advice: "If you find yourself in a hole, the first thing to do is stop digging." Stop trying to manage employee performance through process improvement. But if not process, then what? Performance management is the answer to *what*. But for most companies, *what* is the wrong question. The right question is *how*.

The first step is setting objectively measured performance targets, such as revenue, cost, production, or error rate. Supervisor or manager ratings are *never* objective measures.

At first glance, it might seem easy to objectively measure performance in some jobs but impossible in others. With a little perseverance, managers can find objective measures by answering the questions: "What does this employee do?" and "What value does this employee create for the organization?" If those questions don't produce clear answers, then it might be time to restructure the job.

Once objective performance targets have been set, the real work begins — creating an environment that supports employees in reaching, or exceeding, their targets. This is the heart of effective performance management. Organizations must:

- shift focus from process control to goal achievement
- individually develop each employee's ability to reach the highest levels of performance
- create pay systems that reflect actual performance. In other words, employees who create twice the value as the average worker should earn twice the pay.

Creating the right environment to support maximum employee performance requires shifting from rigid, uniform process application to tailoring the workplace to fit individual producers. This whole idea runs contrary to process-focused quality and reengineering principles. Managers adept in the tools of quality and reengineering must shed their old ways for a new set of management skills if they want to be successful.

Can organizations accomplish a shift of this magnitude? Sure, why not? The real question is, why shouldn't they? The payoff of enhanced financial performance should be all the motivation they need. And a look at recent profit numbers from most companies shows there is cause for concern.

For some companies, it's even a matter of survival. Productivity has risen recently because workers are working longer hours, buoying the financial performance of their companies. But — like the stock market bubble of the 1990s — this kind of short-term strategy is not sustainable. To make real productivity gains — and gain a competitive advantage — the surest route is implementing effective performance management systems.

For most companies, this hasn't happened yet. You'll realize this the next time you call about your phone bill, and you hear the customer service representative use your name at least four times and offer you new services three times — all to meet a quota. You should think, "This company doesn't get it. They still think process control equals management."

HIRING AND DEVELOPING TALENT:
KEY DIFFERENCES   *by Benson Smith and Tony Rutigliano*

December 11, 2003

Selecting great salespeople, and developing them, require distinct tools

More than 800,000 people have taken StrengthsFinder, Gallup's Web-based talent assessment. Since the publication of *Discover Your Sales Strengths*, this trend has been increasing. More and more sales professionals are learning how they can improve their sales performance and increase customer engagement by harnessing the power of their talents. Nothing could make us happier. Helping salespeople improve their performance was the whole reason we wrote *Discover Your Sales Strengths* in the first place.

Recently though, we have been fielding a substantial number of questions from senior sales executives about using StrengthsFinder as a tool to help evaluate sales applicants. Not long ago, a vice president of sales for a large financial institution said to us: "I've noticed that some of my best performers seem to have themes like Achiever, Self-Assurance, Command, Positivity, Relator, or Responsibility. Would it help my organization to use StrengthsFinder to screen candidates, and then hire individuals who had those same themes?"

Broadly speaking, this executive was asking us two separate questions. The first question is: *Is it a good idea to try to hire people who have talents similar to your best producers?* The answer: *absolutely.* The second question is: *Is StrengthsFinder a good instrument to use to make that determination?* The answer: *absolutely not.*

Drawing on more than 30 years of extensive research, Gallup works with companies in two connected yet distinct ways to help them improve their business performance. First, we show businesses how to hire employees whose talents indicate great potential in particular roles. Second, we show organizations how to develop strengths by building on the talents of their existing employees. The connection — talent — is obvious, and it is the common starting point for our selection and development assessment tools. But the outcomes are different, so we use different tools to achieve them.

Using talent to select a new hire

Selection instruments are designed for a very narrow purpose: to help a company make better hiring decisions. These instruments are developed by carefully examining a company's best performers. If a company had a sales force of 1,000 people, we would look at the 100 best performers. We would compare them to a contrast group of another 100 people. Our research team would then look for questions that the best performers consistently answer differently from the comparison group. Eventually, we will isolate the set of items that produces a marked contrast in responses between the two groups. These questions become the basis for a selection instrument. Gallup is able to make a prediction about the likelihood of new applicants' success in their roles based on how they answer this set of items.

The questions used in these assessments — and the answers — tend to be unique, even when the jobs may seem similar. Recently, Gallup developed selection instruments for two different companies in the mortgage brokerage business. Each selection instrument contained approximately 50 items, yet there were only four items that were the same on both assessments.

To be as accurate as possible, selection instruments include questions that have proven to be predictive of success for a particular job within a specific company. This is because the goal of a selection instrument is to make as accurate a prediction as possible regarding an applicant's likely success in that role. If a selection instrument is well-designed, the higher that applicants score on an assessment, the more likely they are to produce at a high level for that role.

After an instrument is developed, the next step is to validate the process. Does the instrument really work the way it is supposed to? The first way to answer this is through a concurrent validity study. We go back into the same sales force and interview a number of people. Our aim is to confirm that those who scored higher on the selection instrument are actually better performers than those who didn't score as high. If this test is successful, we know there is a good correlation between performance and assessment results.

As the instrument is rolled out and used as part of the selection process, we conduct additional "predictive validation" studies. When an applicant gets a high score on the assessment and is hired, we track his or her performance to make sure there is a correlation between the score and how well that person performs in the role. Again, if a selection instrument has been well-designed, the best performers will score higher on the selection instrument than lower performers. Eventually, most companies choose to hire only those sales representatives with high scores on their assessments. This validation process is also essential to make sure that the selection instruments can successfully meet any legal challenge.

Without question, selection instruments can make a dramatic difference in the quality of sales talent a company brings into the organization. It is not surprising that interest in well-designed selection instruments for salespeople is growing rapidly.

Developing a salesperson's talents

A development-oriented assessment such as StrengthsFinder is markedly different from selection tools because its purpose is *not* to assess whether an individual is suited for a particular job or role. Instead, it aims to provide talent insights for developing strengths *within* roles.

Selection instruments are predictive of a person's success in a specific job, but they don't tell us the best way for an individual to perform that job. Two applicants might have an identical score on a selection assessment, but the way they're inclined to do their jobs may be very different. This is where a tool like StrengthsFinder becomes valuable; by understanding their dominant talents, individuals can build strengths that allow them to do their jobs much more productively.

Just as the purposes of selection instruments and development assessments are different, so are the methodologies used to design these instruments. For example, selection instruments use different questions for almost every job. StrengthsFinder, on the other hand, presents the same 180 pairs of statements to everyone. Selection tools provide only a predictive score as an end product. But StrengthsFinder gives much more feedback. It provides the names of actual themes that people can use as a starting point in discovering their talents. And, after years of providing feedback to individuals, Gallup is able to provide considerable information as to how those talents can serve as the basis of strength — the ability to provide consistent, near-perfect performance in a given activity.

If you're trying to get better at something like sales, it's very helpful to know how you're most naturally able to build trust with a customer, to ask for the order, to present information, and to organize your work. Understanding these characteristics about yourself will help you optimize your results by making the most of your dominant talents.

We have found that when sales representatives develop a talent-based sales approach, they significantly increase their percentages of engaged customers. When sales representatives build their sales styles on their dominant talents, their approaches to customers become much more authentic, and the relationships that develop between the customers and the company are much more solid.

What if you have two people who take StrengthsFinder, and they have exactly the same top five themes? If one of those individuals is an excellent salesperson, doesn't that mean that the second individual would also be an excellent salesperson for that same company? The answer, surprisingly, is *not necessarily.* Predictive success in a job doesn't depend on just a person's top themes. Great variation exists in the specific talents — and in the intensity of those talents — within those themes. Themes are only a starting point. That's another reason why StrengthsFinder is an excellent development tool, but not a selection tool.

All about talent

In very real ways, talent is a part of both the selection and development processes. Understanding a person's talents guides employers in making better hiring decisions and helps them bring people who can perform at exceptional levels into the organization. Understanding talents can also help employees refine the way they do their jobs and considerably enhance their performance.

If you are running a sales organization, you should know the answers to two questions: *Is the candidate I am thinking about hiring likely to be as good as my very best people?* And then, *If I hire this person, how can I get the most out of his or her talents?* A good selection instrument designed for a particular sales role can help answer the first question. A good development assessment, such as StrengthsFinder, can help answer the second.

GOOD COMPETENCIES, BAD COMPETENCIES

by Tom Rath

May 12, 2005

Does your organization's program pass the test?

Is Gallup anti-competencies? At a surface level, the answer appears to be *yes*. A few of the organization's thought leaders have publicly railed against competency programs. And the *Gallup Management Journal* has published a number of articles that are highly critical of competencies.

In light of this, I decided to investigate this subject in more depth, and I uncovered surprising results. As you might have expected, Gallup's top researchers and management experts have experienced frustration with bad competency programs. Many of the programs they encounter force employees to spend the *most* time in the areas where they have the *least* natural talent. And very few competency programs are truly performance-based. One expert went as far as to say, "I am not against them, but I do think 90% are misguided. Over the last 10 years, I have seen great competency programs, and they work. But they are rare."

Across the board, people I interviewed were against *bad* competencies, not *all* competencies. If a competency is, by definition, something *proven to drive performance that can be developed*, then Gallup is actually a heavy user of competencies. When you look deeper into Gallup using this definition, you see:

- managers who are held accountable for increasing employee engagement based on 12 core competencies

- executives who are expected to improve on seven basic "demands" of leadership

- employees who are rated on, and expected to meet, key client service competencies

With the exception of the label itself, competencies are pervasive at Gallup. So why have we frowned on this widely embraced management concept? One big reason is the wide variation within competency programs.

Most competency programs are struggling. They start with the best intentions, then veer off course as they evolve. Companies begin with a few, strong "core competencies" that quickly turn into a laundry list of vaguely defined and immeasurable items. Employees who are expected to become everything on this wish list suffer as a result. The outcome is dysfunction, and performance can decline. As one Gallup expert puts it, "Competency programs can turn into remedial programs in no time."

That being said, several organizations have rock-solid competency programs in place. Their programs engage employees and fuel financial growth. What are they doing differently? These organizations follow two simple rules that can keep any competency program on track.

If you can't prove it, don't use it

Defining the *right* competencies is everything. If you use your intuition alone, the program will fail. But if you ground competencies in sound science, the programs will pave the road for growth.

For example, if you have a hunch that managers in your organization need to "set clear expectations" for their employees, put this to the test. The best way to test a competency is to conduct the research within your own organization. Survey as many employees as you can, asking them if their managers set clear expectations. Then compare the data you collect to real performance metrics — customer engagement or retention, or better yet, employee productivity. If you find a significant correlation between managers setting clear expectations and performance on the job, you have found a solid competency. If no significant relationship exists, don't use it.

Collecting these data can be a challenge, but it's usually worth the effort. If this is not possible, look to external sources for validation. Remember, organizations have very different goals, values, and missions. So make sure any outside data you rely on is based on a cross-section that includes several comparable organizations. At Gallup, we have tested 12 employee engagement items across a wide range of industries and workgroups. These items have been proven to drive concrete business outcomes and can serve as essential competencies for a manager.

Teach what's teachable

By definition, competency programs aim to identify areas that can be improved with training and other developmental activities. This makes it easy to get started, as virtually anything can be learned to some extent. But herein lies the trap:

- It is relatively easy to acquire *knowledge* — whom you should ask when you have accounting questions, how to access your voicemail and e-mail systems, or how to find the latest press releases from your clients.

- Similarly, it may take more time, but it is also possible to acquire new *skills* — the ability to perform the basic steps of creating formulas in Microsoft Excel, cooking a hamburger at a fast-food restaurant, or ensuring compliance with government regulations.

- However, in sharp contrast, natural *talents* are more stable over time — the ability to be more competitive, to display empathy, or the rare capacity to be very social and "work a room."

If you want your competency program to produce results as quickly as possible, the key is to start by identifying each person's unique talents, because talents provide a strong foundation for growth. Imagine a building. The stronger and more stable the foundation, the taller the building can become. It's much the same for people. When building on a strong talent base, it's possible to achieve more in less time.

Returning to the example of managers who are held accountable for "setting clear expectations," let's see how this plays out. If a manager is naturally very empathetic, help her set expectations for her employees by leveraging her ability to listen. She can use her talent to help employees define not only what they need to do, but how they can accomplish it. If you have another manager who has talents for being very disciplined and analytical, allow him to set expectations by creating smart and detailed written plans for each employee.

The next step is to augment the manager's talents with the right knowledge and skills. The manager needs to know the company's goals and policies (knowledge) to set the right expectations. She might also need the basic skills required to enter each employee's review into a Web-based performance management and review system. Once managers learn these steps, they will have even more capacity for rapid growth.

The key is to leverage *talents* as the multiplier. Organizations with great competency programs not only allow each person to find his or her own route to reaching a desired competency — they encourage employees to start with their natural talents. This makes the journey more enjoyable for the individual and opens the door for exponential progress.

Simply put, the most effective way to make a competency program work is to set measurable outcomes, then let people's talents lead the way.

To learn more about the Gallup Q^{12} items, see graphic "The 12 Elements of Great Managing" in "Feedback for Real" (page 7)

DRIVING ORGANIC
GROWTH IN RETAIL

by Kurt Deneen

August 11, 2005

Leading industry executives report four keys to boosting store-level performance

There are so many measures of success for retailers today that executives must feel like they're trying to hit a moving target. The list goes on and on: same-store sales growth, average-transaction improvement, conversion lift, traffic count, gross-margin percentage, units per transaction.

But according to leading retail executives, one objective overrides all the rest: creating organic growth in stores. As noted in a recent *Gallup Management Journal* article, "Organic growth occurs when an organization . . . creates more transactions with its current customer base and with continuously growing margins."

Just keeping a store's current customer base happy is not enough for retailers to survive, much less thrive. The real challenge is to create customer engagement, because there's a crucially important difference between an engaged customer and a satisfied one. Fully engaged customers spend more, return more often, and are less price sensitive, and they encourage others to shop at their favorite store. In short, they're the key to building store-level organic growth.

But given the day-to-day challenges of running a retail store, developing and growing a core base of engaged customers is a daunting task for most store managers. And the sheer number of shopping options available to customers in today's retail sector further complicates this task. Customers are now asking retailers, "Why should I buy from *you*?"

The increasingly crowded retail landscape is just one of the factors driving the need for organic growth. Another is the speed at which products move from design through production and shipping to a store display. There is simply more competition to be the "first on the block" with the latest product. Big-box discounters have also created a downward pressure on pricing, making the sector more competitive and price sensitive. Not all retailers can — or want to — compete on processes and price, so many are looking for other ways to remain relevant.

Recently, The Gallup Organization hosted several of the world's leading retailers in Newport, Rhode Island, and Banff Springs, Canada, to explore their strategies for driving organic growth. These retailers represent different sectors, including consumer electronics, specialty apparel, auto parts, and home improvement; many have locations worldwide. Although these executives may define organic growth in slightly different ways, their goal remains the same: They all want more transactions with their current customer base. The question on all of their minds is: How can their businesses achieve this aim? The following four key strategies were gleaned from these conversations.

1. Build the best possible teams

Forbes magazine founder Bertie Charles Forbes said, "If you don't drive your business, you will be driven out of business." A key issue in driving business results, the executives said, is building the best possible teams at the store level. Having the right person in the right place at the right time is essential to a store's success.

Finding leaders in the field organization who know how to lead teams and manage a retail location is a challenging task. Great store managers make all the difference: Find them, and you'll succeed; lack them, and your business will flounder, the retail executives said. As in-store processes become more streamlined, retailers will need to help their managers shift from focusing on tactical and administrative elements of their job to driving results through people and product. These store managers will know how to attain results. They'll have a strong presence on the shop floor, coaching their teams to success. And they'll know how to evaluate how product is selling and maximize its placement on the sales floor.

But how will retailers find the managers of the future? The retailers Gallup spoke with are restructuring their selection criteria, seeking to hire store managers who are more strategic and think and act like business owners. These retailers also want managers who are skilled at running multiple business lines, as many are diversifying their product offerings.

The retail executives also said that selecting for talent within specific job functions is a key strategy for generating organic growth; they are looking for associates who "live" the brand and can offer a true service to their customer base. In fact, some are finding their best associates among their customer base, because they come with a built-in connection to the brand. I've observed that West Marine, a leading North American boating supply retailer, staffs its stores with boaters. Customers who are deeply involved in the boating lifestyle most likely appreciate the opportunity to buy their supplies and equipment from a true "salty dog" who can relate to them and share their experiences.

Finding the right cultural mix is also crucial. For example, Hispanics are now the largest minority population in the United States. Retailers at the summits reported that their goal is to staff their stores with a mix of ethnic and social backgrounds that mirrors that of the local population. A home-improvement retailer, for example, has identified female consumers as a growing customer segment and is making staffing its teams with women a priority.

2. Create powerful interactions between stores and customers

To drive organic growth, these retail executives are also emphasizing the customer's store experience — carefully considering everything from the brand offerings in the store to service standards and how they are being executed to personalizing interactions between associates and customers. Customer satisfaction is not enough; a deeper understanding of what inspires a customer to be loyal is necessary for organic growth.

Clothing retailers, for example, understand that customers can buy a shirt anywhere. What customers may really crave when hunting for that shirt is a unique shopping experience. Retailers who can present their product offerings in a unique and compelling way have a distinct advantage in this environment.

In my view, H&M, the European "faster fashion" retailer, has set the tone for affordable fashion. While its price points are similar to other moderate fashion houses, H&M's assortment and store setup is not. H&M's club-style music, displays, and product mix all speak to a younger, more urban customer. That customer wants to look relevant and current and doesn't necessarily want to buy shirts at a discount. What's more important is buying what's "in," and I've observed that H&M presents its products with authority to that customer.

Another key factor in the customer's store experience is creating a trusted and sincere interaction between the customer and the store's associates. To achieve this, retailers are rethinking service standards and measures. Standards are shifting from a traditional "zone selling" approach — in which sales associates cannot leave their assigned section of the store — to "cross-selling," a model that frees associates to walk the store with a customer. Cross-selling creates a more intimate interaction that gives customers a sense that someone personally cares about meeting their needs. The aim is to inspire an emotional attachment to the store — and repeat business from the customer.

3. Transform the transaction

As the retail landscape shifts, organizations must adjust their offerings and value proposition, executives said. This proposition can come in the form of education, installation, or in-store processes. It's not enough, for instance, to sell a home entertainment system; retailers must also add value by teaching customers how to use its features or helping them install it. These value-added services establish the retailer as an expert that offers customers more than products.

The goal of this strategy is to build out business. One organization noted that more than 60% of its revenue growth will come from selling more to current customers. That growth can only be achieved by providing outstanding customer service and a compelling service offering.

Both home improvement and consumer electronics businesses are capitalizing on the "do it for me" movement by expanding related service offerings; some are launching or expanding divisions dedicated to this strategy. Best Buy has been aggressively marketing its "Geek Squad," a team of associates who go to customers' homes or businesses to handle any and all computer-related issues, whether or not the equipment was purchased at Best Buy. The Geek Squad not only gives Best Buy another customer "touchpoint," but I think it also helps position Best Buy as an authority on consumer electronics — and a retailer that offers a strong value proposition to its customers.

4. Emphasize metrics that matter

The process of setting clear goals and objectives, then holding stores accountable for those goals, is a crucial factor in organic growth, the executives said. Simply stating a company goal is not enough to create a cascading effect through the field organization or to guarantee success. What's needed, they said, is a stronger focus on metrics that matter, such as conversion, average transaction, or sales per hour. Too often, stores are inundated with competing messages, such as "Grow your average transaction," "Gross margin is what matters," and "Comparable store increase is the goal." While all these messages are important, the end result is confusion, not growth.

The retailers at the summits, in contrast, said that their goal is to identify clear drivers of success. These drivers varied from retailer to retailer, but the approach was the same: They're sifting through their measurements to determine which metrics matter. Then they're communicating the importance of those metrics to store employees and managers by coaching them on how to help the company meet its goals and assessing associate and store performance against their key metrics, then rewarding associates and managers accordingly.

The executives said that every sales day offers an opportunity for store managers to set clear objectives. The right "launch" to the day helps associates achieve desired results. A positive focused message on service standards and daily goals is enormously helpful in setting up a team for success and can pay big dividends for a retailer.

Getting employees and customers engaged

Gallup research has shown that on average, only 20% of customers in business-to-consumer relationships are fully engaged, or have a strong emotional attachment to a store or company. This poses quite a challenge to retailers — but it's also a significant opportunity. Poor service, messy stores, and lackluster in-store displays won't engage customers — and they won't help boost organic growth. Developing the best possible teams, creating powerful interactions between stores and customers, adding value beyond the transaction, and emphasizing the right metrics, in contrast, are the keys promoting organic growth from the field level on up.

See Related Article

"Good to Great? Or Lousy to Good?" (page 197)

To learn more about the levels of customer engagement, see graphic "How Engaged Are Your Customers?" in "Managing the Value of Your Brand" (page 158)

WHEN TO SAY, "YOU'RE FIRED!"   *by Benson Smith*

November 10, 2005

What successful sales organizations have in common with "The Donald"

Once again this television season, millions of viewers are tuning in to watch America's most famous businessman fire one of his would-be apprentices. As odd as it seems, seeing Emperor Trump give someone the ax now qualifies as entertainment.

Sometimes we cheer. Admittedly, it felt pretty good to watch the villainous and conniving Omarosa get sacked. But can executives learn anything real from *The Apprentice*?

Well, even the most hardhearted businessperson would have to agree that we can all learn something about self-promotion from The Donald; even his hairdo has become famous. He has received the ultimate honor in American society: hosting *Saturday Night Live*. Jack Welch must be green with envy. Sorry, Jack; all you did was deliver outstanding shareholder value and turn around General Electric. Mr. Trump, on the other hand, has found it easier to please viewers than shareholders.

But one thing that's crystal clear about each *Apprentice* episode is that someone is going to get fired. On a similar note, Welch also made it clear that not all of GE's employees could take their jobs for granted. He encouraged his operating units to fire the bottom 10% of employees each year. While this kind of drama may be good for ratings, is it good for business?

Gallup's research and analysis suggest that firing poor performers is not just good for business, it's *necessary* — especially if your goal is to continually improve the quality and performance of your sales organization. The hard truth is that each year, some salespeople need to get the ax.

Looking at your worst performers

Why do we say that? Over the past five decades, Gallup has had the opportunity to study many sales organizations, including some of the world's best. As I reported in *Discover Your Sales Strengths*, we found a considerable range of individual performance between the top-performing quadrant and the remaining groups. Since most of the companies we were studying were growth-oriented, we normally looked at sales increase over prior year as the key indicator of productivity.

When we analyze performance data, we usually exclude sales reps with less than two years of experience, because most salespeople go through a learning curve before they are up to speed. We want to separate learning issues, which usually correct themselves over time, from other more problematic causes of poor performance.

We found that the top 25% of the sales force was responsible for generating 57% of the sales increases. On the other hand, the bottom 25% of the sales force was in negative territory; those reps sold less in the current year than during the prior year.

We also typically find significant range of performance in creating or improving customer engagement levels. A close look at customer engagement scores on a territory-by-territory basis generally reveals that the best sales reps usually have the highest customer engagement scores. On the other hand, it isn't unusual to find bottom-quartile reps eroding engagement.

This is crucial information for sales managers, because customer engagement levels are strongly linked to sustainable growth and future financial performance. If your sales force includes reps who are eroding customer engagement levels, they may also be limiting your company's opportunities to achieve sustainable growth — and negatively affecting your business' future financial performance.

What to do about them

Even though low-performing reps may be selling something for you today, they are ultimately hurting your chances for better results tomorrow. This leads to perhaps the most important question: What can you do about poorly performing reps? And why are they performing so poorly in comparison to your best sales representatives? Gallup's analysis provides an important clue.

Often, our work with sales organizations involves developing a selection system that helps them identify candidates who are most likely to produce exceptional results. In developing this selection system, we determine the talents and attributes that are reliably predictive of success in a particular sales role.

So ask yourself: What talents and attributes are required for success in your sales organization? And what percentage of your current sales force actually has those particular talents? Gallup's analysis reveals that even in good sales forces, we typically find that 30% of sales reps are significantly lacking in the required characteristics. In other words, 30% of your sales force might not have the right talents to be successful at your company.

This doesn't mean that they are bad people, aren't trying, or aren't dedicated to your company's success. What it *does* mean is that they do not belong in sales — at least at your company. Their inability to meet your sales standards will inevitably affect their attitude — and it will negatively affect how your customers view your company. And because they lack the talents required for success, these reps aren't likely to improve even with more experience, training, or management attention. Often, they're trying hard and want to succeed. Consequently, firing them can be a tough decision.

It's always easier for a manager to muster the emotional courage to fire people when they have done something wrong — if they are difficult to work with, or are argumentative, or have cheated on their expense reports. However, it's harder for most managers to fire someone simply because he or she is underperforming, especially when the employee seems to be making a sincere effort. Front-line managers usually need to be prodded to fire these lackluster performers.

The organizations we've studied that handle this issue most effectively do so by developing clear performance expectations, then enforcing them fairly and firmly. Jack Welch's policy of terminating the bottom 10% of performers each year is a good example. Another organization we've studied fired every sales rep who was in the bottom 25% two years in a row. A major brokerage firm recently mandated that if its brokers earned less than $225,000 a year in commissions, they would have to go. Finally, another stellar sales force sets a minimum growth objective of 20% annual growth for sales reps to keep their jobs.

Needed: a clear line

None of these guidelines may be right for your company. It might take intense discussion within your organization to find the right place to draw the firing line. But remember: That line needs to be drawn high enough so that it is effective in weeding out bottom performers, year after year.

By rigidly enforcing this performance standard, you might avoid the potential legal problems that can arise from more arbitrary firings of poor performers. But more importantly, you will be removing performers who have little potential for improvement and who are limiting your company's ability to improve customer engagement levels and future financial performance.

You don't need a television show to do this. You don't need to imitate Donald Trump's gestures — or his haircut. But you do need the will and discipline to determine that every year, somebody will get fired.

THE FUTURE OF
THE INTERNET

Interviewed by Jennifer Robison

April 13, 2006

Vinton Cerf discusses his role in the creation of one of humanity's greatest technologies and what's next for the information age

A *GMJ* Q&A with Google's Vinton Cerf, one of the Internet's creators

Most of the people who invented the great technologies — the telephone, the printing press, and the internal combustion engine, for example — that irrevocably altered the way humans live, work, and even think of humanity itself, share two common characteristics. The first is that they didn't know what they were getting us into back when they were toiling away on their world-altering advances. The second is that they're dead, which is inconvenient.

It's inconvenient because we will never know what they thought about when they were changing the course of humanity, why they did it, and what they wanted out of it — and that's a sad loss to history. In one way, Vinton Cerf, Ph.D., is like those other pioneers. Dr. Cerf, who designed the TCP/IP protocols and architecture of the Internet with pioneering computer scientist Robert Kahn, didn't recognize the impact of his work while he was doing it. But unlike them, and conveniently for us, he is very much alive — and kicking.

Most of us might decide that creating one world-altering contribution to humanity was enough, but Dr. Cerf has been at the forefront of several historic social changes. He led the team of MCI's advanced networking framework architects, which was key to getting individuals and businesses online. More recently, Dr. Cerf joined the senior management team of Google, a company that may yet change the nature of business on the Internet, as well as the business model for all communications organizations. In the meantime, he's received dozens of awards, including the U.S. National Medal of Technology and the Presidential Medal of Freedom.

All of this gives Dr. Cerf a unique perspective on what is arguably the greatest advance of our age. In this, the first of a two-part interview, Dr. Cerf discusses the birth of the Internet, his thoughts on its future and its impact on how the world does business, and the social implications of his invention. But first, he explains why he'd like to lose his most famous title: "Father of the Internet."

GMJ: *You've been awarded countless honors, among them the title "Father of the Internet." Tell me how you invented the Internet.*

Dr. Cerf: First of all, it would be wrong for people to solely attribute fatherhood of the Net to me. My involvement was very much in a collaborative mode, first with Bob Kahn, then later with many other people who participated in the further evolution of the Internet architecture. In fact, Robert Kahn, who is frequently recognized as another father of the Internet, started the project in late 1972 and early 1973 at the Defense Advanced Research Projects Agency. He invited me to work with him on this project in spring of 1973, when I was at Stanford. We had worked together on the ARPANET project [ARPANET was the first experiment in wide area packet switching] in 1969 and 1970, so I knew him. He realized that, when he was trying to figure out how to do this open network idea, he needed somebody who knew something about operating systems and how on earth to get this idea to work across a variety of different operating systems.

I happened to have been a graduate student at UCLA at the time when the first node of the ARPANET was installed at UCLA. My job was to write the software to interconnect a computer up to the ARPANET, and that's how I met Bob Kahn. Then four years later in 1973, when Bob was working on several other demonstrations of packet switching, the first one, the ARPANET, was very successful. So he started looking at packet switching in mobile radio and packet switching on satellite.

Now, you can understand the military interest here, because ships at sea have to communicate over radio, and satellite is particularly attractive because of its wide-area footprint. Mobile radio is needed in tactical communications. So if we were going to use computers in command and control, we needed to be able to incorporate this capability in ships at sea and in mechanized infantry.

So when Bob came out to Stanford in 1973, he was asking me how to get this packet satellite, packet radio, and ARPANET thing to work, how do we get all the networks to interconnect? *That* was the Internet problem. And that was what he and I basically solved during a very intense six months, from March to September 1973, and we came up with the basic design of the Internet architecture and the basic protocols.

So we wrote a paper together, which ultimately was published in May 1974 in the Communications of the Institute for Electrical and Electronic Engineering proceedings. That paper is now a classic, and copies of it have been auctioned off for as much as $4,800, much to my surprise. I don't have any more in my files; otherwise I'd be retiring by auctioning pieces of paper.

GMJ: In 1973, did you imagine anything like this? Did you ever think that this project you were working on would change human communication forever?

Cerf: Well, no. Our work in the early 1970s was all very technologically oriented; it was, "Can we do this? How can we do this? Can we show that it works? Can we standardize it? Can we make it an international standard?" And that occupied a good ten years before we got to the first rollout in 1983 and then another ten years to get to the point where the general public had access to it.

By 1989, however, I absolutely recognized the requirement to commercialize the Internet service. It was very clear by that time that it would not be possible for the government, either in the United States or elsewhere, to fund access to the Internet for the general public. And if I wanted that to happen, and by that time I did want everybody to have access to the Internet, it seemed to me the only way to do that was to build a business engine underneath it, which meant commercializing Internet service.

GMJ: How did commercialization of the Internet begin?

Cerf: Fortunately, the National Science Foundation, which at that time was sponsoring the NSF Net backbone, shared a common interest in pursuing that goal, so they took various steps that permitted commercialization to happen. They made it possible for the government-sponsored backbone to carry commercial traffic, which up until that time was not permitted. Then in 1992, Congress passed legislation that officially allowed that capability as the government carriage of commercial traffic. By 1995, the NSF Net backbone was retired because of the growth of the commercial service providers — the backbone service providers. So by 1989, I was very convinced that the Internet should be a commercial enterprise.

I don't think that I could possibly have envisaged all of the applications that have arisen on the network. It would be simply outrageous for me to make such a claim, and I don't. But it seemed to me that the standards were so open that it permitted just a huge range of experiments and trials to be conducted by very creative people who could find ways of using this network to exchange information and to supply services to interested parties.

GMJ: Do you think business is exploiting the Internet's full potential?

Cerf: Oh, not by any stretch. I mean, we're just barely scratching the surface of what we can do with this kind of communication technology. And I think you can see that almost daily as you look at new product announcements that involve networked devices. So I'm expecting to see many billions of devices using the Net to communicate with each other. This is not just for human communication, which has been tremendously valuable, or human sharing of knowledge, which has also been very valuable, but it can also be used for managing and controlling various devices.

So my entertainment system should be manageable through the network; third parties should be able to offer to me the ability to manage devices around the house and the office and in the car and maybe even on my person. Once these devices are able to communicate with each other, it means that third parties can build software that services those devices, interact with them, and manage them, or provide services to them.

You see this happening already as mobile phones become Internet-enabled and as you see more and more functionality being injected into personal digital assistants. I carry a Blackberry with me — it's a mobile phone, and it's a PDA in the sense that it has a calendar and e-mail. It also has access to the Net. And there have been times when the ability to do a Google search from a Blackberry in some random spot has been extremely helpful — whether it's finding the nearest gas station or a restaurant or telephone number of the hotel that you're trying to get to, or even just exchanging e-mail with someone in order to coordinate where you're going. This kind of capability is very attractive. I think we are only at the beginning of understanding what we can do with communicating devices.

GMJ: That brings up a social point — it can be very difficult to unplug yourself. People call Blackberries "crackberries" for a reason. Do you think electronic communication is supplanting face-to-face communication?

Cerf: No, I don't. There's a certain amount of rudeness that one can associate with Blackberries or mobile phones or similar devices. I mean, sitting in a restaurant with someone and talking to someone else on a mobile phone is a kind of rudeness that we ought to resist. The same thing can be said about sitting there checking e-mail while you should be chatting with someone.

On the other hand, I have found my ability to stay in touch with a much larger number of people to be dramatically enhanced by having these capabilities. For one thing, they cross time zones, so that if I have an idea that I want to share with somebody, I don't have to wait. I just send them an e-mail and don't have to wait six hours because of the time difference. So I'm very attracted to e-mail in part for that reason and in part because it's a group communication medium in addition to a one-on-one medium. I can keep multiple people apprised of what's going on. The younger generation prefers instant messaging to e-mail; they think of e-mail as being old hat. Maybe when they get older, they won't feel that way, but right now the immediacy of interaction with their friends is very attractive. So I see this as simply enhancing social interaction as opposed to inhibiting it.

GMJ: But has it enhanced communication or only broadened it?

Cerf: In my view, all sorts of things have been enhanced by the convenient ability to communicate and to actually multitask. This is an interesting phenomenon. At Google, it's very common to have a meeting, and everybody brings their laptops, and while they're meeting, they're also doing their e-mail. Some have to be warned ahead of time that multitasking is a badge of honor as opposed to an insult, and it's expected that you'll be able to do that. Kids are growing up now very accustomed to multitasking. If you walk into any teenager's room, you'll see a laptop going with a number of instant messaging windows open, a Google search happening, maybe they've got a television going in the background, and they've got their headset on listening to an MP3 that they downloaded. It's very common to see that kind of dynamic. So it's an expansion of the kinds of relationships that we're able to maintain.

GMJ: What do you think about wireless communications? Do you think that's going to make a huge change?

Cerf: I think it already has. You now see on the order of two billion mobiles in the wireless telephony world, and that has brought telecommunications to a cadre of users who never had access to telephony before or who had to wait years to get a wire line telephone. So in absolute numbers, it's made a huge difference. The expansion of functionality of these mobiles to include

Internet applications is an even more powerful force, because it means that people are using wireless communications to get access to information that they never had before. So just on the pure telephony side, which is being augmented now by Internet access, that's important. Wireless access to the Internet has also had some interesting side effects — it's actually changed some of our behavior. We often leave a laptop at the dinner table, and when questions come up that we don't have answers to, we Google it. And it allows for, in some sense, longer and more in-depth conversations to happen because otherwise we just get stuck — you know, who invented X, or where is Y?

GMJ: It turns the Internet into our spare brain. And as such, do you think there's a danger to that?

Cerf: Perhaps. I do worry about how people do things if they don't memorize or can't remember things, because they are very dependent on being able to get access to them online. I am. I mean, I forget people's names now. And at the age of 62, I find my brain cells are starting to work more poorly than they did when I was 22, so I find myself turning to my e-mail in order to remember people's names. I'll do a Google desktop search because I know I was talking to some person about something. Now that's kind of embarrassing, but it suggests that Google is my solution to old age.

See Related Article
"Getting Six Billion People Online" (Part 2 of Interview, page 261)

GETTING SIX BILLION
PEOPLE ONLINE

Interviewed by Jennifer Robison

May 11, 2006

That's the goal of the Net's creator, Vinton Cerf. He discusses that challenge and many others — including Google's wary relationship with the Chinese government — in this wide-ranging interview.

A *GMJ* Q&A with Google's Vinton Cerf, one of the Internet's creators

Vinton Cerf, Ph.D., is a patron saint of techno-geeks everywhere. In 1973, he and pioneering computer scientist Robert Kahn designed the TCP/IP protocols and architecture that made the Internet possible. Since then, he's been part of the cadre that worked to make the Internet ubiquitous by making it inexpensive and easy to access.

But Dr. Cerf has been part of another revolution, one that business leaders have been watching very closely. As a Google vice president and its "chief Internet evangelist," Dr. Cerf designs network infrastructure, architectures, systems, and standards. As Google has patents on some of the most important technological breakthroughs in the Internet era, has issued one of the largest IPOs in history, is challenging Microsoft, and posts profits in the millions, everything Google does is of interest to business. This makes Dr. Cerf's perspective very compelling indeed.

In the first part of this two-part interview, he discussed the invention and future of the Internet as well as the social aspect of what he created. In this, the second part, Dr. Cerf reveals his thoughts on Google's next moves, Wall Street's math error, what he sees as the real threats to the Internet, and what's really going on with Google China.

GMJ: Your job title is "vice president and chief Internet evangelist" for Google. What does a chief evangelist do?

Dr. Cerf: Well, probably what I've been doing for the last thirty years, which is trying to persuade people that more Internet is better than less Internet — or that we don't have enough Internet yet in the world today, and we need more. The current estimate of the number of users on the Net is on the order of a billion, and when you realize that there are six and a half billion people in the world, my reaction is that we have a long ways to go. I also think that we need better kinds of Internet access, increased broadband access, and more symmetric broadband access so that we can send as well as receive at high speeds.

So in my case, an Internet evangelist looks for ways to help stimulate investment in the spread of Internet technology so that more and more people have access to it. There's a good business reason, from a Google point of view, for wanting that to happen, because the more users there are, the more our business model continues to produce revenue because more people who look at the Net and use the Net are exposed to Google advertisements.

GMJ: When Google went public, the business model — even the Dutch auction method — blew people away. Do you think that Google's business model is going to change that of other Internet or communication companies?

Cerf: Well, that's a good question. It certainly has pioneered and demonstrated the utility of online advertising. There were a number of other companies that had tried to pursue that, but Google somehow did a better job of monetizing that particular practice and providing better feedback to the advertisers, which made their product more attractive than that of other competitors. So I think first of all, they were able, in spite of the dot boom and dot bust, to demonstrate the utility of this particular revenue model.

In the long run, I would think that Google would want to expand its revenue opportunities beyond purely advertising. It's the standard diversification argument — that you don't want to have your company be entirely and totally dependent on only one means of revenue generation. But so far, the company has done extremely well in this domain.

GMJ: I don't mean to make the people who didn't buy stock squirm, but if Google decides to diversify, what would it do?

Cerf: Well, first keep in mind that Google's objective is to help organize information and to make it more useful. So it already has an enterprise business where we install equipment or we provide equipment to be installed at enterprises that want to take their corporate data and organize it in the same way that Google organizes the World Wide Web.

Second, Google has been moving in vertical directions, looking at specific segments of information — for example, Google has been organizing information and supporting searches that are restricted to academic content in the research and academic communities. That can be very helpful in promoting research, and it could potentially produce revenue, although at the moment I think it's not monetized.

As Google gets more and more involved with media other than print or text, once again, there may be some interesting possibilities associated with monetizing access to and organizing non-text information. So I think there are lots of possibilities here, and you can be sure Google is considering quite a variety of them.

GMJ: Bill Gates has said publicly that he's gunning for Google's share of the search market. How much of a threat are Microsoft and Yahoo?

Cerf: The threat, I think, is not so much inherent in the companies themselves; it's more a question of how good is their search technology, how good is ours, and how well each of us manage to improve our search capabilities over time. So in a sense, the threat is present not just at Yahoo and Google, but in other places too. Think about where Yahoo and where Google came from. They came from Stanford graduate students. And Stanford is not too far away from [Google's headquarters in] Mountainview, [California], and there are smart people there too.

So I think generally, we don't see the threat as corporate or embodied specifically in Yahoo or in Microsoft, because it is just generally the technology threat that if you fall behind, you fall behind. So we work very hard to improve our own search technologies, and hopefully we can stay ahead of everybody else. I don't sense at a corporate level that Google sees special threats coming from Yahoo or Microsoft. They're simply among the many people interested in the search market, and they're working very hard to improve their products and compete with us.

GMJ: Google's fourth quarter profits last year were up 86% compared to the same period in 2005. This was still below Wall Street projections, and that scared a lot of investors into selling. To me, that sounds like insanity. What does that sound like to you?

Cerf: This is very common in the Wall Street world. If all you do is meet your projected results, you're often punished by Wall Street. Wall Street is already discounting whatever your expected results are, and then they only reward you if you exceed them — at least that's my experience. So we're seeing a classic situation where if we only do as well as we say we're going to do, we get punished.

My guess is that over the long term, markets tend to adjust to the expectations of the investors, and I hope that expectations will moderate towards reality. You can't have 100 percent growth every year for 10 or 20 years — when you do the math, that's an awfully big number. Two to the tenth is a factor of a thousand, and it's hard to imagine a company starting at five billion dollars a year and doubling annually. In 10 years, you'd be at $5 trillion, and I guarantee you I don't think there's enough money in the world to support a five trillion dollar a year advertising business model. So you can't possibly have the sort of returns that continue with the very high rate that they do at the beginning.

GMJ: How has the Internet changed business? And what were the long-term effects of the bubble bursting in 2000?

Cerf: I think that there has been a core of continued economic expansion and a core of continued growth in the user base that has sustained the Internet since the April 2000 crash. So now what you're seeing is that the survivors of that event are much stronger than they were before — what doesn't kill you makes you stronger. So you see Amazon and eBay and Google, among others, all thriving. And I think you start to see more and newer applications arising while the venture capital people more carefully consider their investments than they did before.

During the bubble, anybody who had the word "Internet" anywhere in their business plan had money thrown at them. Many of them didn't understand the difference between capital and revenue, so they spent all their capital, and then they were surprised when they ran out. So I am persuaded that we still have quite a long ways to go before we've exhausted all the possibilities that this kind of communication offers for business.

GMJ: Software presents some challenges, though.

Cerf: Our efficiency in hardware has not been matched by our efficiency in the development of software. We're slow at it; we still build bugs into the systems, and we don't have a good theory of computer science for programming, at least not as good a theory as we have for engineering hardware. And I'm disturbed by that. I think that we should be challenging the computer science departments and the researchers in them to dig much more deeply into an understanding of software and how it's produced. There have been many attempts to do that, but none of them have adequately delved into the real understanding of computing.

I keep challenging the computer science people with the question "Where is the science in computer science?" And there is some — computability, decidability, theory of languages, parsing, and things like that, and maybe a little bit in operating system design. But I feel like we're a very long way from understanding how to cope with the complexity that the software world challenges us with.

GMJ: Do you think things will improve?

Cerf: I don't know. Software is very complex stuff. The network makes it harder, because every device that's on the Net is filled with software that nobody predicted. In other words, the combination of software on your laptop is different from [the combination on] mine, depending on what we downloaded or what combination of software we've installed. So our interactions with each other are experiments, in the sense that if your machine and my machine have never exchanged any information before and now they do, that's a new experiment. So there is an overwhelming complexity associated with networking of computers with unpredictable software. It's hard to judge whether that will get better.

I think that we need a better theory of operating system design that will protect the ensemble of hardware and software from hackers, and I don't mean just hormone-filled teenagers. Some of these people are professionals who are out to steal business secrets or penetrate machines for purposes of gathering information, and maybe they do so on a paid basis. This whole business of disruption and deceit in the network poses a huge challenge for anyone who's looking for a rational and legal environment.

GMJ: Which brings up another issue — what did you think about the United Nations' desire to assume oversight of ICANN [the Internet Corporation for Assigned Names and Numbers]?

Cerf: First of all, I'm glad that you used the term "oversight," because too many people have said the U.S. wants to control the Internet, and of course ICANN doesn't control the Internet. ICANN manages the assignment of domain names and IP addresses and is overseen by the U.S. Department of Commerce, but that does not equate to the Department of Commerce controlling the Internet. Certainly ICANN doesn't.

If you review the history, it's understandable how the Department of Commerce ended up with this responsibility. The U.S. Department of Defense had that responsibility in the earliest days when it was responsible for inventing and operating the core of the Internet. And if anybody had any direct control over the Internet, it would have been me and Bob Kahn, but that was 30 years ago. So I think that the oversight function is one that is understandable from a historical perspective. It has been distorted into and misrepresented as control, and that distortion has been a great deal of the debate leading up to and including the two world summits on the information society.

I want to emphasize, however, that to focus only on the specific job that the Department of Commerce has is to fail to understand the real challenge of Internet governance, which is people's use and abuse of the Internet. Governments normally step in to deal with public policy questions of that sort. These are way outside of the orbit of ICANN. It has very specific and very limited responsibility for maintaining the uniqueness of domain name identifiers and Internet address identifiers. That's really its fundamental responsibility. Governments should be involved in the public policy aspects of Internet that lie well outside of the purview of ICANN.

GMJ: But some governments will do anything to repress the transmission of information that the Internet offers.

Cerf: Personally, I am excited about the possibility that the Internet brings to freedom of expression, and in my heart of hearts, I hope that the Internet will be a very powerful force to encourage or support or enhance freedom of expression. But at the same time, to borrow a Cold War expression, governments are going to behave the way they want to behave. The sovereignty of governments is not something that's going to dissolve overnight. But even in the most repressive of environments, it's always been my hope that if the Internet is permitted in, then it will be the camel's nose under the tent, so to speak.

GMJ: Which brings us to Google China. The public seems to feel there's a disconnect between Google's support of the free transmission of information and the Chinese government's censorship of search findings.

Cerf: The problem, of course, is that the Chinese government is very nervous about open access to the world's information. So the question is, under what circumstances are we able to conduct business there?

We've done several things to try to mitigate what we consider to be a situation which is not entirely satisfactory. First of all, we have agreed to remove responses from our system in accordance with the laws of the Chinese government, but we insisted that when such a removal happens, that we mark the information as having been suppressed. So the users at least are aware that something is missing. The second thing that we chose not to do is to put up services that would involve personal information. So we didn't put up e-mail or other information-messaging kinds of services because we were concerned that we might be legally forced to divulge information that could be associated with individual people.

The other thing I would observe is that there are enterprises outside the United States that apparently have found ways to mitigate the limitations of Chinese Internet access, as it were, and so some knowledgeable Chinese users are able to reach the global services of Google and, of course, the rest of the Internet. There was a great article in *The Washington Post* about that.

GMJ: Very knowledgeable computer people can always get around obstacles.

Cerf: So can knowledgeable teenagers, as near as I can make out.

GMJ: Is Google trying to erode the Chinese government's resistance?

Cerf: Well, no, I don't think Google is being politically active at all. What I am suggesting to you though is that the flow of information is kind of like water — it goes pretty [well] anywhere that it can flow, and over time, information tends to erode barriers. So I don't suggest to you that anything will happen overnight. But over time, I think that Internet technology is going to lead to almost an inevitable opening up of access to information in China, whether the government is entirely comfortable with that or not.

Like many others, I've learned that patience sometimes counts. So does persistence. And if you'll notice, the Grand Canyon was carved by water flowing over the earth. It just took a few hundred million years to do it.

See Related Article
"The Future of the Internet" (Part 1 of Interview, page 255)

ARE YOU FAILING
TO ENGAGE?

by Tom Rieger and Craig Kamins

November 9, 2006

Most companies face barriers that prevent them from fully engaging customers and employees. Here are the key characteristics of those barriers.

After a long, hard journey, a traveler finally arrives at his hotel. It's late, and he's exhausted. When he gets to the front desk, he discovers that the hotel is overbooked. He no longer has a room. The clerk behind the desk shrugs and tells him, "There's nothing I can do."

This is a true story. It may sound painfully familiar to anyone who has experienced maddening frustration with an employee who is supposed to be delivering customer service.

Here are two more stories — also true. They are different scenarios, but, as we will discuss, the root of the problem is essentially the same:

- An escrow agent calls a mortgage service center with a serious problem. They have a closing that afternoon, she says, and have not yet received the closing statement, though it had been requested several days before. The service representative says that the agent's request is in the queue but isn't ready, and he has no idea when it will be done. The agent requests a verbal payoff but is told that the company does not provide them. She asks to speak with a supervisor and is refused. The call ends with the agent, clearly upset, hoping that none of her customers ever use that mortgage company again.

- In a call center, a customer service representative (CSR) needs to transfer a customer to another department. Because it's a holiday, that department is closed. The CSR, knowing that the department is closed, asks the customer to call the next day and gives him the direct number. The CSR was penalized on her quality evaluation for not "trying to transfer the call" even though she knew no one would answer.

What do these stories have in common? In each case, the employee had little leeway to make things right for the customer. Because of the circumstances, rules, policies, practices, and structure of their organizations, these workers were either compelled to do the wrong thing, or, in the case of the CSR, punished for doing the right thing.

Those rules and policies may have been put in place with the best of intentions, but the results were damaging to the customers who were forced to endure negative experiences and to the employees who were forced to inflict them. The results were also bad for business because they destroyed a significant amount of the emotional connection between the company and its customers and employees. And those connections — what Gallup calls employee and customer engagement — are vital for business because they're what drive organic growth.

Barriers to engagement, such as the arbitrary rules in the previous scenarios, do more than turn customers away. They can force workers to "work around" the system to provide good customer service or frustrate employees and drive them away. Worst of all, in almost every case, these barriers are both unnecessary and self-imposed.

Ultimately, despite other substantial efforts companies may be making to build engagement, barriers like these prevent them from engaging their customers and employees. This two-part series explores the nature of those barriers — and shows how companies can overcome them.

Hitting a wall

U.S. businesses have spent millions of dollars measuring and managing employee and customer engagement — or the related topics of employee and customer satisfaction — often using methods that are tactical and reactive. Even when organizations take a holistic and proactive approach, the focus is sometimes limited to a local level: Individual managers and teams receive the data and coaching tools they need to drive improvement in their divisions or workgroups but not the support to overcome institutional barriers.

When that happens, organizations that are measuring engagement may well see a "flattening" of employee engagement scores. Workgroups can do a great deal to improve employee engagement at the local level; one of the most effective tactics is to conduct impact planning sessions. Once teams maximize the gains from this kind of problem solving, however, often what remains are the stubborn, painful barriers that prevent teams from achieving their optimum engagement and productivity.

Removing these barriers is often outside the direct control or influence of a workgroup or its supervisor. For example, although efforts have been made to increase communication effectiveness at a call center, CSRs are still being held accountable for company-wide policy changes they have not heard about. Or a supervisor wholeheartedly supports a new emphasis on training but finds she still doesn't have time to coach and develop her employees.

Ultimately, problems like these cannot be solved by an individual or a workgroup. Unless organizations take responsibility for removing these kinds of institutional barriers, managers and teams will spend a tremendous amount of time and energy dealing with the same problems over and over in their impact planning sessions. To drive sustained improvement in employee and customer engagement — and ultimately, organic growth — companies need a way to systematically identify and address barriers that exist throughout the company.

To help organizations overcome these challenges, Gallup conducted a year-long study of barriers to employee and customer engagement across organizations in the automotive, financial services, public utilities, high tech, manufacturing, insurance, mass merchandising, and government industries. The work spanned several countries, including Australia, India, Mexico, Poland, Thailand, the United Kingdom, and the United States. The study included an in-depth examination of organizations' current policies, practices, and procedures; a review of current initiatives; and interviews or focus groups with top management, middle management, frontline supervisors, frontline employees, and support staff.

The study uncovered about 200 barriers to employee and customer engagement. Even though the industries, countries, and companies were different, those barriers shared several characteristics.

Barriers are outside local control

As noted above, substantial improvements in employee and customer engagement can be achieved by talented employees who are well-managed by capable supervisors and leaders. But even the most outstanding employees must operate within the constraints of their environment. As hard as they try, at some point, these managers and workgroups won't be able to improve engagement when they encounter barriers they don't have the authority to remove.

Barriers are typically imposed by employees who are far away from the front lines. Sometimes barriers are created by workers within the same department, but often they emanate from outside departments, such as marketing, human resources, or the legal team. They could be the result of rules or policies, new programs, resource allocation decisions, or other corporate initiatives.

Whatever the case, the most profound barriers are iron-clad rules and practices that must be obeyed without fail. Supervisors and employees ignore them at their own risk.

Barriers are damaging to employees and customers

Obviously, not all rules are bad. A company must have policies and procedures to avoid unnecessary risk, ensure efficiency, and provide consistent service. As such, these rules aren't necessarily barriers. Some barriers may be the result of other factors, such as infrastructure or resource allocation decisions.

The difference between a barrier and something constructive is that barriers prevent:

- employees from using common sense
- customers from getting the answers they need
- efficiency
- a holistic view of the customer relationship
- the creation of a positive and engaging workplace
- the organization from reacting quickly

Most of all, barriers ultimately prevent financial success.

Amazingly, our research indicates that most employees — at all levels — know that these practices are harmful. Employees often comment, "We are treated like children," "What we do makes no sense," or "No one trusts us." And the damage multiplies.

Barriers put the emphasis on control

No one adds words to customer service scripts just to make customers angry. Including the phrase "Is there anything else I can help you with?" at the end of a call seems to be absolutely the right thing to say.

But what if the CSR could not solve the customer's problem? Or what if the customer just said he was in a hurry and needed to hang up? Under those circumstances, saying "Is there anything else I can help you with?" can actually make customers angry, though it seems like an easy way to appear focused on the customer.

Companies rarely create engagement barriers on the first day they open their doors. As companies grow, though, "control" becomes more difficult, yet it seems more attractive. If an employee makes 10 decisions every hour, a company with 100,000 employees will have *8 million* decisions made by those employees every day.

That can be a frightening thought for executives. One manager of a large pharmaceutical support company said, "We have nearly ten thousand frontline employees. That's too many to control. We can't allow them to say whatever they want."

The key to overcoming this fear is to view the situation differently. Although the company has 10,000 frontline employees, it really has about 850 teams, each with 10-12 customer service representatives. There are about 80 departments that each manage about 10-11 teams. So, no one person needs to worry about more than what 12 people, at most, are doing at any one time. Viewing the company this way makes the idea of "empowerment" a lot less scary.

Barriers can be removed

One professional services executive said, "One of the worst and best things I ever did was buy a crowbar. Now I come home, and my wife, who loves redecorating, will — without warning — have started ripping something apart. At first, it drove me crazy, but as we got into each project, I could see that the original wood underneath was rotting or that the current setup just was not working. And once she explained her vision, I could see how much better it would be when the project was done. I have learned that the same thing is true in businesses. Impossibility often exists only in someone's mind as a defense mechanism. Addressing problems requires work, but in the end, it's worth it."

We sometimes forget that walls can be torn down. Part of the problem is determining who should wield the crowbar and how they should be allowed to use it. For example, one executive of a retail organization said, "Our store managers each get more than one hundred reports a month. But the *good managers* know which three or four they should look at."

In this case, the solution seems obvious: Stop doing the other 96 reports. The problem, however, is that it's unclear why those reports originated, how they are being used, why they are considered important, or who "owns" them.

See Related Article
"Why You're Failing to Engage Customers" (Part 2 of Series, page 274)

WHY YOU'RE FAILING TO ENGAGE CUSTOMERS

by Tom Rieger and Craig Kamins

December 14, 2006

Most companies face barriers that prevent them from fully engaging customers and employees. Here are the five root causes of those obstacles — and how to overcome them.

All companies strive to make the most of two key assets — customers and employees. Yet organizations unintentionally create barriers that prevent them from fully engaging those two groups.

In the first article of this two-part series, we outlined the key characteristics of those barriers, as determined by a Gallup study of barriers to engagement across several industries in seven countries. This article explores the root causes of these barriers and how to permanently remove them to clear a path to greater customer and employee engagement.

The five root causes

Gallup's study identified about 200 barriers and evaluated the root causes of each. Surprisingly, virtually every barrier identified could be traced back to one of five primary causes, regardless of the industry, function, or geography of the company.

The barriers were often obvious and seemingly intractable, as they involved hundreds of variables and many job roles. Understanding the key variables helps companies identify the specific systems, structures, processes, and people in the organization that must change to overcome the barriers. And though the barriers can seem entrenched and complex, the root causes are not.

Root cause 1: fear

The most prevalent root cause of barriers to engagement is fear; at least one fear-based barrier existed in all the companies Gallup studied. While it may seem surprising that companies with rational, disciplined management would be subject to self-inflicted damage due to fear, the data indicate that it likely happens in all companies.

Fear-based barriers restrict employee and customer engagement in several ways. Fear stifles innovation and creativity, limits an organization's flexibility in meeting customer requirements, prevents cross-functional collaboration in addressing problems, discourages empowerment, and causes turnover.

As companies grow, they begin to introduce rules, policies, and procedures that attempt to mitigate concern about loss — loss of control, respect, or certainty that employees will "do the right thing." Checks and balances are required in all businesses, but they can go too far. Examples of *institutional* fear-based barriers include excessive scripting of customer contacts and lack of frontline empowerment.

Managing institutional fear may sound daunting, but it can be done. For example, the customer center of a financial services company decided that rather than scripting its customer center interactions, it would provide guidelines to encourage customer service representatives (CSRs) to use "value added phrases." The key is to establish limits while allowing employees to take some risks to meet customer or internal needs. Risks that succeed should be rewarded; risks that fail, but are attempted within the rules, should be treated as learning experiences rather than as a cause for discipline.

The second source of fear in an organization is at the *individual* level. Even when an organization is struggling, some employees will find power and contentment in the status quo. This leads them to resist change — actively or passively. Typically, fearful employees fall into three categories:

- The reluctant gatekeepers: These employees tend to derail progress or innovation. Often, they are influential players who are more interested in protecting the "old way" than in adapting to a changing environment.

- The risk-averse: These workers are reluctant to challenge inefficiencies or to propose change — in the organization or in their own department — because they fear reprisal or are concerned about how change might affect their role or workload.

- The "speed bumps": These employees aren't necessarily in a position to directly influence thinking in the organization. But they can, through lack of knowledge or motivation, slow down the progress of groups tasked to investigate challenges and enact change.

Managing individual fear is more challenging because this type of fear can't necessarily be conquered by modifications to process or policy. The first step is to ferret out the organizational factors leading to this fear.

For instance, change often inspires fear. One way to counteract this is to improve communication about changes by clearly establishing who is accountable for achieving strategic outcomes. This helps managers and employees look past the initial hardships of change (such as increased or varying workload, or loss of power or valuable connections) while focusing on the eventual benefits of success (such as increased efficiency and productivity, improved customer relations, or increased sales and incentive-based compensation).

Root cause 2: information flow

Like fear-based barriers, information-flow barriers also existed in all the companies Gallup studied. Information-flow barriers can appear within or across departments and from the front line up to management. These barriers limit employee and customer engagement by preventing employees from getting the information they need to maximize their performance.

There are two main types of communication barriers. The first is a *transmission* failure: when information fails to flow smoothly from management to frontline employees or from the front lines back to management. Here are two examples:

- A number of the companies Gallup studied failed to provide their frontline employees with sufficient information to do their job well. This can happen when departments hoard crucial information that other departments may need. Or, system limitations can prevent a holistic view if customer-facing employees cannot access every customer account, leading to missed opportunities and slower service delivery.

- Other companies failed to incorporate frontline input into their decision-making process. One manufacturing plant installed new equipment without input from frontline employees, even though those workers knew immediately that the machine wouldn't achieve its goal. The equipment was pulled from the line at a tremendous cost. Incidentally, there is significant evidence to suggest that involving frontline workers in decision making not only helps reduce turnover, but it also increases revenue.

The second type of communication barrier occurs when employees fail to *assimilate* information or use it effectively. The most common causes of this are a lack of time to process or understand new information or insufficient access to needed facts.

- According to executives in a public utility service center, CSRs in a call center must often absorb and implement more than 50 process changes per week. However, many call centers provide very little time for CSRs to read their e-mail (if they even have e-mail access) or learn about changes in other ways.

- A large national pharmacy and convenience store never has employee meetings, so employees don't always learn about policy changes or new initiatives promptly. When communication does occur, it often leaves out the "why" behind the change. As noted earlier, a failure to explain change initiatives can lead to fear. Without appropriate communication — and time to assimilate it — frontline employees struggle to adapt.

There are many ways to address transmission barriers. A good strategy is to analyze how information flows across an organization — between departments, to the front line, and to management. Mapping communication can pinpoint where information is being lost, blocked, or distorted.

It's just as important to analyze how communication is assimilated. A particular department or group may be receiving information — but are they receiving it when they need it? Do workers have time to read it? Is the technology used to send the message appropriate? Is the message easy to understand, and can employees apply it immediately to their work? Does it conflict with other messages? Is there a way for managers or workers to request additional information, and how quickly is it provided? Addressing questions like these is the key to providing timely strategic and tactical information.

Root cause 3: organizational alignment

Successful communication alone isn't enough to ensure that operations will run smoothly between departments. In many organizations, departments work at cross purposes or fail to understand other departments' strengths. Barriers like these existed in 92% of the organizations analyzed in the Gallup study.

Lack of *goal alignment* was the most common barrier of this kind, found in 83% of the organizations. As companies grow larger and individual fiefdoms become more powerful, some departments set goals that don't necessarily mesh with the goals of other departments. Friction invariably results.

Barriers like these typically appear as conflicts between departments with competing goals: sales and service (customer acquisition versus customer retention), sales and operations (revenue generation versus cost control), human resources and operations (controlling hiring decisions versus living with them). Here are three examples of poor goal alignment:

- Promises made in the sales process can place burdens on the service organization. A balance transfer on a credit card may sound attractive, but customers may become unhappy if they later learn that "low rate" balances get paid off first, while interest on the remaining balance and new charges continue to accrue at a higher rate.

- A call center may have strict goals for handling as many service calls as it can as quickly as it can. However, if the CSRs answering the phones don't share the same goals as the field technicians, the CSRs may be tempted to "just send a technician," even though, by spending a little more time with callers, they could have solved the problem over the phone.

- Important information "left unsaid" in a mortgage loan-acquisition process, such as prepayment penalties, servicing fees, and additional closing costs may create unpleasant surprises for the customer. These surprises then must be dealt with by escrow, closing, and service personnel.

In each of these examples, departments end up working against each other at the expense of employee engagement, customer engagement, and profitability. In each case, the system rewards one group at the expense of another.

Addressing alignment barriers starts with an analysis of the company's goals. Companies that want alignment across all functions must aggressively manage their goal-setting process. Each goal should make a definable contribution to a key business outcome, such as revenue, repeat purchases, or increased customer engagement. Similarly, each employee should make a definable contribution to other departments as well as his or her own.

Goals should not be set in a parochial manner, in which local success trumps corporate success. But neither should department goals be so focused that success on local, tactical goals isn't rewarded at all. Finding the correct mix of local and shared accountabilities with clear links to outcomes greatly improves the odds that alignment barriers won't hinder a company's success. A strong performance management system can help structure goals into appropriate success metrics and incentives.

Another manifestation of friction-based barriers is a lack of a *holistic customer strategy*. It's not unusual for organizations to treat customers more like transactions than like people, but people never see themselves that way. Business banking customers also have personal checking accounts. People with checking accounts also have credit cards. Business travelers also take family vacations. Luxury car buyers may have teenagers who need a more modest automobile. Yet companies rarely are able to cross-reference activity across channels.

Organizations frequently overlook the reality that poor performance in one channel will affect perceptions of the company as a whole, or that excellent performance in one channel may represent an opportunity to broaden the customer relationship in other areas. Both opportunities to improve are lost when the channels don't align.

Improved knowledge management systems can help companies implement a holistic customer strategy. However, employees from different departments also need to provide one another with consistent service. Too often, departments lack insight into how their actions affect other areas of the company, leading to mutual distrust and competing claims that the other departments are inefficient, uncooperative, or just "don't get it." Consistent service to internal customers — whether it's employee to employee or team to team — can help companies identify cross-selling or process-efficiency opportunities that can benefit external customers too.

Root cause 4: money
Money-related barriers existed in 82% of the companies Gallup studied. However, the actual percentage was likely higher, as these types of barriers

may have existed in some pockets of the organization that were not included in each study. There are two main types of financial barriers.

First, people generally do what they are rewarded to do. It follows, then, that improperly balanced *compensation and incentives* can actually encourage the wrong behaviors. For example, if a customer service call center only provides incentives for cross sales and low handle time, CSRs will be highly motivated to rush customers, while pushing as many products as possible as quickly as possible. Worse yet, CSRs might even be rewarded for hanging up on callers before their problem is resolved, forcing customers to call back a second time.

The second type of financial barrier is related to internal *resource allocation* decisions. Budget battles are often won based on the best sales presentation, the loudest voice, or personal relationships rather than on a set of unbiased guiding principles, such as the impact of each budget decision on customers, employees, financials, or risk.

Even when there is a level playing field, resource allocations aren't always aligned with strategy if decisions are too closely tied to the previous year's budget. In that case, departments are unlikely to surrender budget willingly to another, even though corporate strategy or change initiatives make the other department's needs more urgent.

The best way to address compensation and allocation barriers is not necessarily to fight self-interest, as employees and department heads usually gravitate toward the money. Instead, companies should ensure that self-interest is aligned with corporate goals.

For employees, *all* desired behaviors should be rewarded under a balanced incentive system. For example, if a company is focused on both revenue growth and customer retention, it may want to reward sales representatives for total sales and individual account growth. This would reduce a rep's inclination to focus primarily on new sales and to keep him or her from taking the "quick win" if it comes at the expense of the long-term health of the account.

Not all incentives need to be financial. More often than many managers realize, recognition itself can be a powerful reward, especially when the type of position, a union contract, or other circumstances make praise the only way to reward employees. Specific behaviors or outcomes may be treated as milestones toward advancement or promotion, rather than directly rewarding employees through base or incentive pay.

Some allocation barriers may relate to the company's goals. As discussed earlier, a lack of shared goals may generate barriers to engagement by inadvertently pitting one department against another. However, shared goals alone don't guarantee that a company will be free from these types of challenges. Shared goals must be balanced with local and tactical objectives that address the role a business unit, division, or department plays in driving corporate strategy.

Transparency is also helpful. Resource allocation can have a strong impact on employee engagement, particularly if budgeting decisions seem to be based on favoritism or in support of "flavor-of-the-month" initiatives.

Root cause 5: short-term focus

These "quick-fix" barriers existed in 82% of the companies Gallup studied. The barriers included *acts of commission*, or actions taken in the interest of near-term benefits that may have a negative impact on mid- to long-term revenues and profits, and *acts of omission*, which occur when the company takes no action in an area that requires long-term planning or analysis.

Acts of commission are common, particularly in public companies that focus more on quarterly earnings than on long-term horizons. In many cases, these acts involve significant near-term cutbacks. For example:

- To make this quarter's numbers, a company may stop hiring new employees. However, after a few months, staffing shortages may result in overtime, lost customers, and inefficiencies that far outweigh the initial savings.

- A plant may delay needed equipment repairs to save a few dollars in the short term but suffer even greater repair needs and downtime when the machine fails.

Acts of commission are not always the result of cost cutting. Some companies drive employees to the breaking point to generate an increase in near-term sales; others strive to achieve the same sales goal through extreme discounting of their products or services. Both strategies may drive short-term sales while damaging relationships with employees — or undermining customer relationships or the brand.

When it comes to acts of omission, the most common barrier is a lack of succession planning. This goes beyond identifying potential stars for future leadership in the organization. Many companies fail to make a "plan for success" for employees in crucial but less prestigious roles. These barriers also occur when there is an urgent need to "put out the fire" without carefully thinking about how badly you have "flooded the house." For example, resources may be pulled from other projects to handle an emergency, which later causes those projects to fail or miss deadlines.

Given the realities of the marketplace, companies will always struggle with balancing short-term and long-term needs. Adopting a short-term focus is not necessarily a barrier to engagement. To determine whether its near-term actions will have a negative impact on long-term engagement, a company needs to ask itself three questions:

1. *Do these actions achieve a strategic goal?* Some companies must take immediate measures to drive a lagging stock price or to capitalize on an opportunity to grab market share from a weakened competitor. But a myopic focus can also be a symptom of other barriers mentioned above, such as fear, communication breakdowns, or lack of collaboration between departments.

2. *What are the implications of these actions?* There are situations in which a short-term gain is justified, but a near-term focus can become a barrier when mid- to long-term implications aren't considered. Logic and discipline must be added to resource-allocation decisions to avoid these types of barriers. By implementing a set of guiding principles that balance short- and long-term costs and rewards, a company should be able to rationally prioritize long-terms decisions. Guiding principles for decision making may include questions such as:

   • How will this decision affect our revenue?

   • How will this decision affect our costs?

   • To what extent will this decision decrease or increase liability or risk?

   • Will this decision prevent or inadvertently encourage any catastrophic failures that could lead to higher costs?

   • How will this decision affect employee engagement?

3. *What will these actions communicate to employees and customers?* Employees must feel that the company is making the right moves. Consistent communication about change and change initiatives is important, particularly if the company is concerned about maintaining employee engagement. Companies should give change

initiatives the appropriate resources and support even if that in-creases short-term costs.

Pulling down barriers

If organizations want to build and sustain a great workplace that, in turn, builds strong customer relationships, it's not enough to simply measure employee or customer engagement, then hold team meetings to discuss it. Workgroups can meet to identify and address local issues, but institutional systems outside the control of managers and employees can remain thorny barriers to employee and customer engagement. Barriers like these must be systematically addressed by company leaders; organizations that fail to address them may find that they are limiting their ability to achieve strategic targets.

A disciplined, objective approach to identifying and removing systemic barriers related to fear, information flow, organizational alignment, money, and short-term focus can help clear a path toward organic growth.

See Related Article
"Are You Failing to Engage?" (Part 1 of Series, page 268)

THE FOUR DRIVERS
OF INNOVATION

by Shelley Mika

January 11, 2007

Top executives and business experts reveal the keys to making your company more creative

A couple of decades ago, when economists forecasted the highest earning countries across the globe, many put their money on Japan as the leader, Germany as the runner-up, and the United States in third place for the largest GDPs in the new millennium. But now that we're seven years into the 21st century, it's clear that those economists lost the bet: The United States' GDP is currently $12.3 trillion, exceeding the current GDPs of Japan and Germany by about $8 trillion and $10 trillion, respectively.

So what happened to make the United States' output soar above economists' predictions? According to some leading executives and management thinkers, the answer is innovation.

In fact, many argue that innovation is the most important driver of macroeconomics today. That's why a group of senior executives and business experts gathered recently in Chicago to discuss innovation, leadership, and the new economy of creativity, knowledge, and invention — and how to focus these amorphous concepts into real business dollars. Their insights are relevant to executives from businesses large and small, global and local.

Interpreting innovation

Opening the event, Gallup Chairman and CEO Jim Clifton gave an overview of the history of macroeconomics, making it clear that business leaders are playing in a much different game than they did in the past. Economic centers once formed where resources like cattle or steel were plentiful. Now, these centers emerge where innovation is happening, he said.

Everyone can probably imagine what innovation is. We've seen it in Web sites like MySpace and YouTube and in each iteration of the iPod, and we'll see it again the day a noncombustion engine relieves many nations of their dependence on oil.

But, often the term *innovation* gets confused with *creativity*, according to Barry Conchie, principal leadership consultant at Gallup and a speaker at the event. "Let's be clear: Innovation and creativity are not the same thing," Conchie said. "Creativity may spur innovation, but there's an element of action missing there."

The difference is that innovation actually brings ideas to life. "You can't get innovation without a groundswell of creativity," Conchie said. "But you [must] turn creativity into something that has an impact beyond the conversation you had about the idea." Innovation is more than an idea — it takes place when great ideas actually happen and make their mark on the world.

In the past, most businesses have focused on continuous improvement of their products and services to maintain a competitive edge. But in today's economy, that's not always enough, Clifton said. As the agricultur-alists of the past had to literally break new ground to expand their trade, today's businesses must come up with new ideas, rather than settle for marginally better ideas. In Clifton's words, "*Better* doesn't work anymore. *Different* does."

If innovation is today's hot commodity, how can business leaders harvest it? They must create conditions in which innovation can thrive in their companies. Below are the four drivers of innovation, as identified by executives and thinkers who spoke at the event.

Driver #1: Finding and fostering talent

According to Clifton, four types of people drive innovation: inventors, en-trepreneurs, extreme individual achievers in their fields (such as the arts, entertainment, or sports), and super mentors. "The theory is that where these people settle is where new economic empires will be built," Clifton said. "And they go where there is other talent like them."

Marla Mayne, senior vice president of retail lending at U.S. Bank, knows the importance of hiring the right talent — people who, based on the way they naturally think, feel, and behave, are likely to be top performers in their field. Her company was looking for sales talent, but even some of the most experienced salespeople weren't superb performers. "One gentleman had results and more than ten years of experience. But just because your stock did well before doesn't mean it will in the future," she said.

That's when Mayne realized she needed to focus on hiring only what she calls "A's" — the very top talent in sales. Rather than having a staff of 50% A's, she asked herself how she could hire a greater percentage of top performers.

Using selection practices that identify candidates who are most like the best in their roles based on their natural talents, Mayne was able to identify and hire top talent. "We're hiring an 'A' team, and we'll have one thousand loan officers outproducing a company with three thousand loan officers," she said.

Mayne found out that experience doesn't matter nearly as much as talent. Now, she and her management team focus primarily on talent when selecting salespeople. "We can teach them the business, [but] not talent," she said.

Once you've hired these employees, how do you make the most of their talents and foster innovation? Based on Gallup research, Conchie said, employee engagement is highly related to the ability to innovate.

THE THREE TYPES OF EMPLOYEES

ENGAGED employees work with passion, and they feel a profound connection to their company. They drive innovation and move the organization forward.

NOT-ENGAGED employees are essentially "checked out." They're sleepwalking through their workday, putting time — but not energy or passion — into their work.

ACTIVELY DISENGAGED employees aren't just unhappy at work; they're busy acting out their unhappiness. Every day, these workers undermine what their engaged coworkers accomplish.

Gallup recently asked American employees to rate their workplace on four items:

- My current job brings out my most creative ideas.
- My company encourages new ideas that defy conventional wisdom.
- I have a friend at work who I share new ideas with.
- I feed off the creativity of my colleagues.

For all four items, the percentage of engaged employees who strongly agreed far outnumbered the percentage of not-engaged or actively disengaged employees who strongly agreed. Clearly, creating an environment where employees are engaged can yield a higher crop of creativity, Conchie said.

Mike Morrison, dean of the University of Toyota, said that one approach to engaging employees is to "incubate" their ideas. "You can't wait by the phone for a breakthrough idea," he said. "You need knowledge, technique, and motivation. If one [element] is missing, you can't have an innovative environment."

Morrison said that when people are relaxed, ideas begin bubbling to the surface. So at Toyota, they periodically take people out of their typical office environments and let them develop ideas in places where the pressure is off and they can brainstorm without the demands of the workplace competing for their attention. The company also provides those people with lots of information and reading material on the subject at hand, hoping to inspire them to create bigger and better ideas than those that already exist. These incubation periods yield the breakthrough ideas Toyota is looking for, Morrison said.

Driver #2: Managers matter

Let's not forget that creativity needs action to become innovation. Companies must do more with their employees' creativity than just acknowledging that an employee has a good idea. That's why *managers matter*.

Looking at the four categories of innovators, often the inventors, entrepreneurs, and high achievers would be nothing without that last category: super mentors, Clifton said. "When it comes to innovation, mentors play a key role, because they're the people who say, 'That's a great idea. You can make a lucrative business of that,'" Clifton said. Super mentors inspire their protégés and help them connect with the people who can couple action with their ideas — as some of the best managers do.

In Mayne's case, managers were integral to U.S. Bank's success with its loan officers. Although the bank was hiring A-level loan officers, it found it wasn't able to keep them: U.S. Bank still saw a 60% turnover rate among this crucial group.

To remedy the problem, Mayne decided to assess the manager talent among her staff. It turned out that half of her regional managers were from the "B" or "C" pool. Once Mayne used selection tools that identified people who are most like the best managers — increasing her regional management staff from 4 A-level managers to 25 — she started keeping those coveted A-level loan officers. More importantly, she started seeing results. "When you put talent in a fully loaded environment, you get performance out of people," she said.

Now Mayne's team operates with fewer people, but its retention is up, and so are its numbers. Mayne found that loan officers who are:

- A's completed 794 more loan applications per month than B's
- A's closed 624 more loans per month than B's
- A's closed $66 million more in loans than B's

In addition, when loan offers were divided into two groups by engagement levels and compared, A's in the top half closed 8 more loans per month than A's in the bottom half. Similarly, A's in the top half closed 9 more loans per month than B's in the top half.

At U.S. Bank, hiring the right talent, then making sure that talent was engaged and led by the right managers, made for a lucrative combination.

Driver #3: Relationships matter too

Talented managers usually understand the importance of relationships. "An emotional commitment of one person to another makes a difference. But the control a manager has to enhance or limit [an employee's] contribution to innovation is the most powerful factor," Conchie said. "It's important that [relationships are] cultivated from manager to manager and employee to employee. But we know that the [quality of the] relationship between a manager and an employee affects the ability to leverage that relationship. A bad relationship is a sure-fire way to kill innovation."

A relationship with customers matters too. In the new economy, improving a business model is more complicated than assembling a piece of hardware on an assembly line. To move forward — to develop the most creative ideas, and most importantly, enact them — a company must understand the needs of its customers, and that takes a good relationship. "In order to stay ahead of the game, you have to think of a way to connect with customers that makes you different," Conchie said.

Driver #4: Keeping the right leaders

If leaders are so important in driving innovation — both in terms of thought leadership and fostering creativity in the people they lead — what happens when they step down? Often, retiring CEOs choose their successors based on instinct or on an assumed company lineage, Conchie said. He shared an example of a manufacturing company that was facing the imminent departure of its CEO. To continue its growth, the company needed a leader with the right kind of talent. But as Conchie said, "The CEO already had a point of view. He was picking the people he admired, not people who could replace him. But you shouldn't think about succession planning without thinking about the loss of talent when the CEO leaves."

As the company set out to evaluate the performance of its key candidates, it learned that those who would typically be considered for the position didn't match the talent profile needed to succeed as CEO. When they assessed potential candidates for their drive to execute and their management, relationship, and direction talents, a different group stood out. Operating on these data, the company chose a successor whose talent profile projected success — and it worked. In just four years, the company grew to $1.1 billion, and its stock price doubled.

To select the right leaders, Conchie said, companies must ask three key questions:

1. How objective is your company's assessment of current performance and leadership talent potential?

2. Is your company's succession management focused on lining up individuals for positions, increasing overall leadership capability, or both?

3. Is leadership team talent assessed or measured as a precursor to all leadership hiring decisions?

When companies begin asking these important questions, they can begin a formalized process for hiring leaders who are more likely to succeed. And when a data-driven performance review meets a talent-based succession planning model, it creates a powerful combination that allows companies to choose successful leaders — and innovators — who can make a solid future for their organizations.

What happens without innovation?

In today's fast-paced marketplace, if a company keeps offering the same product, a rival can easily race past with a better one. And yet another competitor will blow them both out of the water when it invents something altogether different and better — something innovative. To remain competitive, companies must consider how to find and keep visionary leaders and how to foster innovation and creativity in their employees, the executives and experts at the event agreed.

On the global stage, innovation could mean the difference between the United States keeping a tight grasp on economic leadership or eventually slipping behind countries like China and India, as some economists have predicted. But, those fast-growing countries also face the same challenge.

"Right now, does China have innovation, or does it just make the lowest cost products?" Clifton asked. "If it's bankrupt in terms of innovation, its economy is just as likely to be a bubble as the dot-coms."

See Related Article
"Start Finding Tomorrow's Leaders Now" (page 212)

PROBING THE DARK SIDE OF EMPLOYEES' STRENGTHS

by Brian Brim

February 8, 2007

Can their talents actually alienate colleagues and hurt your organization?

I spend a great deal of my time speaking, writing, and teaching about how organizations can leverage employees' talents to improve business performance. Because some executives and managers don't fully understand the impact that a strengths-based approach can have, they may write it off as "fluff" or simply regard it as a "rose-colored glasses" approach to people.

As those executives and managers begin to learn more, they realize that this approach helps them see their employees — and themselves too — as they really are. When organizations take a strengths-based approach to managing their employees — when they hire, develop, and deploy people in ways that help them maximize their innate talents — their employees can make powerful, positive contributions that can drive the business forward.

On the other hand, when companies begin using strengths-based management, employees don't magically become perfect in their jobs. Nor do those employees cease having problems or struggles at work. A strengths-based approach, however, does allow organizations to begin to understand *why* employees may be struggling. Managers can then use that new understanding to help employees learn how to channel their talents productively to achieve real change — and real results.

Is Matt overbearing?

To dig deeper into this, we need to think about a question I hear all the time when I give talks about strengths: "Is there a bad side, or a 'dark side,' to strengths?" When people ask me this, I usually ask them exactly what they mean. In fact, I recently had this conversation with Matt, a manager in a retail company. Matt mentioned that, on occasion, his coworkers felt he had taken over meetings or conversations, and he'd been asked if he could "tone down" this behavior a bit.

Matt had recently taken the Clifton StrengthsFinder, an online assessment that measures a person's talents in 34 categories called "themes" then
reveals the user's top five themes. Matt's results showed that Command
is one of his dominant talent themes. People particularly talented in this
theme generally feel little discomfort in imposing their views on others;
once they've formed an opinion, they feel compelled to share it.

Matt wanted to know if there was a downside to having Command as one
of his top themes. He was essentially asking, "Can too much Command be
bad? And if so, how do I dial it back?"

These are fair questions. People with a lot of Command talent have a strong
presence. They can take control of a situation and be decisive. It's easy to
see how, if the talents are applied incorrectly, a negative perception of those
talents could emerge.

I explained to Matt that Gallup's definition of strength — *the ability to
consistently produce a nearly perfect positive outcome in a specific task* — can
help clarify what he's experiencing. The key to this definition, I said, is the
phrase "produce a nearly perfect positive outcome."

If people are saying that Matt has too much Command, what they're really
thinking is that Matt hasn't figured out how to leverage the talents in his
Command theme in a positive manner. Matt's colleagues shouldn't blame
his Command talents if he appears to be pushy or domineering. Rather,
they — and Matt — should understand that he is not applying those talents productively to his job.

I also explained to Matt that it's nearly impossible for someone to "tone
down" their top talent themes. Instead, he should focus on refining those
talents and learning to use them in a more sophisticated way. Learning
to use his Command talents more productively could be Matt's key to
strengths development and increased success. He can also help others
move beyond seeing him as "bossy" or "opinionated" and help them appreciate what his most powerful talents contribute to the organization.

Does Susan ask too many questions?

Here's another example: Susan is a researcher at a consulting firm. Analytical is one of her top talent themes. Susan loves to probe problems and
ask many questions. Her colleagues say that Susan continually "peels back
the onion." This is a tremendous asset to her organization, as her in-depth
analyses add real value for the company's clients.

The downside is that she sometimes doesn't know when to quit, and she can drive her colleagues crazy with what they perceive as her "endless questions." It also doesn't help that her e-mail messages, filled with data and analysis, can run many pages.

When thinking about Susan's talents from a strengths-based perspective, it's helpful to return to our original question: "Is there a bad side, or a 'dark side,' to strengths?" Again, if you look at Gallup's definition of strength — *the ability to consistently produce a nearly perfect positive outcome in a specific task* — the answer is no, because a strength is about producing "a nearly perfect *positive* outcome."

On the flip side, if you were to wonder whether Susan was applying her talents in a negative way, the answer is clearly yes. Again, Gallup's definition of talent — *a natural way of thinking, feeling, or behaving* — helps clarify this. If Susan's Analytical talents lead her to wear people out with her persistent questioning, then she is applying those talents in a negative way. This is also true when Matt's Command talents manifest themselves in pushiness or in domineering behavior.

The key to a strengths-based approach to managing employees is to help people like Matt and Susan understand their natural patterns of thought, feeling, or behavior so they can apply them in a *positive and productive* manner. When Matt uses his Command talents to be productively decisive without being pushy or overbearing — and when Susan channels her Analytical talents to ask questions that make her consulting firm more valuable to its clients (without driving her teammates nuts) — their talents can contribute powerfully to the workplace.

In these moments, Matt and Susan are using their greatest talents to produce "a nearly perfect positive outcome," and there is nothing bad, or dark, about that.

See Related Article
"How Ann Taylor Invests in Talent" (page 220)

CONTRIBUTING AUTHORS: BIOGRAPHICAL NOTES

Scott Ahlstrand is a Principal of Gallup.

Vandana Allman is a Principal Leadership Consultant for Gallup. She is the coauthor of Gallup's book *Animals, Inc.: A Business Parable for the 21st Century* (Warner Books, 2004).

Alec Appelbaum is a writer based in New York.

Raksha Arora is a Senior Consultant for the Gallup World Poll.

Brian Brim is a Principal and leader of Global Client Education for Gallup.

Wei-Li Chong is Vice President, Organizational Effectiveness, Ann Taylor Stores Corporation.

Jim Clifton is Chairman and CEO of Gallup.

Barry Conchie is a Principal Leadership Consultant for Gallup.

Steve Crabtree currently leads the production of published material for the Gallup World Poll, a groundbreaking worldwide survey launched in 2006. He contributed to writing *Building Engaged Schools* (Gallup Press, 2006), Gallup's book on education reform. He is a regular contributor to the *Gallup Management Journal*.

Kurt Deneen is a Senior Consultant for Gallup.

John H. Fleming, Ph.D., is Principal and Chief Scientist — Customer Engagement and HumanSigma for Gallup. He is coauthor of *Human Sigma: Managing the Employee-Customer Encounter* (Gallup Press, 2007).

Jerry Hadd, Ph.D., is a writer for Gallup.

James K. Harter, Ph.D., is Chief Scientist Workplace Management and Well-Being for Gallup. He is coauthor of the *New York Times* bestseller *12: The Elements of Great Managing* (Gallup Press, 2006).

Bill Hoffman is a Partner with Gallup.

Stefanie Julier is a consultant for Gallup.

Craig Kamins is a Senior Consultant for Gallup.

Emily A. Killham is a Senior Consultant for Gallup.

Jerry Krueger is a writer for Gallup.

Jack Ludwig is a Senior Methodologist and the Director of Research for Gallup's Poll Social Audits.

William J. McEwen, Ph.D., is Global Practice Leader for Gallup's Brand Management practice. He is the author of *Married to the Brand* (Gallup Press, 2005) and coauthor of the *Harvard Business Review* article "Inside the Mind of the Chinese Consumer."

Shelley Mika is a former writer for Gallup.

Glenn Phelps, Ph.D., is a Senior Consultant for Gallup.

Tom Rath leads Gallup's workplace and leadership consulting practice. He is coauthor of the #1 *New York Times* bestseller *How Full Is Your Bucket?* He is also the author of *Vital Friends: The People You Can't Afford to Live Without*. His latest book, *StrengthsFinder 2.0* — based on the assessment that has helped millions around the world to discover their strengths — is already a #1 *BusinessWeek* bestseller.

Tom Rieger is a Principal for Gallup.

Jennifer Robison is a writer based in Lincoln, Nebraska.

Tony Rutigliano is coauthor of *Discover Your Sales Strengths* (Warner Books, 2003).

Lydia Saad is Senior Editor with The Gallup Poll.

Benson Smith is coauthor of *Discover Your Sales Strengths* (Warner Books, 2003).

Vijay S. Talluri, D.B.A., is a former research director for Gallup.

John Thackray is a writer based in New York.

Teresa J. Tschida is Global Practice Leader, Financial Services Industry for Gallup.

Rodd Wagner is a Principal for Gallup. He is coauthor of the *New York Times* bestseller *12: The Elements of Great Managing* (Gallup Press, 2006).

Mick Zangari is a former senior consultant for Gallup.

ACKNOWLEDGEMENTS

Scores of talented and supremely dedicated writers, editors, researchers, Web designers and technicians, marketers, and executives have helped us publish the *Gallup Management Journal* every month, and they have all played a vital behind-the-scenes role in this volume. Our thanks and gratitude go to this extraordinary team of world-class professionals, which includes:

Kelly Henry, who is the world's best copy editor and who always pushes us to achieve perfection.

Darren Carlson, Catherine Heron, Ben Klima, Cheryl Knight, Trista Kunce, Bryant Ott, Paul Petters, Theresa Prystanski, Julie Ray, Mark Stiemann, and Alyssa Yell, all of whom offer outstanding editorial support and insights.

Kelly Slater and Carolyn Madison, who are superb editorial team leaders.

Jennifer Robison, a brilliant and imaginative writer and reporter who has produced countless articles for this publication, both as a bylined author and as an editor and rewriter.

Yvonne Sen and David Osborne, who work tirelessly on behalf of our subscribers, and Eric Nielsen, who helps push the *GMJ* message out to the world.

Laurie Dean, Julie Fienhold, and Shannon Malousek, who play key roles in supporting our internal customers, as does our project manager, Tim Dean.

Molly Hardin, Chris Johanowicz, Collin Stork, Christopher Purdy, and Tommy McCall, who provide outstanding design and graphics.

Rachel Johanowicz, who ensured that the production stayed on track and on schedule. And Beverly Passerella, who played a key role in helping assemble its contents.

Beth Karadeema, who did first-rate work on the design and typography of this book and its cover.

Stephanie Oswald, Matt Johnson, Mike Jaros, and Kim Ideus, who, along with many others in Gallup's technology lab, make up the world's best technical team.

Jessica Korn, who, as a brilliant and determined founding Editor in Chief, made sure the *GMJ* was highly successful and admired right out of the gate.

Gallup's Chairman and CEO, Jim Clifton, and our Chief Marketing Officer and Executive Publisher, Larry Emond, who dreamed of making this publication a reality years ago and who have always inspired and challenged us to make it better and more compelling. There never would have been a *GMJ* without their vision and determination.

And last but not least, the thousands of Gallup associates who touch this publication. From the interviewers and researchers who gather the data to the copy editor who puts the final touches on the content, nearly everyone who works for Gallup contributes in some way to the *GMJ*. We couldn't possibly list them all, but we couldn't publish the *GMJ* without their help. And we most certainly cannot imagine a world without them.

— *Geoffrey Brewer and Barb Sanford*

LEARN MORE

To stay up-to-date on the latest insights into Gallup's research on employees, customers, brands, leadership, and organizational performance, visit the *Gallup Management Journal* at http://gmj.gallup.com, where management experts regularly contribute articles and company profiles.

Readers of *The Best of the Gallup Management Journal 2001-2007* can receive a six-month trial subscription to the *Gallup Management Journal*. Simply go to: http://commerce.gallup.com/ma/code/, then follow these instructions:

- If you already have a Gallup membership, enter your user name and password, then click "Log In."

- If you do not have a Gallup membership, click "Create an Account" and enter the required information. Click "Submit Registration," then log in to continue. Enter your user name and password, then click "Log In."

- Enter the promotional code **BestofGMJ**, then click "Continue."

- Review your order, and click "Submit Order" if the information is correct.

For assistance, e-mail galluphelp@gallup.com.

ABOUT THE EDITORS

Geoffrey Brewer is the Editorial Director of Gallup Press, which publishes books and the *Gallup Management Journal*. He is the editor of *The New York Times* bestsellers *12: The Elements of Great Managing* and *How Full Is Your Bucket?*, which reached #1 on the business list. He also edited the #1 *Wall Street Journal* and #1 *BusinessWeek* bestseller *StrengthsFinder 2.0*. Brewer was previously editor-in-chief of *Sales & Marketing Management*, a strategy publication for senior executives, and a contributing writer on management for *The New York Times*. He is a seven-time recipient of the Jesse H. Neal Editorial Achievement Award from American Business Media. Brewer lives in Brooklyn, New York, with his wife, Regan Solmo, and their son, Henry.

Barb Sanford is the managing editor of the *Gallup Management Journal*. Sanford also contributes her writing and editorial expertise to the book publisher Gallup Press. She was an editor for *Discover Your Sales Strengths* and *Married to the Brand* and for the bestsellers *12: The Elements of Great Managing* and *How Full Is Your Bucket?* In addition to her work with the *Gallup Management Journal* and Gallup Press, Sanford writes and edits for Gallup's corporate marketing team. She is actively involved in the International Association of Business Communicators and has served in leadership roles at the chapter and regional levels. She lives in Lincoln, Nebraska, with her husband, Howard, and daughter, Elizabeth.

MORE BUSINESS BOOKS FROM GALLUP PRESS

Human Sigma: Managing the Employee-Customer Encounter
This book reveals that there are right and wrong ways to assess and manage the health of a company's employee and customer relationships. The rigorous new approach described here offers a new perspective on organizational performance that hinges on five core principles that all great companies must embrace.

StrengthsFinder 2.0
Gallup introduced the first version of its online assessment, the Clifton StrengthsFinder, in the 2001 bestseller *Now, Discover Your Strengths. StrengthsFinder 2.0*, a #1 *Wall Street Journal* and #1 *BusinessWeek* bestseller, unveils the new and improved version of this popular assessment and language of 34 talent themes, as well as hundreds of strategies for applying your strengths.

12: The Elements of Great Managing
The long-awaited sequel to the bestseller *First, Break All the Rules, 12* follows great managers as they successfully face a host of challenges in settings around the world. Written for managers and employees of companies large and small, this *New York Times* bestseller explains what every company must know about creating and sustaining employee engagement.

Vital Friends
This book challenges long-held assumptions people have about their relationships. And its landmark discovery — that people who have a "best friend at work" are seven times as likely to be engaged in their job — is sure to rattle the structure of organizations around the world.

Married to the Brand
Many marketers are great at wooing a "first date" with consumers, yet lousy at creating a lasting marriage between buyer and brand. *Married to the Brand* tells the story of what makes profitable brand relationships work — through the eyes of the consumer, not the marketer.

How Full Is Your Bucket?
Filled with rich discoveries, powerful strategies, and heartwarming stories, this #1 *New York Times* bestseller is sure to inspire lasting changes and has all the makings of a timeless classic.

Gallup Press exists to educate and inform the people who govern, manage, teach, and lead the world's six billion citizens. Each book meets Gallup's requirements of integrity, trust, and independence and is based on Gallup-approved science and research.